Master Conductors

on Orchestral Score Reading

Master Conductors on Orchestral Score Reading

Maja Metelska-Räsänen

Maja Metelska-Räsänen

Master Conductors on Orchestral Score Reading

Copyright © 2025 Maja Metelska-Räsänen. All rights reserved.

No part of this book may be reproduced in any form or by any electronic or mechanical means including information storage and retrieval systems, without permission in writing from the author.

Published by Met-Music Publishing
www.metmusicpublishing.com

ISBN 978-952-65063-2-6 (paperback)
ISBN 978-952-65063-3-3 (hardcover)

Contents

Preface	ix
Introduction	xi
1 Historical Perspectives	1
Hermann Scherchen and the Ideal Conception of a Piece	3
Sir Adrian Boult's Systematic Technique of Score Reading	5
Symbols and Markings in Nicolai Malko's Method	9
Nadia Boulanger's Teaching of Score Reading	15
Eugene Ormandy and Inner Hearing of the Score	18
Ilya Musin and the Process of Reading the Score	20
Conductor as Interpreter in Eugen Jochum's Phenomenology	23
Erich Leinsdorf and Faithfulness to the Composer	25
Gunther Schuller and the Quest to Know the Score	29
Sir Georg Solti's Reflections on Score Reading	32
Creative Score Reading in Witold Rowicki's Aesthetic Approach	34
Stanisław Skrowaczewski on Interpretation and Recordings	36
2 Contemporary approaches: interviews	39
Challenges in Score Reading – *Antoni Wit*	41
Realization of the Score – *Jorma Panula*	47
The Score's Logic and Layers – *Osmo Vänskä*	64
The Architectural Metaphor – *Charles Olivieri-Munroe*	77
The Magnifying Glass – *Anna-Maria Helsing*	90
Score Internalization and Layout – *Tito Muñoz*	98
The Daily Routine of Score Reading – *Philippe Bach*	113
Open Sound Image and Leadership – *Maria Badstue*	125
Context and the Dramatic Arc – *Tomas Djupsjöbacka*	134
Teaching Score Reading – *Ilona Dobszay-Meskó*	146

Polyphonic Voices and Moving Clefs – *James Sherlock*   154

A Flexible Sound Image – *Chloé Dufresne*   164

Transpositions and Score Reading – *Vlad Vizireanu*   177

Zooming into the Score – *Eero Lehtimäki*   179

3   Results of the Score Reading Questionnaire   193

4   Conclusions   211

Overview   213

Score Reading Methods   215

The Stages and Focus of Score Reading   218

The Composer's Language and Background of the Piece   222

Score Reading Tools and Orchestral Imagination   224

Transpositions and Other Challenges in Score Reading   227

Marking the Score   230

Listening to Recordings   232

Score Reading and Conducting   235

Bibliography   239

To my parents,
with gratitude for their support,
and everlasting inspiration

Preface

My deep interest in the subject of score reading arose through my experience as a conductor and my work with conducting students. From the very beginning, it became clear to me that score reading involves far more than simply decoding and imagining pitches, rhythms, and harmonies. To gain a broader understanding, I sought insights from master conductors, musical authorities, and experienced professionals. Exploring different methods, techniques, approaches, and preferences – both historical and contemporary – led to new discoveries and valuable information, along with fascinating perspectives on the subject.

I extend my heartfelt gratitude to the conductors who participated in interviews for this book – your wisdom, reflections, experience, viewpoints, and anecdotes on score reading are truly inspiring. It was a privilege to engage in conversation with you. I also offer sincere thanks to the conductors who completed the Score Reading Questionnaire, the results of which are presented in this book, for generously sharing your views, experiences, and advice on score reading. I would also like to thank my husband, Otto Räsänen, for his unwavering support in my research, his passion for orchestral music, and his help with the publication of this book.

This book was written and published with the support of a grant from Suomen tietokirjailijat ry (The Finnish Association of Non-Fiction Writers). I am very grateful for this recognition. The book includes my own English translations of texts originally spoken or written in Finnish, Russian, and Polish.

It is my sincere hope that this book will bring greater insight into and understanding of the many aspects of the conductor's art of reading orchestral scores. Within the score, hidden beneath the surface of the notation, lies a wealth of ideas, treasures, and beauty. Through this book, I aim to draw more attention to and encourage deeper appreciation of the conductor's art of reading orchestral scores, while also contributing to its development. It is an essential part in the work of a conductor, who brings the score to life with the orchestra. The journey of score reading continues, and each musician who engages with a score ultimately chooses – and carves – their own path. May this book serve as a valuable resource for those interested in reading orchestral scores and performing orchestral music, offering both knowledge and inspiration.

x

Introduction

Score reading is a fundamental and pervasive element of the conductor's musical work – extending beyond rehearsals with the orchestra and the outcome of a single performance. It begins before the conductor enters rehearsal, continues throughout their collaboration with the orchestra, and remains relevant afterward. This book serves as a source of methods, techniques, and approaches to score reading, offering advice and guidance for student conductors and other readers of orchestral scores. It emphasizes the idea that the conductor's art is an expression that originates in the act of reading the score.

The goal of this book is to provide insight into and a deeper understanding of the specific aspects of the conductor's art of reading an orchestral score – ultimately bringing the music to life in rehearsal and performance with an orchestra. It explores the aesthetics and philosophies of master conductors, drawing on both contemporary and historical voices. In doing so, it documents current score reading tendencies and knowledge within the broader context of past achievements. A central aim of this book is to present the perspectives of conductors across generations – from historical figures to today's experienced and emerging professionals, from various countries and conducting schools – in order to examine the similarities and differences in their approaches to score reading. It brings together a rich and diverse range of viewpoints on the art of score reading.

Among the topics addressed in this book are how conductors read, analyze, memorize, and interpret orchestral scores; create a sounding image of the score in the mind; uncover the composer's intentions; and decode transpositions. The book reflects on the challenges of score reading and provides solutions validated by the experience of professional conductors. Special attention is given to musical style and the ambiguities of musical notation. It also explores how score reading methods and techniques have evolved with the modern tools now available to conductors, such as audio and video recordings, MIDI files, metronomes, tuners, software programs, smartphones, tablets, and digital manuscripts. The book reviews significant literature on the art of conducting in relation to score reading, with the aim of building on the best traditions of the past while taking into account the demands of new music and the possibilities offered by modern technological advancements. While much of the existing conducting literature focuses on the conductor's communication with the orchestra and manual technique, this book emphasizes the conductor's work with the score as essential preparation for conducting the orchestra.

Today's conductors perform music from all eras, including baroque, classical, romantic, modern, and contemporary works. As they read scores, they engage with a wide range of musical styles, bringing them to the present and, in the case of recordings, to future audiences. They navigate both written and unwritten performance practices and traditions. When reading a score, the conductor must make musical decisions not only about what the music will sound like, but also how to realize it. Through score reading, the conductor rediscovers the musical past and creates new paths of understanding for the future.

The book seeks to answer questions related to score reading, such as: What is the best and most efficient method to read scores, if one exists? How can fluency and proficiency in score reading be achieved? What steps are necessary to understand a score in depth? How can a conductor uncover meaning and the composer's intentions hidden behind the notes? What should be considered in a thorough reading of a score? What are the key steps in score analysis, and in what order should they be approached to prepare for conducting? How can transpositions be decoded efficiently? In what ways does listening to recordings influence score reading? How can we know how the composer intended the music to sound, and what do their markings in the score signify? How does a conductor memorize the score, and is this relevant to their work? How have score reading methods and approaches evolved over time? What are the current tendencies and practices? Which elements should the conductor focus on when reading a score, and in what order? Is playing the piano or another musical instrument a necessary skill for reading a score? Can singing support the score reading process? Is there a specific technique to score reading? What role does score reading play in a conductor's work, and how is it connected to conducting and the performance of a piece? This book explores these and other questions from multiple angles and perspectives. The results of the author's research in this field are presented throughout the book.

Chapter 1 explores historical approaches and methods of score reading as practiced and recommended by 19th- and 20th-century conductors and conducting pedagogues. Chapter 2 features interviews with master conductors from around the world, all carried out by the author of this book during

2023–2024. Chapter 3 presents the results of the Score Reading Questionnaire, designed by the author and completed by forty professional conductors in 2024. In Chapter 4, the author reflects on the material presented in the book – the historical development, the current tendencies in score reading, and how the insights gathered can benefit conducting students and be applied to their work as conductors.

Score reading has often been regarded as a kind of secret knowledge – passed down from the master conductor to their apprentices – or as a deeply personal and private activity. Through this book, identified and explained are the teachable elements of this art: components that can be studied, practiced, and mastered to achieve proficiency. The richness of material stems from the desire to learn from the masters of conducting, drawing on the best traditions and ideals of both the past and the present. Each generation of conductors has contributed to the development of the art of score reading, and today's masters will shape its future.

This book is intended for conducting students, musicians, music lovers, and anyone interested in score reading, orchestral music, artistic creation, interpretation, and performance. It aims to support students and inspire future conductors, and to deepen the understanding of the conductor's art.

1 Historical Perspectives

Hermann Scherchen and the Ideal Conception of a Piece

In his famous *Handbook of Conducting*[1], published in 1929, the German conductor Hermann Scherchen (1891-1966) dedicates a section to the topic of score reading, where he offers guidance and advice for the student conductor. He emphasizes that a conductor must have a powerful musical imagination and a complete internal understanding of the music before bringing it to life with an orchestra. This process begins with reading the score and forming an ideal conception of the piece in the mind, and continues with its realization in performance.

According to Scherchen, score reading is a preparatory stage during which the conductor creates a mental musical image of the piece – the ideal conception of the work. He underlines the importance of the vision of the piece deriving solely from the score, and not from listening to the sound of the orchestra. When reading the score, the conductor should hear the music inwardly as clearly and completely as the composer did when creating it. In Scherchen's view, perfect knowledge of the score includes coordinating the melody, harmony, rhythm, dynamics, and architecture of the piece. An analysis of melody consists of determining its structure – "the centre of gravity, the driving forces, the curving-points."[2] As a result of score reading, the conductor can deduce the correct tempo, style, and technique required for the performance of the piece.

Reading the score in portions is Scherchen's recommendation – for example, ten measures at a time – so that the melody, harmony, rhythm, instrumentation, dynamics, and all other indications relevant to performance become embedded in the conductor's mind and ear. Learning one portion of the score influences the reading of the next. He notes that the conductor's role extends to reading scores and interpreting music from various historical periods, which also requires broad cultural and stylistic knowledge. Conductors must be able to distinguish between the characteristics of a musical era and the unique voice of an individual composer.

---

[1] Hermann Scherchen, *Handbook of Conducting*, trans. M. D. Calvocoressi (Oxford: Oxford University Press, 1989).
[2] Ibid., 7.

Scherchen emphasizes that all of the conductor's activities are spiritual – a principle that also applies to the art of score reading, which is therefore influenced by the conductor's personality. Because of this, each conductor's mental image of the piece is slightly different. The inner hearing is shaped by the conductor's unique perspective, making every interpretation personal, as the conductor "stamps his own personality upon the music."[3]

The ideal musical conception of a piece is defined by Scherchen as a "perfect inward singing,"[4] which naturally arises from within and is uninfluenced by external obstacles. In his approach, perfect clarity of conception is the first condition for the materialization of a musical work. The conductor's preconception of the piece determines the technique of conducting and inspires the technique of orchestral execution – not the other way around.

To communicate the ideal conception of the piece to the orchestra, Scherchen stresses that the conductor must know the score so thoroughly that they can conduct it from memory. During performance, the conductor's eyes should be directed toward the players and not the score, as conducting is carried out through gestures and eye contact. Consequently, the conductor will be effective in performance only when fully independent of the printed score. Scherchen also points out that, when conveying the ideal conception of the work to the orchestra, the conductor does not need to notate nuances – such as dynamics, tempo, phrasing, expression, or other markings – in the orchestral parts, as all of these can be communicated through conducting.

In Scherchen's philosophy, conducting is the act of giving sounds shape and manifesting the inner image of the music clearly and flawlessly to the audience. The conductor strives to realize this ideal image with the orchestra. To accomplish this, they need to unify the multiple personalities of the orchestra to serve the realization of that image. The goal of conducting is to achieve absolute unity between the ideal musical conception of the piece, resulting from reading the score, and the sounding realization of it with the orchestra during performance.

---

[3] Ibid., 2.
[4] Ibid., 2.

Sir Adrian Boult's Systematic Technique of Score Reading

Sir Adrian Boult (1889-1983) shares insight and advice on score reading in two of his books: *Handbook on the Technique of Conducting*[5], written in 1920, and *Thoughts on Conducting*[6], from 1963. The first was designed for his conducting students at the Royal College of Music in London, as well as for organists, schoolmasters, and amateur orchestra conductors, offering instruction on the conductor's technique of "greatest simplicity and economy of means."[7] The latter book further develops these ideas and is meant for conducting students and general readers. He values an approach that is both economical and effective.

In Boult's view, the aim of the conductor's score reading is to comprehend the score as a whole – "a splendid elevation"[8] of music from the beginning to the end of the piece. As the first step in reading a score, he recommends doing a quick run-through without the piano – at the tempo that seems appropriate for the music (1920), or at a slightly faster pace (1963). In this newer approach of using a rapid tempo, Boult suggests doing several run-throughs – especially in the case of a modern score – not with the goal of hearing the score, but to observe its shape, balance, keys, and climaxes. He compares this reading to looking from a high hill, airplane, or bird's nest at a distant landscape. The purpose of this method is to grasp the architecture of the whole piece in sound – with a sense of balance in keys and climaxes, but not yet all the details, examination of which comes afterwards.

The second step is to examine the harmony in detail, especially focusing on difficult chord progressions. It is useful to use a piano at this point, particularly for challenging passages in modern music. Perfect pitch is helpful in recognizing wrong notes. The harmony may be read either page by page, by individual instruments or instrumental groups, or from another point of view. Boult emphasizes that at all moments of analysis, it is essential to

---

[5] Sir Adrian C. Boult, *Handbook on the Technique of Conducting* (Oxford: Hall the Printer Limited, 1920).
[6] Sir Adrian C. Boult, *Thoughts on Conducting* (London: Phoenix House, 1963).
[7] Sir Adrian C. Boult, *Handbook on the Technique of Conducting* (Oxford: Hall the Printer Limited, 1920), 7.
[8] Sir Adrian C. Boult, *Thoughts on Conducting* (London: Phoenix House, 1963), 7.

maintain a perspective of the whole piece. Therefore, it is beneficial to interrupt this detailed examination by repeating the first step of score reading.

The third step of score reading is to analyze the bar phrasing, which Boult calls "bar rhythms."[9] He connects measures into longer phrases and periods – for example, four bars of 3/4 becoming a single phrase in 12/4. He emphasizes that this is especially important in music with a fast tempo. This approach simplifies the piece in the conductor's mind and aids in memorizing it. According to Boult, as a result of score reading, the conductor should know the score by heart in the sense that they could write out a condensed version of it or play a reduction on the piano while imagining the instrumentation. However, they do not need to know each instrumental part from memory to conduct the piece.

After these fundamental steps, the conductor should return to the big picture of the score and reflect on the shape and structure of the whole piece, as if trying to fit it onto just two pages side by side. The details of the score should always be examined from the perspective of the whole. Thanks to this, the conductor won't become overwhelmed by them. Boult is against marking the score, except for unexpected bar groupings – such as a three-bar phrase in a four-bar passage – and important entries of instruments after a long rest. He recalls Sir John Barbirolli saying he preferred "to spend the time learning the music rather than scribbling in it."[10] Boult sees the risk that conducting from a marked score might result in all performances being the same, because the conductor "will think only of the marks and forget the music."[11]

The next step of the conductor's score reading process is to form an "emotional plot of the work noting the alternation of moments of excitement and calm."[12] The conductor needs to locate the point of highest intensity in the piece (usually there is only one in each piece) and gradate the climaxes accordingly. Attention should also be paid to descriptive words from the composer that refer to the character and atmosphere of the piece. It is very important that this emotional plot be a clear and definite idea, because the conductor chooses the tempo for the piece based on it before conducting the orchestra.

---

[9] Sir Adrian C. Boult, *Handbook on the Technique of Conducting* (Oxford: Hall the Printer Limited, 1920), 18.
[10] Sir Adrian C. Boult, *Thoughts on Conducting* (London: Phoenix House, 1963), 12.
[11] Ibid., 12.
[12] Sir Adrian C. Boult, *Handbook on the Technique of Conducting* (Oxford: Hall the Printer Limited, 1920), 18.

Boult remarks that in faster music, it is easier to determine the tempo, because it depends on the players' skill and the acoustics of the performance space. In slower movements, however, the tempo is often harder to figure out. He recommends basing it on a passage of faster notes that appears later in the movement, so that the tempo can be maintained. If the composer provided metronome markings, Boult emphasizes that they should be considered carefully. However, he does not see a need for using a metronome during score reading or conducting, because in his view, all tempos can be deduced from a ticking watch by subdividing 300 clicks per minute to receive tempos of 150, 100, 75, 60, and 50.

Concerning transposing instruments, he explains that there are two methods of reading them: one is imagining them in a different C clef with an adjustment of accidentals (he notably excludes the F transposition from this and does not mention the use of treble and bass clefs for substitution); the other is to move the entire part up or down by the appropriate interval. He emphasizes that the conductor should pick one of these methods and stick to it consistently. If the conductor is not fluent in reading C clefs, they should use the interval method.

Boult encourages conductors to develop and use visual memory when reading a score – to mentally embed the view of the page into the mind. In this way, eyesight helps internalize and absorb the piece. However, this presents limitations if the edition of the score is changed, or when conducting from a piano reduction. The latter should be avoided, especially because the balance of instruments is distorted. He recommends using only one edition of the score, to which the conductor becomes accustomed. Using several editions can be, in his opinion, confusing.

According to Boult, the best way to form one's own perspective on a piece is to listen to how others perform it – live or in recordings – always following along with the score. He encourages conductors to check the orchestral parts before rehearsals to ensure that they are clear and consistently marked with expression indications, rehearsal letters, and numbers. The conductor should confirm that all necessary markings are present beforehand, so that valuable rehearsal time isn't spent writing them in – nothing should need to be added during rehearsal. Bowings for the strings, breathing marks for long passages in the winds, and extra expression marks should be added beforehand by the conductor or section leaders, and only slightly modified, if necessary, in the first rehearsal.

Boult underlines that it is crucial to know the score thoroughly before making any interpretive decisions. A state of "half-knowledge" is dangerous, as it leads to embellishments rather than conveying the essential message of the piece. The conductor's work during rehearsals and performance is built upon the structure of the piece and the ground plan they created in their process of score reading.

Symbols and Markings in Nicolai Malko's Method

Nikolai Malko (1883-1961), the conductor and pedagogue, is the author of treatises on conducting, in which he also discusses matters of score reading. His motto is: "The *truth* is in the *score.*"[13] He calls the score reading process the "rationalization" of the score and "practice on a silent keyboard."[14] It is the mental side of conducting – the conductor's personal, preparatory work – that forms the basis for the performance. Without this preparation, the conductor would be "like an actor coming onto the stage without having read his lines beforehand. He would repeat the words of the prompter automatically, understanding only later their sense and meaning."[15]

The score, according to Malko, is the conductor's guidance chart and the only clue as to how the music should sound. In reading the score, the conductor "communes" with the mind of the composer, who is the creator of the music. While reading, the conductor actively uses their imagination to plan the performance and to solve potential issues in advance. The conductor's goal is the music.

In Malko's view, one way to get to know the score – to learn the music and the notes – is to play it on the piano, which becomes a substitute for the orchestra: "On the piano, one can project the orchestral music like a colorless photographic picture of an otherwise colorful landscape."[16] When the conductor reads a score on the piano, they transpose instrumental parts to the correct pitch and octave. Malko emphasizes that, while reading the score on the piano, the conductor should always actively imagine – with their inner ear – the sound of the orchestra and the color of each instrument.

After reading the score mentally, Malko recommends that the conductor further familiarize themselves with the music by listening to recordings. He insists on this order of activities because, otherwise, the conductor – under the influence of a recording – might become an imitator rather than a creative artist, which would paralyze their individuality. For students, he sees

---

[13] Nicolai Malko and Elizabeth A. H. Green, *The Conductor and His Score* (Englewood Cliffs, NJ: Prentice Hall, 1975), xi.
[14] Ibid., 14.
[15] Ibid., 12.
[16] Nicolai Malko, Conductor and His Baton: Fundamentals of The Technic of Conducting (Copenhagen: Wilhelm Hansen, 1950), 20.

listening to recordings of leading orchestras and conductors as a valuable learning tool, and they can – even should – imitate fine examples from these recordings. In his opinion, following the sound of the recording can be beneficial, as it is also a part of conducting – for example, in accompaniments. He advises listening to many recordings of the same piece, so that there is no unconscious acceptance of the good and bad characteristics of a single recording. Otherwise, the student "accepts the mistakes and the 'traditions' without question."[17]

The starting point of score reading for the conductor, in Malko's method, is to examine the instrumentation, which is visible on the first page of the score – indicating what kinds and how many instruments are needed for the performance. Next, the conductor translates the symbols in the score into sound. These symbols represent the composer's ideas and intentions. Malko insists that the conductor must always respect the composer as their author, and that the conductor's goal in score reading is to understand the content of the music, not just to know the notes. This requires performing a wide range of score analyses: style, emotional character, overall form, phrasing, harmony, techniques, and performance challenges. Later, when conducting, the conductor's gestures should express the composer's directions embedded in the score – and their meaning – to the orchestra.

Malko recommends reading scores from a broad, panoramic view before going into the details – first look at the whole forest, and only afterward examine the individual trees. The process is similar to reading a book. A necessary means of approaching the score, which plays a very important role in his score reading method, is phrasal analysis – the grouping of bars. Malko states that "Phrasing is the syntax of the score,"[18] and the conductor should carefully "count out" their phrases. He explains that a phrase begins when some kind of change appears in the music – for example, a new melody, rhythm, harmonic sequence, dynamic, or instrumentation. In the case of an upbeat, he suggests counting the phrase from the following measure[19]. Sometimes composers – for example, Mozart – use an interlocking phrase, where the end of one phrase is the beginning of another; in such situations, Malko advises that the conductor should give priority to the new phrase. In

---

[17] Nicolai Malko and Elizabeth A. H. Green, *The Conductor and His Score* (Englewood Cliffs, NJ: Prentice Hall, 1975), 12.
[18] Ibid., 35.
[19] Determining whether something is an upbeat or not, and where the measure group begins, can be challenging for the conductor – especially in fast tempos, as, for example, in the *Scherzo* of Beethoven's *Third Symphony*.

complicated pieces, he recommends drawing a separate graphic scheme of the measure groupings, showing the interrelationship of phrases and measures. He underlines that phrasal analysis supports the conductor's understanding and memorization of the score; it clarifies the structure in the conductor's mind and helps them notice subtleties and hidden surprises, such as added or omitted measures. As a result of phrasal analysis, the conductor reaches a broader understanding of the whole piece.

According to Malko, the conductor's role is to "*lead* a phrase and build a structure out of phrases."[20] He recognizes two types of phrases – those with an onrush (forward direction) and those with a backlash (a terminal feeling). He compares the continuous forward motion and ever-changing character of music to life itself: "Music is never static. It flows through time."[21] The shape of a phrase is clarified by the conductor through dynamics and tempo. He notes that, in score reading, the conductor also needs to pay attention to expression – the character changes from phrase to phrase – to ensure an inspired artistic performance. This is achieved through the technical means of tempo, dynamics, and articulation (*legato, non-legato*). At transitional points, it is important not to break the musical line.

Next, the conductor has to consider the style of the piece – "the exactness with which a composer's intentions are conveyed."[22] Malko insists that, to understand style, the conductor must know and feel the composer's personal approach, the general period, and the music of the composer's lifetime. Although not everything is written in the notes, this does not give the conductor the right to distort what the composer wrote or to rebuild it in a different way. Harmful performance traditions should be actively resisted.

Malko gives substantial attention to marking the score, which, in his view, serves primarily for reading and learning the score – not for conducting it. He advises using only pencils (not pens or markers), as they can be erased in case of changes. Handwriting in the score should always be clear and careful, without obscuring or covering any of the music.

In Malko's system there are two types of markings – those that don't change the music, and those that change the sound. The former are intended for the eyes. In the range of instrumentation, they include abbreviations at the beginning of the staff in case of disappearing staves or before a page turn. To separate multiple systems on one page, he uses a short double-line

---

[20] Ibid., 22.
[21] Ibid., 22.
[22] Ibid., xi.

mark. He notates the punctuation of phrasing and measure groupings below the bottom line of the score, and the sequence of phrases is marked under the first measure. Cues are marked as abbreviations in the top margin directly above the beat; simultaneous entrances of several instruments are shown as a column of abbreviations in the margin, starting with the most important instrument on top; sequential entrances are marked with an upside-down letter L for each instrument, in red or blue depending on the dynamic. For dynamics, Malko uses specific colors: he encircles *piano* in blue and *forte* in red. Additionally, he draws red half-circles for *sf* and red-blue half-circles for *fp*; he underlines *crescendos* in red and *diminuendos* in blue. For dangerous places in the music, he uses a special *nota bene* marking (NB) to alert and remind the mind.

The second type of markings in Malko's scores – those that alter the sound – are meant for the conductor's ears. In terms of instrumentation, these include adding or removing notes as a consequence of the historical development of instruments, especially winds. For example, in Beethoven's time, some notes were not playable, but today they can be added. He notes that conductors may also double instruments (indicated with a letter D next to the instrument) or omit them – not altering the composer's ideas or the composition itself, but rather adjusting the intensity of sound or the notation. For instance, winds may be doubled in the case of a large string section.

Malko recognizes two kinds of dynamic markings in the score – the overall dynamic of the orchestra and the dynamic of an individual instrument within the orchestra. According to him, the conductor has considerable freedom to adjust the dynamic markings in the score to balance the instruments, although this should be done with "fine musical sensitivity,"[23] because, as he explains: "No composer can ideally balance his score. He can state his general idea, but player and conductor have to work together to produce the score in the fullness of its beauty by intelligent dynamic artistry. The things the composer wrote must sound – if it were not so, he would not have written them. An orchestral dynamic as indicated by the composer is a dynamic of resultant sound."[24] It is the ear of the conductor that balances the melody, counter-melody, and accompaniment against each other, so that the composer's idea is clearly presented in the orchestral performance for the audience to enjoy. For example, he recommends that when a melody is accompanied by sustained notes marked *forte* or *forte fortissimo*, the dynamic of

---

[23] Ibid., 47.
[24] Ibid., 48.

the sustained notes should be dropped immediately after the attack. The conductor can also adjust the dynamics to shape the music, "to explain and deepen the musical sense of the score."[25] He emphasizes that there are subtleties of dynamics not written by the composer but needed for an artistic and inspired performance. In making such decisions, the conductor must be careful not to contradict or rewrite the composer's musical ideas.

Malko refers to the conductor's "improvements" to the score as "retouches" – for example, to create greater climaxes, more effective endings, heightened suspense, or stronger emotional effects. These, he cautions, need to be applied with extreme care. Some scores already contain such "retouches" made earlier by the editor, and it is important to recognize what originates from the composer and what does not. Markings that change the sound of the score also include the conductor's corrections of mistakes made by editors or by the composers themselves. Malko points out that some editions may contain numerous errors. He advises the conductor to proofread the orchestral parts against the full score before rehearsals, in order to find any potential mistakes – a step that will save time during work with the orchestra.

In his writings, Malko also addresses the topic of bowings, which he compares to breathing in a choir. When choosing bowings, the conductor needs to take into account the individuality of the orchestra – different bowings may be appropriate for different ensembles. For instance, he observes that Russian orchestras used to favor long and expansive bow strokes, while German orchestras preferred a shorter, more economical bowing style. He emphasizes that in tutti passages, uniform bowings across all string sections ensure a unified interpretation. What matters most to him is the naturalness of the bowings. For non-string players, to determine bowings, he recommends Nikolai Rimsky-Korsakov's method of whistling: "A feeling of breathing in would result in an up-bow marking and breathing out, a down-bow."[26] He explains that scores contain bow phrasing and bowing slurs, which are not the same: the former carries greater musical significance, while the latter is a technical means to realize it. In the case of a long phrasing slur, musicians may change bows at different times to achieve the desired *legato* effect.

While there are many useful markings a conductor can insert into the score, Malko is opposed to adding those that refer to conducting gestures,

---

[25] Ibid., 49.
[26] Ibid., 68.

as well as repeating the same markings. The ultimate goal for the conductor, he writes, is "to breathe life into the symbols on the printed page"[27] and, together with the orchestra, deliver the best possible performance of a piece to the audience.

---

[27] Ibid., 11.

Nadia Boulanger's Teaching of Score Reading

Nadia Boulanger (1887-1979) was a renowned teacher of conductors and composers from around the world. A master of score reading, she would sight-read full orchestral scores at the piano, reaching into the smallest details of the music. We learn about her teaching methods through her articles, lectures, and the recollections of her students. Unfortunately, she never published her own treatise on music.

Boulanger's score reading skills were legendary, both in tonal and atonal music. One of her students recalls a situation in which Boulanger, after receiving the score of the newly written *Perséphone* by Igor Stravinsky, played it for the students on the piano with one hand – transposing from the score – and conducted with the other[28]. The ability to play scores at the piano was something Boulanger also demanded of her students. If a student said they were not a pianist, she would reply, "It doesn't matter, play it anyway."[29] Another student, Mario di Bonaventura, recalls that during his studies with Boulanger, he gradually improved his piano playing skills and understood that in score reading, the goal was to "play the music, rather than the notes."[30]

An important method of score reading in Boulanger's teaching was to sing through the piece. She would ask students to read Johann Sebastian Bach chorales and fugues by singing one of the voices and playing another. She placed the highest importance on melodic lines, with particular focus on counterpoint. This approach to score reading strengthened the students' linear, horizontal hearing of the music. As part of their studies, conducting students would also orchestrate pieces and perform score analyses.

A central principle of Boulanger's teaching was the *grande ligne* – the idea that notes, like words, connect in a long line to express greater meaning. All the details of the score should be read in the context of the whole piece. She explained, "One syllable, one note, one note value is nothing,

---

[28] Léonie Rosenstiel, *Nadia Boulanger: A Life in Music* (New York: W. W. Norton & Company, 1998), 254.
[29] Philip Glass, *Words Without Music: A Memoir* (New York: Liveright Publishing Company, 2015), 137.
[30] Léonie Rosenstiel, *Nadia Boulanger: A Life in Music* (New York: W. W. Norton & in Company, 1998), 344.

and unfortunately the complexity of musical language often leads us to deconstruct, to focus on small things rather than on big ones, on detail rather than on the whole."[31] Her focus was first on the architecture of the piece, and then on its harmony.

Students of Boulanger learned to transpose music into any key at sight and to read transpositions fluently by mastering all seven clefs. This skill was developed, for example, through the practice of reading Bach chorales in which each voice was written in a different clef, or through exercises with frequently changing clefs. Reading in seven clefs was also a foundation of Boulanger's method for teaching music to children. According to this approach, a chosen line on the staff could represent any pitch depending on the clef, allowing music to be written without ledger lines. She emphasized the close connection between transpositions and clefs: "I contend that it is impossible to transpose correctly something which is a little difficult if one is not able to employ the clefs. You can transpose and the harmony comes right on, but in order to do something precise, it can only be done with the employment of the clef. This is the best."[32]

When reading a score, Boulanger looked for the inner logic of the piece – the "supreme order" by which it was governed. While sight-reading new compositions or skimming through scores, she would immediately notice details that were inconsistent with the overall structure of the piece or the composer's style. She could recognize the different solutions composers used for similar musical problems – a skill she also taught her students. Recalling his two years of study with Boulanger, Stanisław Skrowaczewski expressed admiration for her score reading skills: "Nadia was an extraordinary phenomenon. Her mind could be compared to a computer: she heard everything and had an excellent musical memory. She could sight-read a complex atonal score."[33] He remembered that while leafing through a score, she would immediately find weak spots, mistakes, and solutions that were not logical within the composition.

---

[31] Nadia Boulanger, "Concerts Colonne," *Le Monde musical 30, no. 11 (1919),* reprinted in *Nadia Boulanger: Thoughts on Music,* ed. and trans. Jeanice Brooks and Kimberly Francis (Rochester, NY: University of Rochester Press, 2020), 101-102.

[32] Nadia Boulanger, "Teacher's Lecture" (original English text, 1925), in Nadia Boulanger: Thoughts on Music, ed. and trans. Jeanice Brooks and Kimberly Francis (Rochester, NY: University of Rochester Press, 2020), 391.

[33] Agnieszka Malatyńska-Stankiewicz, *Byłem w niebie – mówi Stanisław Skrowaczewski w rozmowie z Agnieszką Malatyńską-Stankiewicz* (Kraków: Polskie Wydawnictwo Muzyczne, 2000), 47. Author's own translation.

Boulanger shared the view of Ravel and Stravinsky that the performer should, first and foremost, realize the score, not interpret it. She emphasized: "All that is needed is to play exactly what is written, exactly as he wrote it, and the effect the composer wants will be produced. It already contains the emotions that you are to feel. [...] The expressiveness of the music is the result of the succession and choice of notes, of rhythms, of tone-colours, and of dynamic marks made by the composer in his score and not added afterward by the performer."[34]

Boulanger was also famous for her incredibly broad knowledge of repertoire and various styles. As a performer – primarily a conductor, pianist, and organist – she concentrated on communicating the score to the audience. For her, the background of the piece and the life of the composer were of secondary importance compared to reading the score, though she acknowledged that such context, while not necessary, could help in discovering the character of the piece.

To achieve a deep understanding of a score, Boulanger emphasized the importance of recognizing the musical structure of the piece. She would say: "What is usually lacking in performance is the establishment of overall structure, and that is perhaps the most essential thing. Therefore, find the great, architectural elements, give them all their rightful importance, and watch the harmonic motion."[35]

Among Nadia Boulanger's students are many esteemed conductors, including Daniel Barenboim, John Eliot Gardiner, Igor Markevitch, Rico Saccani, Stanisław Skrowaczewski, and Antoni Wit.

---

[34] Nadia Boulanger, "Lecture for the British Broadcasting Corporation, *Music of the Week*" (original English text, 1938), in *Nadia Boulanger: Thoughts on Music*, ed. and trans. Jeanice Brooks and Kimberly Francis (Rochester, NY: University of Rochester Press, 2020), 418.

[35] Léonie Rosenstiel, *Nadia Boulanger: A Life in Music* (New York: W. W. Norton & Company, 1998), 264.

Eugene Ormandy and Inner Hearing of the Score

Eugene Ormandy (1899-1985), in his famous essay *"The Art of Conducting,"*[36] elaborates on the complex and demanding nature of the conductor's work, the first level of which involves personal study associated with score reading.

According to Ormandy, the conductor's purpose in reading the score is to "hear" it in their mind in the form of orchestral sound. To achieve this, the conductor must possess a thorough knowledge of the orchestra's colors and timbres. They must also understand the historical background of the piece and apply a deep knowledge of its stylistic conventions in order to build an interpretation. The piece always exists in a context; it is not separated from external influences. Stylistic validity should especially be applied to musical elements such as tempo and dynamics.

The conductor's work on the score is both technical and artistic, and at this stage they realize their role as a "musician, historian, stylist, orchestrator, and listener."[37] In the process of score reading, the conductor evaluates the music, balances "the many strands of the musical line,"[38] and creates a mental aural concept of the piece's architecture – an internal model by which they later guide the orchestra in rehearsals and performance.

Ormandy encourages conductors to make sensitive retouches to scores. In his view, performing older music usually requires the conductor to make instrumental adjustments and, at times, delicate rewriting of entire passages. This need arises due to changes in the construction and sound of instruments, the larger size of orchestras, and the increased technical skill of orchestral musicians.

In Ormandy's view, when imagining the sound of the score – "listening" inwardly to the piece – the conductor must adopt an objective attitude toward it. In shaping the musical flow and "spacing its climaxes,"[39] they should consider how the audience will receive and experience the piece. During the performance, the conductor identifies with the music, drawing

---

[36] Eugene Ormandy, *"The Art of Conducting"*, *The Conductor's Art,* ed. Carl Bamberger (New York: McGraw-Hill, 1965).
[37] Ibid., 252.
[38] Ibid., 252.
[39] Ibid., 253.

on the understanding developed earlier through score reading and personal study.

Ilya Musin and the Process of Reading the Score

Score reading is the focus of several sections of Ilya Alexandrovich Musin's (1903-1999) final book, *The Language of a Conductor's Gesture*[40]. In this treatise, Musin underlines the analytical nature of the conductor's score reading process, in contrast to the practical work of the instrumentalist reading their orchestral part. He gives advice on score reading, which he sees as a preparatory homework for the conductor, done as a separate task from conducting. The more thoroughly a conductor reads a score – with special attention to the accompaniments – the more productive they will be in working with the orchestra.

The goal of score reading, according to Musin, is to master the musical work and comprehend its "entire deep essence."[41] To achieve this, the conductor needs to unravel the composer's intentions and feel them as if they were their own musical thoughts. The most important aspect of mastering a score is understanding the content of the music and the development of its musical form. This can be accomplished only by reading the score. Musin warns against trying to get to know the piece through recordings, as listening to them is a passive process that reveals only the external aspects of the music.

In the process of reading the score, the conductor needs to discover their own emotional reaction to how the notes are connected. These emotions are then conveyed to the orchestra and the audience through conducting. Musin compares musical notes to words in a sentence – a series of notes achieves a new and greater meaning than a single word. This is something the conductor needs to consider while reading the score. Every conductor will arrive at a different emotional response to the content of the music, depending on their musical background, culture, and understanding of the notation.

The method of mastering the score recommended by Musin is memorization. Using this approach, the conductor gains deeper insight into the musical content of the score and develops a better understanding of the dynamics of its formal development. Memorization of the score is achieved through detailed and perceptive performance analysis. He emphasizes that

---

[40] Илья Александрович Мусин, *Язык дирижерского жеста* (Москва: Музыка, 2007).
[41] Ibid., 98. Author's own translation.

mastering the score is not about being able to write it down from memory – although some conductors, including Arturo Toscanini, have practiced this. According to Musin, as a result of score reading, "the conductor must remember not the musical text, but the music."[42]

Musin advises beginning score reading with a general picture of the music, and only then moving on to specific details. According to his method, the conductor first focuses on structural elements and constructs a plan of the piece – a kind of map. They divide the piece into sections and read each one separately. The next step is to compare the sections, especially in the case of reprise and exposition. Musin likens score reading to walking through an unfamiliar city – after looking at the map, we already anticipate what we will see, recognize the buildings, and walk toward them, not away from them.

In Musin's method, after grasping the form of the piece, the conductor concentrates on the details of the score – motives and elements that form phrases and sentences. At this stage, it is important to consider performance issues, such as trying out different tempos and dynamics, and to begin feeling the emotional content of the music. By reading small fragments repeatedly, the conductor memorizes the score. After this, they attempt to conduct the piece without the orchestra, as motor skills help them find the correct gestures needed to express the music. Finally, to check their knowledge of the score, the conductor may listen to a recording of the piece – preferably many recordings by different conductors, rather than just one. As a result, they may revise their performing intentions.

Musin recommends that, while reading the score, the conductor creates a plan for how they will work with the orchestra during rehearsals and tries to foresee the potential challenges in advance. Depending on the characteristics of the orchestra and the acoustic conditions of the hall, they may need to make adjustments to the score. These retouches come from the conductor's understanding of the piece's texture. It is important to consider practical matters such as bowings, which the conductor may sometimes need to change – either to clarify the composer's intentions or to reflect their own performance choices.

When revisiting a familiar score, Musin insists that the conductor read it as if it were a new piece, since "over the years the conductor sees more and

---

[42] Ibid., 101. Author's own translation.

more of what he had not noticed before."[43] In this situation too, score reading must be thoughtful and careful, not limited to the external aspects of the music. To understand a score, one must possess not only specific knowledge of the piece, but also general knowledge of structure, principles of formal development, style, and performance traditions. The conductor is the interpreter of the score – they "must not only know the piece thoroughly, but also interpret it."[44]

---

[43] Ibid., 101. Author's own translation.
[44] Ibid., 103. Author's own translation.

Conductor as Interpreter in Eugen Jochum's Phenomenology

The German conductor Eugen Jochum (1902-1987), in his philosophical text *"About the Phenomenology of Conducting,"*[45] describes the conductor's experience of reading a score and the process of creating a sounding image of the score in the mind. In his writing, the conductor is the interpreter of the score, standing between the composer and the performance of the piece. As a spokesperson for the composer, the conductor submerges themselves in the composer's work and nature: "The strength of an interpretative talent is determined by the extent and depth of this capacity."[46]

During the private process of score reading, which can take place in full isolation, the conductor creates an "independent inner image of the work,"[47] performs a detailed analysis of the piece, and identifies with the will of the composer. This is then immediately followed by the conductor's work with the orchestra, where they transfer their inner conception of the piece to the ensemble, refine certain aspects if necessary, and bring it into physical reality.

Jochum explains that the most organic way to create an inner image of the piece is by adopting a passive attitude toward it – abandoning oneself to the music – and reading the score repeatedly. Through absolute pitch, the conductor can hear the music directly, without the use of a piano. At first, the conductor concentrates on the general aspects of the music – the "facts" – and only later on the details, such as tempo relationships and the character of the themes.

As a consequence of reading the score, the piece begins to live on its own in the passive mind of the conductor, almost entirely independent of their conscious will and "shaping impulses."[48] The tempo of the piece finds itself. Only after the conductor has formed an "emotional field of tension"[49] with the piece can their personality and conscious engagement with it begin to

---

[45] Eugen Jochum, *"About the Phenomenology of Conducting,"* in *The Conductor's Art,* ed. Carl Bamberger, (New York: McGraw-Hill, 1965).
[46] Ibid., 258.
[47] Ibid., 258.
[48] Ibid., 260.
[49] Ibid., 260.

emerge. This is when the conductor performs a detailed analysis of the score.

While analyzing the score, the conductor examines aspects of the piece such as the themes – their structure, relationships, and transformations – the construction of the form, and the resulting relationships of key, dynamics, and orchestration. The conductor identifies the tempos, their relationships, and any necessary modifications, which have to be carefully balanced and considered in relation to both the overall structure of the piece and the local function of each tempo. Sections perceived by the audience as having a steady tempo often require the conductor to make subtle, imperceptible variations in order to achieve "the vitality of the musical flow."[50] In the nuances of tempo lies the art of the conductor's interpretation. The conscious phase of the conductor's private preparatory work also includes the process of memorizing the score.

When reading the score, the conductor considers how to transmit their knowledge and interpretive ideas to the orchestra. Then, in rehearsal, they inspire the musicians to achieve their highest artistic performance. Each player has to feel that they are actively shaping the music, supported by the conductor's leadership, which unifies the orchestra's diverse talents and temperaments. In this way, the conductor brings vitality to the interpretation. At the same time, they have to ensure that the realization stays faithful to the score and to the composer's intentions.

---

[50] Ibid., 261.

Erich Leinsdorf and Faithfulness to the Composer

The subject of score reading is addressed in Erich Leinsdorf's (1912-1993) book *The Composer's Advocate: A Radical Orthodoxy for Musicians*[51]. According to Leinsdorf, the conductor should read the score accurately and fluently, using both knowledge and imagination, to understand not only what is written but also how the piece sounds in a way that is true to the composer's intentions. He emphasizes that in score reading, the context of the piece must be taken into account, including the performance traditions and the language of the composer. The conductor's judgment needs to be grounded in an understanding of the historical background of the piece. It is a misunderstanding to play only what is written in the score, because notation is limited and musical values are relative. Additionally, he observes that scores may contain errors and misprints, so it is necessary to consult manuscripts and early editions of pieces to clarify the material.

To learn basic score reading skills, Leinsdorf recommends reading and playing four-part pieces in various clefs, especially from Johann Sebastian Bach's *Art of the Fugue*. The goal of this practice is to develop the conductor's ability to hear multiple voices simultaneously and to understand transpositions. Score reading exercises should be played at an even tempo, without stopping or slowing down, to maintain musical continuity. Leinsdorf highlights the connection between reading old clefs and transpositions: the A transposition can be replaced by the soprano clef, the F transposition by the mezzo-soprano clef, the D transposition by the alto clef, and so on. He supports score notation with transpositions because it helps recognize an instrument's range and aids communication between the conductor and the orchestra – the conductor sees the same notation as the orchestral musicians.

In Leinsdorf's method, fluency in score reading can be achieved by learning what to look for in the score and how to interpret it, as well as by acquiring knowledge of the traditions and the social environment surrounding the composer. He is particularly critical of overmarking scores with excessive annotations, which he sees as signs of insufficient study and refers to as "traffic signals." These markings may help in memorizing the score but

---

[51] Erich Leinsdorf, *The Composer's Advocate: A Radical Orthodoxy for Musicians* (New Haven and London: Yale University Press, 1981).

do not contribute to learning the music. Leinsdorf also argues that proper understanding of a composer's performance directions requires knowledge of foreign languages, especially in opera and choral scores. For this reason, it is important to always read scores in their original language to be able to refer directly to the composer's instructions. In longer descriptions, translating individual words is not sufficient, as the meaning may differ. Leinsdorf concludes that only with knowledge of the language can a conductor understand the composer's intentions.

He emphasizes the importance of studying composition, harmony, counterpoint, and form to grasp the underlying logic of a work. According to Leinsdorf, to read a score, it is not necessary to play it on the piano or another instrument, as many composers worked without one. He encourages developing the inner hearing and reading scores mentally and visually instead. In his view, a conductor must sing the score to understand where breaths occur between phrases, which also influences tempo choices.

It is the conductor's duty, Leinsdorf stresses, to dedicate themselves to investigating the composer's mind – their ideas, aims, decisions, dilemmas, and the ways in which they solve musical problems. A conductor identifies with the composer's personality much like an actor identifies with a character they portray. To achieve this, Leinsdorf believes that it is necessary to examine the entirety of a composer's output and to revisit works regularly, always with a fresh approach. To understand orchestral scores, a conductor must study all musical genres, including instrumental, vocal, and chamber music. Comparing different versions of a composer's work – including transcriptions – is also informative, as it enables the conductor to trace the composer's development and to recognize the decisions and revisions made to the piece.

Central to Leinsdorf's message is the idea that no work exists in isolation: "It is the result of a composer's development and of music's continuing history."[52] To understand newer works, one must study older ones. There are infinite connections between pieces. Composers learned from their predecessors, often engaging in musical borrowing and adaptation. Leinsdorf highlights Johann Sebastian Bach as a key figure in musical history, whose symbolic use of musical gestures laid the foundation for later composers.

On the subject of musical traditions, Leinsdorf distinguishes between the authentic practices of the composer's time and interpretive habits that developed later. For music written within strong performance traditions, many

---

[52] Ibid., 28.

expressive details were left unmarked in the score, assumed to be understood. He insists that conductors must study and internalize these "unwritten laws" – such as those related to ornaments, dotted rhythms, or articulation signs like the dot and accent – and recognize that not all notation is to be taken literally. A common mistake, according to Leinsdorf, is made in interpreting the *alla breve* time signature. He explains that it refers to the next higher rhythmic unit, which means it is not always in two. Leinsdorf also emphasizes that in dance music of folk origin, the notation is similarly approximate to that found in jazz. To understand such traditions, he recommends reading musical treatises, for example Carl Philipp Emanuel Bach's *Essay on the True Art of Playing Keyboard Instruments* and Leopold Mozart's *Treatise on the Fundamental Principles of Violin Playing*.

Tempo, in particular, receives extensive treatment in Leinsdorf's writings. He views it as a structural and expressive component, not a fixed numerical value. He notes that tempo markings often vary across editions and that metronome indications, while helpful, must be weighed against the character of the music and its internal relationships: "The words indicating tempos are always secondary to the notes when a conflict is apparent."[53] Tempos within a musical piece are relative and interrelated, closely tied to the work's overall structure. However, Leinsdorf warns that these relations should not be over-theorized. Rather than seeking rigid rules, he encourages conductors to choose tempos from the perspective of the piece's overall message and to cross-reference the score with the composer's other works. This comparative method of studying a composer's complete output helps clarify tempo relationships across phrases, themes, movements, and, on a larger scale, leads to a deeper understanding of the composer's markings and intentions.

Leinsdorf also discusses issues such as balance between instruments, the impact of concert-hall acoustics, ensemble size, and bowing decisions, all of which need to be considered in score reading and performance preparation. He argues that dynamic markings are relative and shaped by context and performance conditions, rather than being absolute instructions. Leinsdorf maintains that bowings are part of the conductor's interpretive vision of the piece and closely tied to the sound of the orchestra. In nearly every piece, he contends, there is one primary climax that the conductor should recognize as the emotional high point. A conductor must also con-

---

[53] Ibid., 109.

sider articulation and balance within the wind instruments. The overall balance of the orchestra is influenced by the ensemble's seating arrangement. In setting balance, Leinsdorf mentions a universal law: "the long note is louder than the short."[54] Adjustments to the score, including reorchestration or rebalancing, are sometimes necessary and do not contradict the aim of serving the composer – provided they align with the work's expressive goals and are carried out with good taste, knowledge, imagination, and reverence for the composer.

Concerning the use of recordings, Leinsdorf advises against relying on them during the process of score reading. He believes that recordings stand in the way of the conductor's ability to connect directly with the composer and to develop a personal relationship with the piece. While listening to recordings can be helpful at later stages of a conductor's work, Leinsdorf insists that interpretations must first be built independently – through the eye and the mind.

---

[54] Ibid., 199.

Gunther Schuller and the Quest to Know the Score

The conductor's reading of a score holds significant importance in Gunther Schuller's (1925-2015) philosophy of conducting, as presented in his book *The Compleat Conductor*[55]. The art of conducting, according to Schuller, is about achieving the most accurate acoustic result from the orchestra through physical gestures, which are a manifestation of the conductor's profound, detailed knowledge and emotional connection to the score. Schuller regards the score as a kind of sacred document that embodies and reflects the composer's creation – one that, through careful reading, becomes a source of inspiration for the conductor's re-creative imagination, enabling the translation of abstract notation into a vibrant performance with the orchestra.

The art of conducting is a collaboration between the conductor and the composer – even if the composer is no longer living. It is an interpretive, re-creative art. The conductor serves as a medium through which the composer's score is expressed. In reading the score, the conductor retraces the steps of the composer's creative process in order to understand the music and, as a result, form an authentic interpretation that derives directly from the score. The conductor's attitude toward the music notated in the score should be characterized by humility, love, commitment, and freedom from personal ego. Full respect for the content of the score is essential, which is why the conductor must engage in a never-ending quest to study the score and strive to know absolutely everything about it – "essentially why every note and every verbal annotation in that score is there, what their meanings and their functions are in the over-all work."[56] While complete knowledge of a score is not possible – since we can never be entirely certain of the composer's full intentions – it remains a necessary goal.

The conductor performs a thorough study of the score – what Schuller calls a detailed "score analysis" – which he considers the only path to gaining the knowledge and understanding necessary to reveal the piece's meaning and essence. This analysis includes a wide range of musical elements – the tools used by the composer – especially the functions of pitch, intervals,

---

[55] Gunther Schuller. *The Compleat Conductor* (Oxford: Oxford University Press, 1997).
[56] Ibid., 10.

and harmony; motivic and thematic content; rhythm, tempo, and tempo relationships; phrase and period structure; overall form; material hierarchy; homophonic and polyphonic textures; instrumentation; and dynamics. All elements in the score are interrelated, and the conductor's reading should be integral, synthesizing them into a unified understanding. In reading the score, the conductor should not only recognize the obvious elements but also look for the peculiarities, such as an unusual note, original orchestration, or unexpected voice leading. As a result of score analysis, the conductor will know what should be realized in performance – and just as importantly, what should be avoided, such as unnecessary exaggeration or misplaced emphasis. When preparing to conduct, the conductor's ears need to know what to listen for and what to hear.

There is no such thing as a single correct interpretation, but respect for the score and a thorough knowledge of its content can lead to a great one. As Schuller writes, "The secret of great artistry and true integrity of interpretation lies in the ability to bring to life the score for the listener (and the orchestra) through the fullest knowledge of that score, so that the conductor's personality expresses itself *within* the parameters of the score. It illuminates the score to the fullest."[57] Although musical notation has its limitations, Schuller emphasizes that there is far more in the score that is objective and precise than what is vague, undetermined, or left open to the performer. The notation reflects the composer's conscious choices and musical instincts. Since the time of Beethoven, composers have become increasingly detailed and reliable in their notational practices.

Developing an interpretation that is faithful to the score is not an easy task – especially in matters of tempo, dynamics, and articulation – as it requires great discipline from the conductor. While fidelity to the score still allows for interpretive freedoms, any interpretation that does not emerge directly from the score risks becoming a misinterpretation or superficial reading. The dangers of an over-personalized interpretation include attempts to "help" the composer, clarify the score, or bring out certain details – often based on the conductor's preferences rather than the composer's intentions. All interpretive decisions must be informed and guided by a clear and comprehensive understanding of the piece as a whole.

Schuller gives special attention to the matter of tempo, as it most significantly influences the shape, continuity, and character of a piece. In his view, verbal tempo markings refer to a range of metronome values:

---

[57] Ibid., 24.

largo/largamente (40-60), *adagio/lento/grave* (48-66), *andante/andantino* (56-90), *allegretto/allegro/allegramente* (88-144), *presto/prestissimo* (132-180). Tempo depends on the mood, texture, and density of the music – and in vocal music, also on the text. Tempo and musical content are interconnected; the composer had a specific tempo in mind when writing the piece. Metronome markings serve as useful clues in determining the relative tempo. Not all tempo modifications are indicated by the composer in the score, but they should still be realized and carefully balanced. The character and essence of a piece are also influenced by the conductor's choices regarding dynamics, articulation, phrasing, and bowing. Like tempo, dynamics are comparative within a piece and do not represent fixed or absolute levels.

In addition to reading the score, Schuller recommends that the conductor study the background of the piece and examine the factors that influenced its creation. This information supplements the knowledge gained from the score but cannot replace it. Conductors must also study both good and bad performing traditions. According to Schuller, "The study of performing traditions must be tempered by study of the score, although conversely the study of the score may also be informed by a study of the accumulated attendant traditions."[58] Good traditions are those that arise from the score, while bad traditions often originate from technical limitations or bad habits of the performers.

Regarding the method of score reading, Schuller believes that piano playing is not an essential skill for a conductor. However, playing piano transcriptions and reductions can support the process of reading and learning scores. Schuller also addresses the topic of memorizing the score, warning against surface-level memorization. He encourages conductors to know the score by heart while still keeping it on the stand for security and comfort.

---

[58] Gunther Schuller. *The Compleat Conductor* (Oxford: Oxford University Press, 1997), 61.

Sir Georg Solti's Reflections on Score Reading

In his Memoirs[59], Sir Georg Solti (1912-1997) reflects on the process of reading orchestral scores and the modifications he made to his method over the course of his life. He describes himself as an "architectural" conductor because he carefully plans his interpretation before working with the orchestra – unlike conductors who prefer to improvise in front of the ensemble. Before conducting, he envisions the shape of the music from the beginning to the end of the piece. He gives special attention to tempo and its modifications, and to elements which should be brought to the foreground, such as melody, harmony, and rhythm.

In his view, there is a direct connection between score reading and conducting. Thorough and detailed knowledge of the score is essential to becoming a great conductor; grasping only the outlines is not enough. The conductor must know the score intimately in order to teach it to the orchestra. Solti emphasizes that "when you go before an orchestra, you need to have a clear idea in your mind – a sound-image – of what you are trying to achieve."[60] This image reflects the conductor's dream, which they strive to fulfill through their work with the orchestra. As he puts it, "rehearsals exist in order to try to realize dreams."[61] The conductor's goal in working with the orchestra is to make the orchestra produce the sound that they imagined while reading the score.

The main obstacle to realizing this dream, he stresses, is an incomplete sounding image of the music in the mind of the conductor and the lack of confidence that arises from it. When the conductor knows exactly what they want, their body language – regardless of the level of their manual technique – will communicate it to the orchestra. When the conductor believes in what they are doing, the orchestra will follow. The same orchestra will sound differently with each conductor. As Solti remarks: "For me, the fight is with myself, not with the orchestra. If I can solve an interpretive problem in a way that satisfies me, then I am able to get the orchestra to achieve it."[62]

---

[59] Sir Georg Solti, *Memoirs* (Chicago: A Cappella Books, 1998).
[60] Ibid., 206.
[61] Ibid., 206.
[62] Ibid., 207.

Solti's most significant training in score reading and conducting took place at the Franz Liszt Academy of Music and during his work as a piano coach at the Budapest Opera in the 1930s. While working as a répétiteur, he played numerous piano scores of operas and worked with such conductors as Arturo Toscanini, Erich Kleiber, Fritz Busch, and Bruno Walter. He admired their interpretations and adopted the philosophy that the conductor's role is to serve as the interpreter of the music, faithfully realizing the intentions of the composer.

Due to his lack of visual memory, Solti describes his score reading process as slow, often taking weeks or months. Yet, this limitation became a strength, as it forced him to read every note in a score carefully and learn the score in great detail, a process he believed was crucial for effective conducting. He notes that a great deal of work is required from a conductor to arrive at an interpretation of a piece.

Later in life, Solti observed changes in his approach to score reading. In his early years, he focused mostly on the form of a piece, but with time and experience, he began to pay closer attention to detail. His earlier method involved going through the scores and marking all important elements – such as tempi and dynamics – in red pencil. He would then listen to a recording of the piece, either his own, the composer's, or one by a respected conductor, following along with the score.

In the last fifteen years of his life, however, he changed his method. When returning to pieces he had previously conducted, he would begin again with a clean, enlarged score to avoid needing glasses. He would sit at his desk with anticipation as he opened the score, and let the notes lead him to the composer. He viewed score reading as a dialogue between conductor and composer. To preserve a fresh perspective, he deliberately avoided listening to his earlier recordings of the same piece, though he occasionally listened to others' interpretations, using them as "catalysts" in his own study. His primary focus was on "developing ideas directly from the printed score"[63]. The daily routine of beginning each morning with score reading remained a constant in his life.

---

[63] Ibid., 205.

Creative Score Reading in Witold Rowicki's Aesthetic Approach

The Polish conductor Witold Rowicki (1914-1989) shared his insights and observations on conducting, score reading, and the nature of music in his book *Notes of a Conductor*.[64] According to Rowicki, the conductor's creative process begins with the very first look into a score. From it, the conductor draws thoughts and feelings – much like a painter observing a landscape or a model, moving from perception to emotion, reflection, and finally to expression. Everything in this process is connected, and the ability to form associations is essential. The conductor then communicates these internalized thoughts and feelings to the orchestra through posture and hand gestures.

When reading the score, the conductor uncovers, explores, and interprets the thoughts and intentions of the composer encoded in the notation. Through contemplation, they "compose the work within themselves,"[65] reaching a point where the score is no longer needed. The conductor transforms the score into live music during rehearsals with the orchestra. This is where the shaping of the music occurs. Rowicki encourages student conductors to observe orchestral rehearsals to understand how the score becomes music.

In Rowicki's aesthetic, "the score is a *created nature*, and its realization in sound is a *becoming nature*."[66] It is the conductor who breathes life into the score, reviving the music in performance – and this should be done, he insists, "with full breath and no hesitation"[67] on their part. He compares the score to a painted forest, which comes alive only when you walk and meander through it. Music, in his view, is the result of a compromise between the composer and the performer. It is not merely a sequence of sounding tones, but something that "belongs to the realm of the spirit and intellect, whereas sound belongs to the physical world and the senses."[68]

---

[64] Witold Rowicki, *Zapiski dyrygenta* (Warszawa: Oficyna Wydawnicza przybylik &, 2014). Author's own translation.
[65] Ibid., 131.
[66] Ibid., 86.
[67] Ibid. 124.
[68] Ibid. 43.

Rowicki also reflects on the difficulties composers face in notating their ideas – especially in contemporary music. He argues that the primary purpose of score notation is to provide clarity for the orchestra musicians who will perform the piece, rather than to assist in the conductor's search for the composer's intentions. For this reason, the conductor needs to make a special effort to reach beyond the surface of the notation and look behind the notes. Rowicki warns against two attitudes toward score reading: believing one has fully understood the score, or falling into a state of euphoria.

In Rowicki's opinion, all scores require improvements from the conductor for the benefit of the performance. Being faithful to the notation does not guarantee a good performance, and it is not enough to play the notes for the music to emerge. The conductor engages in a struggle to realize both the composer's and their own ideas. This includes discovering the emotional dimension of the music, which is composed into both the details and the overall form of the score. Expression emerges not only from the interaction of musical structures but also from the method of execution – how each note, phrase, and the entire piece is brought to life. Rowicki places great importance on bowings in the string section, viewing them as crucial to the ensemble's unity, musical quality, and expression. He would prepare his own bowings and send them in advance to the orchestras he worked with to save valuable rehearsal time.

According to Rowicki, listening to recordings does not reveal how the music was formed or shaped by the composer. Recordings can serve an educational purpose only in learning about the musical repertoire and comparing differences in interpretation. They remain products of the recording process – like a photomontage of the original creative performance and a piece of "finished" music. Relying too much on recordings, or adopting established interpretative stereotypes, can cloud the conductor's ability to read the score with fresh insight and independent judgment.

Rowicki opposes the notion of "stylistic correctness" or the idea of a single "stylish performance". In his view, great artists can perform the same piece in many different styles and still achieve brilliant results. Every conductor, like every musician, has a unique performing style. What determines the success of an interpretation is the aspect of time – it reveals whether the tempo, interpretive details, and musical expression have been correctly realized.

Stanisław Skrowaczewski on Interpretation and Recordings

Stanisław Skrowaczewski's (1923-2017) describes his approach to score reading in the conversation-based book *I Was in Heaven*[69]. As a child, he would read a vast number of scores on the piano, either by himself or in four-hand arrangements with his mother, without yet having the intention to conduct. In this way, he also learned about orchestration – a skill he applied when composing pieces for orchestra. For example, when he was nine, he composed two symphonies and an overture in the style of Mozart. He remembers constantly listening to music on the radio during his childhood and joining in by playing along on the piccolo flute. Thanks to all this, he became familiar with many pieces and practiced score reading at the piano from a very early age. Later, this would give him "divine peace, the feeling that the music lives within me."[70] When he began conducting, he already knew much of the standard orchestral repertoire by heart, including works by Haydn, Mozart, Schubert, Beethoven, Brahms, Bruckner, Schumann, Wagner, and Strauss. He continued to read and master orchestral scores throughout his life.

The most important elements Skrowaczewski focuses on when reading a score are the form, structure, harmony, and line of the music. With an intellectual and experience-based approach, he searches the score for sense, continuity, internal connections, unity and beauty. If a piece is merely linear, without harmony, it does not interest him. Harmony is essential to him – even in atonal music – because it "gives linear solutions special value."[71] He evaluates it and checks the vertical sonorities. Skrowaczewski does not trust the composer's metronome markings, due to the evolving capabilities of instruments and the possible euphoria on the part of the composer, which might lead to an excessively fast indication. What matters to him are the proportions and logic of the piece – the discovery and understanding of

---

[69] Agnieszka Malatyńska-Stankiewicz, *Byłem w niebie – mówi Stanisław Skrowaczewski w rozmowie z Agnieszką Malatyńską-Stankiewicz* (Kraków: Polskie Wydawnictwo Muzyczne, 2000), 47. Author's own translation.
[70] Ibid., 83. Author's own translation.
[71] Ibid., 110. Author's own translation.

which is a key task for the conductor. Without this, he believes, the performance would be a misinterpretation.

Skrowaczewski mentions that he prefers and enjoys conducting scores by heart. Knowing the score by heart allows him to have a vision and a condensed image of the piece in his mind. It gives him an advantage in feeling his own interpretation and sensing the continuity of the piece's development, and it is also helpful for managing tempo changes. He finds conducting from the score limiting, as it requires good eyesight, constant visual tracking of the notation, and page-turning, which are distracting. In the case of accompaniments, however, he has a rule to conduct with the score, because he has experienced situations in which soloists made mistakes and skipped several measures. In such moments, the score serves as a kind of protection – he can whisper the measure number to the orchestra to save the performance.

When preparing for a concert, Skrowaczewski listens to recordings. He is interested in them from a historical point of view, tracing both old performance traditions and new trends. He analyzes and compares how different conductors have performed the piece. Especially interesting to him are cases in which the composer themselves recorded a work – such as Rachmaninov – or when a conductor recorded the same piece at different stages of their life. Skrowaczewski does not listen to recordings for inspiration or to learn an interpretation; rather, he analyzes and compares them historically, tracing the continuity of traditions and the development of interpretations. Sometimes he finds enormous differences between recordings. For Skrowaczewski, listening to recordings is "a journey into the history and tradition of music,"[72] which allows him to formulate and establish his own perspective.

When performing the same piece again, Skrowaczewski begins by analyzing his previous recording, not by reading the score. He accepts some of the solutions he used before and rejects others. He forms his interpretation of the work only when rehearsing with the orchestra – observing the musicians' level, listening to the acoustics of the hall, and responding to his own feelings at that particular moment in life. These factors influence his choice of tempos and their proportions. Once he establishes an interpretation, he maintains it through subsequent rehearsals; he believes that this consistency in the conductor's approach is essential for the orchestra to understand the interpretive concept. He strives to create a new interpretation of the piece

---

[72] Ibid., 79. Author's own translation.

for each performance, rejecting repetition, which he finds boring and unsatisfying. Creating something new each time is possible because, as he emphasizes, "Music is born now, in this very moment."[73]

---

[73] Ibid., 88. Author's own translation.

2 Contemporary approaches: interviews

Challenges in Score Reading – *Antoni Wit*

Interview[74] on 20 February 2024

Could you recommend any preferred method for reading a score, learning it, and as a consequence, understanding it? How should one work on a score?

I can tell, how I do this. Despite the existing vast availability of recordings, I try – and I'm quite consistent in this – to study or familiarize myself with the score without the help of recordings. Only after I have an image [of the score in my mind], I confront it with a recording, because, as it often turns out, I might have done some mistakes. I play the piano quite well, thus I often try to play the score as if I were making a piano reduction, though it is only for my educational purposes. It is not a true piano reduction, but one that gives me an idea of everything that is happening in the orchestra. Of course, with 19th-century scores this is relatively easier, whereas with 20th-century scores it is often not very easy. Nonetheless, even if it is not possible to create a piano reduction, I delve deeply into it for having a good understanding of the harmonic content of the piece, which is later coated in its proper instrumental form.

Going into more detail, do you begin your work on a score by reading individual instruments, groups of instruments, or the whole, and which are the elements you particularly focus on?

In general, I don't read individual instruments, because a score always exists as a whole, as a blend of sounds. Therefore, the harmonies are very significant, though melodic lines need to be followed, too. In polyphonic scores this is a challenge, but honestly saying, there are not very many truly polyphonic scores, and the homophonic texture is more prevalent.

You mentioned about playing the score on the piano – does the piano help you in creating a mental image of the orchestral sound?

---

[74] Interview originally in Polish; translated by the author.

Not of the orchestral sound, but of the content, especially the harmonic one. Sometimes these harmonies can be very complex, and their connections can be very intricate, too.

Do you find any challenging issues or difficulties when reading scores from certain composers?

I consider scores from around the mid-19th century particularly challenging, such as those by Berlioz or Wagner. They often use four horns, each in a different transposition, yet the resulting music is quite simple. This can be quite thankless and time-consuming, especially since we are used to transpositions in F, or even in E and E-flat. However, the 19th-century scores can have horns in D-flat, in B, and practically every transposition imaginable, sometimes yielding very surprising results. A notable example is the beginning of the second act of *Don Carlos* by [Giuseppe] Verdi, where four horns, each in a rare transposition, play in unison for eight measures, which is something not immediately apparent [from the notation].

In many old textbooks on score reading there is a focus on reading transpositions by clef substitution.

That makes sense, under the condition that one knows clefs well.

And in cases when the music is more chromatic or atonal, would you also use such substitutions?

Well, that reminds me that there are, unfortunately, pages in scores which are extremely difficult.

Exactly. When changing the clef, the key is considered, but if the music is atonal, it can be a challenge.

Reading with the help of clefs works well, for instance, with horns in E or E-flat. I only regret that during my time at the Academy of Music, no one taught me about this perspective, which is fundamental. You need practice and fluency to read such horns smoothly, as there are also changes in various chromatic and enharmonic signs. It is crucial to be accustomed to it. Therefore, it would be good if a score reading student first mastered clefs, as it is a foundation and aid at every stage.

Nowadays, many students rely on recordings to help themselves read scores, sometimes even from the very beginning of their score study. What role, in your opinion, do recordings play in the process of working on a score?

It is quite clear that turning to a recording means a huge shortcut. In case of conductors, there is always a danger that a particular recording might impose a certain interpretation. If it is a piece that we are unfamiliar with, that interpretation might seem definitive, even though it might not be, leading us to copy aspects of that recording – which I consider as a big mistake. Why? Because it is often just a replication of the external characteristics like tempo, *rubato*, tempo modifications and changes, instead of something that comes from the conductor's own preferences and intentions. But without these, the result can be random or even grotesque. I recall here one exam from the time when I worked as a professor of conducting. A romantic piece was conducted by a student, very poorly. During a later discussion with her professor, I asked him whether he was approving such an interpretation, and he, somewhat helplessly, admitted that the student convinced him, "saying that she had been listening to Bernstein's recording." And this is how it looks – such a typical mistake, because Bernstein's interpretations are often far from the score, but they are infused with his own individuality. In case of a conductor who copies the external traits of an interpretation but is not able to fill in the substance – it results in a caricature – which was evident during that exam.

Could you advise on how to practice score reading to achieve proficiency and be more efficient in this process?

The main thing is to develop fluency in reading notes. I'm not sure by which method this could be achieved, because I wasn't taught one. While on a scholarship in France, I learned that the French have such methods. One principle is that when reading a piece, even at a slower tempo, it should be done without stopping. This is difficult because it requires continuous reading without pausing to figure out what the notes are. In France, this aspect was heavily emphasized.

When a conductor creates their own interpretation of a piece, how crucial is it to refer to different sources like the composer's letters, comments, or musicological references? In what degree this kind of knowledge helps in the conductor's work? Does the conductor begin work starting from the score, or is it more beneficial to gather earlier as much information as possible to understand the piece, the composer, when creating the interpretation?

What you are saying might be very useful, maybe even necessary. I must admit that I have never started my work on a score from such descriptive sources. I assume that all, what the composer intended to write, is in the score. However, despite the precise notation – ambiguities are inevitable, and they exist in the music of many composers. I have a unique experience in this regard, having conducted many contemporary pieces in the presence of their composers – like [Krzysztof] Penderecki, [Wojciech] Kilar, [Henryk Mikołaj] Górecki, [Krzysztof] Meyer, and also Olivier Messiaen, Sofia Gubaidulina, Arvo Pärt.

It was interesting to experience what attitude the composers had toward their work. Each composer had a different approach, even diametrically opposed. Some composers, as Lutosławski and Messiaen, tried to be very precise in their notation, yet even in their works there are things that raise uncertainties or questions. How precise was Lutosławski's notation is proven even by metronome markings, which he inserted into his scores. Often he indicated tempos that don't align with divisions on a traditional metronome, for example 172 or 55. But Lutosławski wrote these after his deeper thought, and when performing his own pieces, which I know about, he conducted the written metronome markings exactly. This shows that he heard the music very precisely before writing it down.

What preparatory processes relating to the score should a conductor undertake to be ready to conduct an orchestra?

When preparing a rendering of any score, I often conduct at home without any music playing, imagining the music flowing in real time. Each conductor eventually develops their own, let's say individual, method, and then a test of this is the live performance of an orchestra. But a preparatory test can be also listening to a recording, because in our times it is hard to avoid it, and it would be unthinkable not to listen to the existing recordings. While listening to a recording, a confrontation between what I imagined and what is in the reality takes place, plus of course [a judgment], does it somehow suit me. Among the evaluated factors the most important is the tempo. First of all, this is the factor on which the conductor has direct influence, such as on almost none of the other elements of music, and, from the other side, the tempo is something extremely important and often determines the success of a performance.

Are there things that are not written in the score, but a conductor needs to consider before conducting the orchestra?

There are certainly things that, although being written, may not be well understood by the conductor. I can give here an example of such a Lutosławski dilemma. If a melody is played by two instruments, say a flute and a clarinet, and the composer indicates *mezzoforte* for one and *mezzopiano* for the other, does it mean that the one marked *mezzoforte* is more important and should play louder, or, knowing from experience that in this register this instrument is weaker, there is written a higher dynamic for it. This is very easy to imagine, for example the lowest notes on flute have, let's say, such a constant dynamic, they cannot be too quiet, and not at all possible too loud – thus even if we write *forte*, relatively the sound played in this register by a clarinet, or especially by an oboe, will be much louder. And here is the dilemma – did Lutosławski, by writing for one instrument *mezzoforte*, and for the other *mezzopiano*, want to indicate that the instrument with *mezzoforte* is more important, or he just wanted to even these natural differences of instrumental volume? We can say that this dilemma in fact is unresolved.

I encountered a situation in a Messiaen score, where the composer wrote pianissimo for brass instruments and piano for clarinets but added a verbal comment that the clarinets should play in the background of the brass instruments. Therefore, such a balance was planned by the composer, and even though clarinets have a higher written dynamic, they are supposed to sound quieter than the brass instruments.

As you see, apparently he felt the need to provide those additional clarifications.

This was related to balance of instruments. For a conductor a fundamental issue, as you mentioned earlier, is the choice of tempo. Reading the score, based on which elements in the score can the conductor find out the right tempo for the music?

It is difficult to provide here a precise verbal explanation. From one side, the descriptions in scores, especially in composers like Brahms, are quite specific. Is it *Andante* or *Andante sostenuto*, *Allegro* or *Allegro con brio* – we translate it somehow to ourselves, but it is always "digested" by our own musicality and there's never a guarantee that the composer perceived it and heard it in just the same way we do.

Would you like to add anything more about score reading?

I regret only that in common the level of score reading stays, as it seems to me, much lower today than fifty years ago, primarily because of the easy access to recordings, which remove the necessity for conductors to imagine the score without relying on existing auditory models. Thus, I fear that this discipline is right now not on such a high level, even among conductors, as it should be and was fifty years ago.

In the book *Conducting – A Matter of Life and Death*[75], Professor Antoni Wit explains that work on a piece he often starts "by scoping the score, generally flipping it through"[76]. He recommends Leonard Bernstein's advice that next time you take "a score you've previously conducted, you should study it from the beginning, as if it would be a new piece."[77] He believes "every conductor should be able to play the score on the piano,"[78] following Henryk Czyż's teaching to "find beauty in the music."[79] After an initial phase with the score, Professor Wit visualizes the entire score and considers the performance side of music, predicting "where there might be challenges for the orchestra – and of what type."[80] Eventually, he listens to recordings of the piece – especially his own, but also by other conductors – "not to imitate, but to find various solutions, that I like, and draw conclusions."[81]. He highlights the usefulness of conductors preparing their own orchestral materials with specific details, including bowings, which "influence the quality and character of the orchestra's sound."[82] Professor Wit is meticulous in learning scores and prefers to conduct from memory, using scores only in case of conducting accompaniments.

---

[75] Antoni Wit, *Dyrygowanie – sprawa życia i śmierci – Antoni Wit w rozmowie z Agnieszką Malatyńska-Stankiewicz* (Warszawa: Czytelnik, 2021).
[76] Ibid., page 411. Author's own translation.
[77] Ibid., page 411. Author's own translation.
[78] Ibid., page 412. Author's own translation.
[79] Ibid., page 412. Author's own translation.
[80] Ibid., page 412. Author's own translation.
[81] Ibid., page 412. Author's own translation.
[82] Ibid., page 100. Author's own translation.

Realization of the Score – *Jorma Panula*

Interview[83] on 15 September 2023

Would you have any advice on score reading for conducting students?

I've written sometimes – or I have this one paper, but nothing else. I just shared it like this, only with the students. Nothing has been published[84].

One of the questions students often ask concerns the use of recordings for score reading, since they are so easily accessible. What do you think about the role of recordings in reading scores? Should they be used, and if so, when?

No recordings at all, just the score. Otherwise, it goes in through the ear, and people start to mimic. When it gets [into the mind], it's imprinted there, and it affects their own, they end up copying unconsciously. That's why: no recordings.

How can we create a mental image of the score and develop the ability to imagine the orchestral sound?

First, when you open the score, read the lines. What instrument, what key (if there is one), and what time signature – those are the first things. Then you start reading it at the indicated tempo, *Moderato*, *Allegro*, in your own *Allegro*. There is no need for a metronome – never think about it, have your own metronome. Mozart didn't have one, neither did Haydn. Others added [metronome markings] later. Well, Bartók wrote metronome markings, and Stravinsky too, but Stravinsky didn't follow them when he conducted, so it doesn't matter.

Is it acceptable that performances differ from the written metronome markings?

The metronome marking doesn't mean anything. If it says *Allegro molto*, then that's your *Allegro molto*. What is *Allegro molto*? It can be anything.

---

[83] Interview originally in Finnish; translated by the author.
[84] After the interview, Professor Jorma Panula shared several of his materials with the author, which are referenced below.

It is the conductor's own *Allegro molto*. Otherwise, it's like a gramophone. And then, when you start reading, you read at that tempo. You turn the pages, read the whole section. Then it gets photographed in your mind. It is there.

When reading the score, do you play it on the piano, or sing it?

No, no.

Do you imagine the notes?

Yes, just silently. If I'm on a plane or a bus, you can't sing there.

I remember you saying about this in masterclasses – when you sing, you focus on just one thing, but without singing, you can concentrate on a larger number of things at the same time.

Yes, and in tempo. Then, when you look at it a second time, you remember many things along the way: *Aha, yes, I saw that, I heard that, that's how it goes.* So, you read it several times, and it stays there *[touches head]*. The next movement, the same way. And then, you can leave it for a month. When you come back to it, it has been "incubating", so to speak. Incubation – you remember much more. That's how it gets into your head.

Is it so that during the second reading, we go a bit deeper into the score, see and understand more?

Right, you see what you saw the first time, but now much more. Always more and more as you read it again. For some conductors, one time is enough, for others, it is not.

It is a challenge for students to decode transpositions...

Yes.

When reading old score reading books, you often see the clef substitution method – for example, that an E-flat transposition in treble clef can be changed to bass clef with an octave and key adjustment. But in chromatic and atonal music, this method becomes difficult.

No such thing, you just do it directly.

With the horns in F, should we think a fifth down?

Yes, just a fifth down.

And the same with the clarinet in B-flat, a major second down?

Yes. You just have to read and remember. If it is in F, you'll see it over time. This is just about habit, year after year, and then it becomes natural.

When we have different simultaneous transpositions – as for example in Berlioz's **Romeo and Juliet***, where the horns are in four different transpositions that change constantly, and together form chords – should we think, for example, that the E-flat horn sounds in E-flat major and the E horn in E major at the same time?***

That is too complicated.

So, it is about the transposing intervals?

Yes, that's it.

When you read a score, do you think about layers, such as melody, harmony?

It is a whole. You read the whole score *[shows horizontal movement with hand]*, but at the same time you hear it vertically – harmonies *[shows vertical movement with hand]*. This is how the music moves, how it sounds. You either see it or hear it.

How important is balance?

Balance is important. The composer writes the music, but the composer does not always hear everything.

Does the conductor need to make changes?

Yes. Let's say, with Mozart you don't need to make many changes, but with Beethoven – yes, and with Brahms and Romantic music in general, it is necessary, because nowadays instruments are different. For example, the F horn in Vienna back then had a smaller sound. Now we have the double horn with B-flat horn, which is much louder. You can't play the nuances that are written, because when they see *fortissimo*, it becomes "whoooom" – awful. You can't play like that; you have to change everything nowadays. Balance. In Sibelius's music you have to adjust it all the time, and with Brahms as well. Even with Wagner, but he already knew a lot about this.

When we read the score, we also want to understand it. What is the most important for a conductor, or conducting student, to analyze when reading the score?

I've written an analysis of all the Brahms symphonies and the Sibelius symphonies as well. Every bar: "Be careful here, it is too loud there, it has to be played softer", "Here, this part should stand out, but this part should be quieter."

Can students attending your masterclasses learn this from you?

Yes, but it is best if they read it beforehand. With no talking during rehearsals – I don't like that. It wastes too much time. If they have only twenty minutes to rehearse, there is no time for talking. The proper language is body language, this is their language *[shows hands]*; but in Germany and America, they talk far too much. Show what you want, instead! There's no time.

But what happens before the conductor goes in front of the orchestra? What do conductors need to do to be prepared, to have a clear vision of the piece for the rehearsal? When they get in front of the orchestra, might they need to change that vision?

The first time the orchestra plays, conductors do their best to communicate the vision they have.

They start from their own vision, don't they?

Yes, and in some places, they have to exaggerate to make the orchestra notice. If you play normally, like in a concert, it won't work. Then the second time, things change.

Does a conductor need to be a musician who is able to hear the score and form a vision of the piece from reading it?

Yes, and the conductor must know a lot before standing in front of the orchestra.

Is it important for the conductor to gather knowledge by reading books and other written sources to understand the composer's style?

Yes, of course – the history, the background.

Do they understand the score better this way?

Yes, to understand the composer's soul.

Is it good if the conductor also thinks about bowings?

Yes, but if the conductor is not a string player, the best is to ask the concertmaster. You discuss it beforehand, because one set of bowings won't necessarily work for the next orchestra. The bowings depend on the sound of the orchestra. Berlin plays very differently from Finland. You can copy them, but it won't always work.

Is it best if the conductor has played in an orchestra?

Absolutely.

That would help...

With the overall sound. Those who have played in an orchestra are privileged. And those who come straight [to conducting], they can't imagine the sound because they haven't heard it. It is very difficult for those who only play the piano, because it is not an instrument of the symphony orchestra.

But if we play chords on the piano to check the score, is that a good idea?

Yes. If it doesn't sound right, you can check the harmony. Sometimes, when I start from the very beginning, we go slowly through the piece. I conduct like this – one, two, one, two – *What is the harmony, what is the chord?* You must know right away. Many people don't know how to read a score.

Is this also important when there are many layers, like in Mahler or a polyphonic work?

It is the same. You have to know the whole thing. New music is even more difficult because you need to know how it sounds. Even the composer doesn't always know everything.

In case of new music – is it a good idea to listen how the computer software plays it first?

Well, you could do that.

Would it be better to have more rehearsal time with the orchestra?

There is no time. If it is a premiere, you'll have three days of rehearsal – no more.

Are there certain decisions the conductor needs to make when reading the score, like about articulation, phrasing, breaths?

Those are all part of it.

You mentioned tempo earlier.

Yes, it goes in the tempo; you must hear the phrasing. The conductor must know the score completely by heart, in that sense. You need to know in advance what is coming next. You have to hear it ahead of time. The conductor is ahead, then playing comes after.

To learn the score by heart, does the conductor need to return to it?

Yes, when you read it again, you remember more and more each time. Read it so many times that you remember it.

Do you work on one phrase or one section at a time?

It depends. You need to know how much rehearsal time you have, since there are other pieces as well. Ten minutes of modern music and then half an hour of something else, and then a solo – you have to calculate how much time each piece will take. Difficult pieces take more time. If the orchestra doesn't pick it up right away, you work on it one section at a time, slowly at first, then at full tempo. It goes slowly, but nowadays orchestras play everything. Even in Finland, sight-reading has improved a lot compared to the past. But if you go to London, they know how to do it, and you have to play the music correctly right away.

Is the conductor's own interpretation, own vision, possible to realize then?

Interpretation, or rather realization – interpretation is not really the right word. Ravel said, "Don't interpret my music, realize it." That's it – you must realize the music as it is written, not interpret it. You must interpret that this is a G, and it is *mezzoforte*, nothing more. The tempo must stay the same. You need to realize the music with the orchestra, not interpret it.

To understand the composer's language – is it good to read other pieces they composed, because the same markings can mean different things with different composers?

Exactly. That's why you need to know the composer's language. Each composer has their own language. Sibelius and Chopin are different.

What do you do when you have a difficult piece like Stravinsky's Rite of Spring, where there are so many layers at the same time? If you try to play it on the piano – Stravinsky even made a version for two pianos – it is very difficult to play it as one person.

You can't play it.

Is it therefore so that you have to choose or practice two layers together, then add a third? What do you do when there are a lot of figurations?

First, what you want is the foundation – the bass, the cello – separately. Then the woodwinds, then the brass. You can read these separately: this group, that group, then the next one – strings, winds, brass. And only then do you combine them all together.

Combining can be difficult...

Yes, it is. And there's no need to rehearse everything if the strings have it difficult. Here is a difficult place, at letter B – everyone is playing, but it is not necessary. You just need to rehearse what is difficult, that group, only the strings. And there – only the winds, no strings. Often what happens – it is just tutti, tutti, tutti...

Earlier, when the conductor reads the score, do they need to think about what is difficult and what needs to be rehearsed?

Exactly, you need to know that. That's why you must know the instruments. You must know what clef it is in. And if you can play several instruments, even better.

And how does a conductor get the result they want?

You need to know that there is a difficult spot coming up and focus on the group that has it. The others might only have long notes, but here there is something rhythmically challenging. You rehearse that spot, then come back to the whole. There are often too many sounds in rehearsal – too much is played unnecessarily. Everyone is playing, but it should only be that one group. That is more relaxed for the orchestra, and they won't get tired.

Do musicians understand their role in the music better this way, and play better together?

Yes, exactly. There are a lot of these situations. For example, if the brass is far away, and there is an upbeat, they can't hear anything because they are far away. But the strings can hear the brass – it is easier for them.

The conductor needs to hear the score, have their own vision, but also think about what to rehearse and how to work with the orchestra. It isn't just about what to do, but also how to do it. How do we achieve all of this?

Young conductors, when they are rehearsing, do tutti, tutti, tutti all the time. Then they focus on a completely different issue, like the second flute –

"Let's do it again," so the second flute gets it. But not everyone needs to play – just that group. They don't realize this; they don't know how to rehearse. That's why you should do it this way – it is rehearsing technique. The hardest thing is rehearsing.

Does a score reading technique also exist?

Yes. If you play through everything first and then want to analyze, take only the strings and read that, or the woodwinds, or the brass. The foundation is always important – the bass line; the bass must be heard. Is it the contrabasses, the bassoon, the tuba, or something else – you need to hear that. Harmony and the bass are important. The theme, of course, has to stand out when you find it. What is the first theme, what is the second theme – you need to recognize these when you read the score. There's a lot happening, even in just four bars. Everyone is playing at once, so you have to hear it. If the second violins and second clarinet are playing the same thing, you have to hear whether they are together. If one is late, you have to rehearse it.

Young conducting students mostly like to listen to recordings. If we have already read and studied the score, is it a good time to listen and see what conductors who have recorded the piece do? Can we learn something from recordings?

Yes, but first you need to have your own understanding, your own vision of the whole. Then you can listen a little – to compare, for example, if the tempo matches. Mostly just the tempo. Then the sound, the balance. But first comes your own vision. When you listen, the most important thing is the tempo – to find the tempo. And then you're surprised, because someone did something that is not even marked – you have to reject that. You must be loyal to the composer – the composer's message as purely as possible. If it is Ravel, you know that it is exactly right. But with others, it isn't always so clear. You only learn this later. Brahms's tempos are good, but then someone might do these big things – because this is Romantic – and stretches it, slows it down; be careful, that's not it. Do not imitate. If you don't know why, then why slow down? First, stick to what's written. That is strict. There is no such thing as interpretation – only realizing the score for the orchestra.

Is the conductor's focus on how it sounds?

It is about the ear – the ear is for music, not here *[points to the head]*.

How can fluency in score reading be achieved?

You must read slowly, so the harmony is included as well. The theme, the harmony, the bass – it all has to be heard at once. Then you can say, *Aha, there's something here to fix!* You have to hear it.

When string players read a new piece, they often first play it slowly, then in tempo, and then from memory. Is it the same way a conductor imagines a score?

Yes, exactly. The harmonies have to come together – then the whole picture. You rehearse a section, whether it is ten bars, from one repetition to another, or a particular phrase. First go slowly, so that everyone gets it. After that, you can continue and start again. Then you move forward and return to the beginning to get the whole picture – you can't stop.

Because music is flowing?

Just as the composer intended. Only after that has been done can you move forward. And you have to count the time. If there is no longer time for rehearsal, you must go for the whole.

Is there anything else that comes to your mind about score reading – anything you think is also important?

This is the practice – how to rehearse and how to read the score. First, the whole picture – the entire section. Then you repeat it so many times that you begin to hear the harmonies. Either you check it on the piano, or you go through it like this *[shows a horizontal and vertical movement]* – and you grab the harmony: *Aha, that's the harmony!* But all the while, even if you're going slower.

Read it slowly and continue?

Slowly at first, until it begins to come together. You find all the notes that are important. If a harmony is missing a third – *Who has it?* When the third is too loud, then you have to point it out. For example, if the third is in the trumpet and the second violins, but it's marked *piano* – the trumpet is playing too loud. You need to adjust the balance. These balance issues come up in Brahms and in many other pieces, where the harmony doesn't balance out evenly. But with Mozart, it is pretty good – when you take a harmony from there, it sounds right. But often, especially with the horns – which are too big nowadays and always too loud – you have to remember to tone them down a bit. Sometimes the bassoon too – back then, they had small French bassoons, even until the 1960s, but now there are German Heckel bassoons, which have a much bigger sound. You have to take all of this into consideration when reading the score. Top orchestras – they know. Horn players, bassoon players know. All of them need to be careful.

Do musicians adjust the balance themselves?

Yes, they know and they do. However, brass players often don't adjust – and they are too loud.

Richard Strauss said the brass is always too loud.

Yes, yes. That's how it was back then, but nowadays they know better. Even in Finland, it's gotten pretty good, though there are still some egotistical people: "Here it says *fortissimo*" – yes, but it is relative. In this acoustic, with a small orchestra, you have to play a *fortissimo* that's softer. That's all new for them.

Toscanini said that forte sometimes means piano – do we have to keep that in mind?

The acoustics dictate everything.

We can't really imagine the acoustics in advance. Is that why we need to listen carefully and make real-time adjustments during rehearsals?

Exactly. That's why you rehearse. If you rehearse in one place and then move to the concert hall – it is completely different. In Budapest, for example – I've been to Hungary many times – the rehearsal space is different from the concert hall, and you only get the general rehearsal in the hall. Those three hours are not enough. But if the musicians have played there before, they know what *forte* and *piano* sound like in that space.

The rehearsal hall and the concert hall should be the same?

Yes, but having the same place is not always possible. Everything is alive through the ear. You have to rehearse everything by ear. Not just "Here is a *forte*" and "There is a *forte*," but then it turns out to be something else. It is living – it has to be heard. But there are many conductors who don't change anything – they play the same way, and they beat the same way, no matter what.

The balance on recordings is different, but if you go to a rehearsal, when someone else is conducting, you can listen and observe?

Yes, you can't rely on recordings, because it is all done with microphones – it is nothing like a live performance. That's why I tell my students to go to orchestra rehearsals – that's where you learn. But usually, no one is there. When I was studying, I was at orchestra rehearsals every day. Back then, they were held at the university. Two orchestras played there – one started at 10 a.m., and the other at 2 p.m. When they switched, the custodian would adjust the layout. I sat through all of them – three hours and three hours – and during the one-hour break, I worked on my theory exercises for the conservatory, for the Sibelius Academy. I read, did all my assignments there.

Did you have a score with you?

Always. Always a score – otherwise, there is no point. You have to know: *Aha, why is the conductor correcting that? Was there a mistake, or something else? And why aren't they correcting it?* You need to understand – if it's because of a lack of time, they just have to move on. But make a note: *Hey, be careful here.* Don't just stop and talk – you save time this way. If you stop and start explaining, it becomes egotistical on the conductor's part.

Does the conductor develop through their own conducting in the process of rehearsals and concerts? Understand and imagine more, improve their ear and rehearsal technique, so that life experience makes the conductor more knowledgeable and more effective in their work?

Yes, it is like that. Then, with the orchestra, you tell the students to pay attention. At letter B, for example, there is a problem here, and another one over there. Warn them in advance, so they notice: "Aha, yes, there was a mistake there." You have to know this in advance. That's why I point out the difficult spots.

You train their ear as well?

Exactly. Then afterwards, you discuss it – and watch the video, of course. That's the most important thing. Video is the most important of all. You see and hear the mistakes too. It doesn't lie. If someone says, "Yes, but I did it," you can say, "Okay, let's watch the video" – then they go quiet. When you are focused on something, you don't notice everything. But when you watch it on video – it is clear. You were focused here, but you made a mistake over there. You can't grasp the whole thing. Maybe you were concentrating on a horn player or the strings – and you forgot something else. This is what practice is for. There is nothing you can do in advance, and no book can teach you. It is all about practice – everything.

So, reading the score is an important part, but only one part of the conductor's work, which involves much more that they still need to do?

Yes, the "whole world", indeed. Reading the score is homework. You need time for that. You have to give it time – unless you are one of those [eidetic types]. Abbado was one – he could read the score straight away. Mehta too. They had photographed it. Saw it once, and it went in. But there are not many like that.

Reading requires practice, it takes time?

Yes. That is why you have to read and read, think and think. You can read on the bus, on the plane. Just read. This kind of practice *[waves hands]*, dry one, has no use.

Conductors don't need to practice with the hands?

No. You just need to know how to conduct and where to give clear beats. You need to know those, but you don't need *[shows hand movements]* – that is unnecessary.

If the conductor is a good musician and understands the phrasing, that helps?

Exactly. And the bowings too. For example, Brahms's slurs are not bowing slurs.

Are they phrasing slurs?

Musical phrases – long ones. They can't be played with a single bow stroke. It's the same with Sibelius and others – you can't play them like that. And if the orchestra has 12 first violins, or only 6 or 4, it's a completely different bowing. That has to be done beforehand. Otherwise, you waste time and then, "Oh, we'll have to redo the bowings," and the winds are left waiting.

Should it be done beforehand or during the break, but not within the time of rehearsal?

Exactly, there is no time. Maybe for a few important adjustments, but it shouldn't take more than ten seconds.

Is it good for conductors to have their own orchestral material?

If they can. But with new music, there is no such thing.

It takes time to prepare your own material, and conductors need to make sure all the bowings are correct?

Yes. But if they have their own material and then go to another orchestra, the players might say, "No, this is not for us." And then – well, this is what happened to Paavo Berglund. He was here [in Finland] and specialized in Sibelius's bowings. Then he went to London – and during the break, they took his material away.

They had their own bowings and wanted to use them?

Yes, his idea didn't work. You have to know the orchestra's level. Bowings are a whole different world.

Why are they so important? Is it because they give shape to the phrases?

Yes, because if you take the musical phrase *[demonstrates a long slur]*, the bow won't last and it will end in a *diminuendo*. The musical phrase comes first. If it is too long, then you change the bows.

The phrase requires this change?

Yes, the phrase is the most important – the musical phrase. Bowings are just technique. And it is not about the technique – otherwise, the music changes completely. No, it has to follow the music.

Next, there is also the matter of color. For example, in Debussy's music – how do you get the color, this Debussy sound, to come through? Do you need to know the composer's language?

Yes, you need to know the style of the winds – how they played back then. Let's say Debussy was in rehearsal and he listened – "No, no" – and he rewrote it. That is how Debussy's style comes out – a lighter touch on the strings. But here [in Finland], the strings are pressed too much. In Hungary, the Czech Republic, Poland, and Russia, for example, there is a heavy bow. In England and in Sweden – they have a lighter touch. It is a different style.

From the different playing style comes a different color?

Yes, it is the style – lighter playing, and not too much *vibrato*. In Sibelius, there is never a lot of *vibrato*. In France, however, there is much more *vibrato*.

So, a conductor needs to understand the playing style?

Yes, that's why the composer goes to the orchestra rehearsals and says, "Yes, that's good," or "No, do it like this." Stravinsky was never satisfied – "No, no, no." Here in Finland, Erik Bergman was like Stravinsky – "No, no, no." Debussy would go to his rehearsals, listen for ten minutes, and if he was satisfied, he'd leave. If the atmosphere was right, he was happy.

The conductor needs to know in detail what was important to the composer?

Exactly, yes. That is why you need to read. Many composers have written. Debussy wrote a lot – he was also a music critic. He wrote many books. Stravinsky, too.

Poetics of Music, An Autobiography, *conversations with [Robert] Craft… Which comes first – should we look at the score first, or is it better to read about the composer before starting to study the score?*

It is better to read the background first.

Before we start reading the score?

Yes, of course.

That way we would already be placed in the composer's world of music?

Otherwise, you won't understand why, in all the world, the composer wrote like that. But when you know the composer's life story, it helps a lot. What kind of life did the composer have? Where and how did they live?

Sometimes the composer was also a performer, and they had their own performance style.

Yes. Mozart played himself and wrote for that.

All of these things go into the conductor's preparation before they go in front of the orchestra? All of this is important and must be taken into deep consideration?

Yes, exactly. You need to know all of it. Sometimes people come from Asia, and they don't know the background. Then they go to Vienna to study – and I doubt they read much. Over there, at the conservatory, they don't talk about these things. You have to read for yourself. But there is not enough time.

Can conductors use this knowledge to understand the score – and then apply it in their conducting?

Right. If it is a completely new piece by a composer you've never heard of, it is a good idea to say a few words about the composer to the orchestra as well – what kind of person the composer was. That only takes two minutes.

Is it a good idea to explain to the orchestra, for example when we have a piece by Messiaen, what the piece is about?

Yes, but not like [Sergiu] Celibidache, who would talk for half of the rehearsal. Everything he said was very fine and full of stories, but it didn't help the music. Background and knowledge – yes, that is interesting. But then the orchestra [sighs], "Okay, okay," and asks, "Is it an upbow or a downbow?" – and that is what matters.

Nowadays, there is a lot of noise in the surrounding world, which affects conductors too. Do they need silence to read the score and imagine the music?

Yes. But some people from Asia always listen to the music they are about to conduct. They listen to it constantly. It is already in their head when they go to conduct, but they're still listening, all the time. It's terrible. That means they don't understand anything. They are just copies, clones – there are thousands of them. It's a shame. When a problem comes up – how do you solve it? They do not know. "Well, Karajan did it this way, and someone else did it that way," they say. But how do you solve it? "Um, um, um." Next one: "Um, um, um." And there is only one who can actually do it.

If you understand why Karajan did something – what his musical reasons were – then can you go that way?

Yes, if you understand it and agree with it. But you don't have to. There are many good things, but also some places where – *no, no slowing down; no, the nuance is wrong.* Look at the original first, and only then will you see why he did it. There are many factors. Don't change anything immediately. If you do make a change, ask yourself why, and stick to your decision. If you want to change it tomorrow, then change it.

Does reading the score require time to really think it through?

Yes, right. Otherwise, you are like a weathervane, always changing. Before you get in front of the orchestra, there is a lot of work to be done. One piece can take thousands of hours. You can't say exactly how long it takes – it is different for everyone. Everyone absorbs music differently. Many young people today only focus on the effects. Big *crescendos*...

Fast, loud sounds?

Too fast, and everything is just about the surface. No music.

I remember you saying, that the head shouldn't be in the score during conducting, but the score should be in the head, right?

Yes, don't keep your head in the score, the score needs to be in your head. That is exactly it. You can't see anything otherwise. Contact – contact is the most important thing. And if you ask the orchestra, they will say, "We didn't see – the conductor's head was always buried in the score, we didn't see their eyes." They want contact. That is why I say – "Next one."

So, conductors should be ready – know the score so deeply and hear so clearly in their mind that, during rehearsals, they can focus on making contact with the musicians?

Yes, exactly. And show it like this – clearly, an entrance, a cue.

Professor Jorma Panula has written several texts and materials for conducting students, which include guidelines on score reading. He views the work of the conductor as tripartite: "the endless study of the score, rehearsing the orchestra, and performing the rehearsed music."[85] The first requirement for leading an orchestra is learning the score – "I assume you know the scores and their secrets. To many the score looks like a secret code."[86] Already for the first rehearsal, "the conductor must come in front of the orchestra thoroughly prepared with their knowledge of the score,"[87] and "have a comprehensive understanding of it."[88]

The point of a concert, he emphasizes, is to convey "the composer's message, through the orchestra to the audience,"[89] and the conductor should not add their own interpretations to the pieces – "At this point, I must protest as a teacher. I often say that generally, the composer is also musical, so trust their taste and bring it to life in an audible form."[90] Professor Panula also cautions against imitating CD and video recordings, because "the orchestra musician will notice immediately, and the authority is gone."[91]

---

[85] Materials by Professor Jorma Panula, shared with the author.
[86] Jorma Panula, *Some Hints to the Conductor.* Text shared with the author.
[87] Jorma Panula, *A Masterclass for Conductors*. Text shared with the author.
[88] Materials by Professor Jorma Panula, shared with the author.
[89] Ibid.
[90] Ibid.
[91] Ibid.

Studies in conducting, he insists, should begin with musical literacy: "Learn to play on the piano or your main instrument in four clefs, starting with a classical quartet. Next, transposing wind instruments."[92] A conductor should have knowledge of instruments, their technique and historic use, as well as compositional and performance styles, and acoustics. In the directives for organizing conducting studies at the Sibelius Academy, Professor Panula includes "score playing using your own instrument."[93]

---

[92] Ibid.
[93] Jorma Panula, *Directives for conducting studies at Sibelius Academy,* 1992. Text shared with the author.

The Score's Logic and Layers – *Osmo Vänskä*

Interview on 6 September 2023

Could you share your thoughts, insights, and any advice on orchestral score reading?

This is an important topic, and every single conductor has their own method of studying and analyzing scores. For me, studying "older" scores such as Beethoven, Schubert, Brahms, etc. is a very different process than studying a newly composed score.

With the works from the more standard repertoire, there are often dozens of recordings available to hear on CDs, YouTube, or Spotify. For pieces I know well, I generally just study my already marked-up score. For things I am learning from scratch, I listen to several recordings and hone my own individual interpretation. After years of score study, I have a very specific method of marking my score, and the process is much faster than it used to be. Even now, however, I sometimes change my interpretation when I revisit a score, so I always have a big eraser nearby.

When you receive a score from a living composer, you must find your own way to understand what is written. I am a terrible pianist, so I use the piano only for brief examples, to grasp the harmonic world and what it sounds like in specific sections. Most of the time, once you get an idea of what the composer is writing, you don't need to hear every single harmony because it is like eating the same kind of soup – you recognize some ingredients, but it is usually about the overall flavor. When you know that the composer has used a notation program such as Sibelius or Finale, it makes things much easier. You can always request an MP3 file which allows you to hear exactly what the piece, as a whole, sounds like.

Does a computer program help with score reading?

I don't use a computer program when I am studying a composer's score, however I use it when studying the scores I compose myself, which I am doing more and more lately.

When one creates a score using a program, the printed parts are generated from it, ensuring that every marking that is in the score also appears in the parts. A long time ago, before the computer era, you had a hand-written score, and then you had to check the parts for mistakes – sometimes, there were many! This is a major advancement in the notational system: computer composing programs ensure that the musicians receive exactly the same music as the conductor.

Studying any kind of music, the first thing one needs to find out is the tempo. Tempo is the most important element because if the music doesn't swing – whether slow or fast – it becomes flat and boring. The tempo doesn't always need to be exactly the same as the composer writes it in the score; composers provide only guidelines for conductors. In my case, I often find the tempo by singing or playing the phrases – I also frequently use my clarinet for this – and they should sound natural. You start with that, and then you identify the sections: this is one kind of music, that is another.

Do you recognize the sections of the music at this stage?

It really depends on the piece.

The next thing I focus on is changes in the beat patterns – for example, when a piece starts in 4/4 and then shifts to 3/4 or 3/8. How is it going to be in this tempo? Do I need to show half notes or quarter notes? Eighth notes or quarter notes? I always write the beat pattern in my score above the notes.

Then, very important for me is deciding on and marking phrases. I use the 'x' mark – an 'x' without any number indicates a 4-bar phrase, 'x5' a 5-bar phrase, and 'x6' a 6-bar phrase. This is my way of going a little deeper and understanding is this a 3-bar phrase, a 4-bar phrase, is it 2 + 2 or 4 + 4.

In all music, whether an "old" score or a work by a living composer, these two elements – beat patterns and phrases – are fundamental. After that, one needs to study the score thoroughly before the first rehearsal to minimize surprises. There will always be some unexpected things, no matter how well you have studied the score, but hopefully, they will be manageable and not too significant.

Has access to recordings influenced the way you work on scores?

Yes, but only more recently. I must admit that I once believed what Panula said, "Do not listen to any recordings, because then you are losing your own way!" Wanting to be a diligent student, I followed this advice, and too late – far too late – I realized that this was a mistake. How does one learn to conduct a Mahler symphony? If you try to sit down and read it all, it is just impossible, because these are long pieces! My current method is to listen to as many recordings as possible – but always with the score in hand. If you can find 10, 15, or even 20 recordings, that is good. For me when I listen, in my head it is mostly, "No, I don't know how you can do it this way – it is not in the score, you can't do that!" The process of listening to recordings is not about copying how someone else did it, but about developing your own understanding of the music.

Is it about recognizing differences from the score?

Recognizing whether a recording follows the score and seeing where the differences are. I call this process "learning away," meaning recognizing what is actually in the score and trying to steer away from traditions and conductors' individualized opinions. For me, the most important thing is written in the score itself because that is how the composer wanted to leave their piece for us. My job is to follow what they wrote, and I am happy if I can truly do so, even in cases where I don't understand why it is written that way because it is not my piece to change. I have sometimes asked – what do we think when we visit a museum and look at paintings? As a conductor, I think of the score as a painting. Imagine saying, "Oh, I don't like that yellow there – I would have changed it to brown. And this one? No, this red isn't good, it should be black." That is what we are doing to the scores when we don't follow what the composers are saying.

When a composer writes *accelerando*, it is our duty to do it. How much *accelerando*? That is more up to our own interpretation. But I cannot go against the score, even if some famous conductors or recordings do – no way. That is the essence of it. In my experience, I can only begin making my own decisions about any famous piece – let's say, Mahler symphonies, which are among the greatest challenges for a conductor – after I have heard enough material to understand how they can be conducted and how different people interpret them. That is why it is so important to always have the score on hand. Without it, you may hear something you like, but if it is not in the score, we are going against the composer's wishes.

It is not the piece itself.

When I have listened to 15 or 20 recordings of a piece, I reach a point where I feel – okay, my tempo should be this, these are the most important things that we need to hear, and those other lines should be less prominent.

Access to recordings influences the way we approach reading scores. Does listening to recordings lead to a wider and deeper understanding of the score?

Absolutely. In my opinion, deep understanding cannot come without all those layers. I learn how others have done it, how they understand things, and that helps me find my own way without copying.

Before opening the score, do you read what was written about the composer?

At my age, I'm fairly familiar with the composers' lives, but I definitely did a lot of reading back in my younger years. So much music is about life, death, love and other human situations and emotions.

Let us talk about Mahler again – I have now completed the whole cycle of recordings. His music is so much influenced by his life experiences. The fact that his wife Alma found someone new while she was married to Gustav Mahler – that happens in life. It is not only between Alma and Gustav; there are millions of similar stories. I think music is about something that is a personal experience yet happens everywhere – you turn on the TV and see recognizable situations within minutes. It doesn't need to be specifically about Alma – of course, it could be about any of us. That is why we love this music and feel that it is our own – because we are in the middle of all those emotions. That is why I would say that it doesn't hurt to know about the composer's life, but if the music is written by a skillful composer, the emotions will come from the music itself.

I would still like to ask a question about working with the text of the score. The old handbooks focus on reading transpositions using clef substitution, but some conductors prefer to read transpositions with the transposing interval instead. Perhaps the approach differs between older and newer music. Do you use clef substitution for reading transpositions?

As a wind player, I am used to transposing, so I just flip a switch in my brain and know which interval to use when naming the notes. It is a very helpful skill to have!

The purpose of studying is to give you an idea of how the music unfolds. One needs to find the easiest and most natural way of working because studying, in any case, takes a very long time. If someone is a skilled pianist, that is a great method, but if not, one must find another way. The goal is to make the music sound in a way that speaks to the listeners – to you first, then to the players, so they understand how the conductor wants the music to speak and sing. One has to reach the point of being clear about one's vision of the piece, and there are a million different ways to go about doing that.

You mentioned that it is important to figure out the composer's language from the score, as this makes the whole piece easier to understand. How can we get to know the characteristics of a composer's language and get deeper into a score?

Each composer has their own unique voice. Some composers are very rhythm-based, some focus a lot on creating beautiful melodies, some pieces, especially nowadays are meant to be quite robotic. The easiest and fastest way to get to know a composer's "language" is to study as many of their works as possible.

One of the most fundamental things to figure out with each composer is their use of rhythm, articulation and texture – is the music dancing or more serene? When it comes to people playing the bass instruments – their role impacts the melody. In a band today, the bass and percussion usually take care of the swing, even in rock music. Then, you have players responsible for harmonies, those who lead the melody or sing it. Essentially you need to take an X-ray of the music to find out everyone's role and what propels the piece forward. Often, in rehearsals or concerts, when I focus on the rhythmic element, I have to conduct differently than when I turn to the melodic lines, and my motions need to give information to both groups, so that everything comes together.

I have been thinking of these elements as musical layers – a melody, a second melody, then the harmony, the bass...

For me, layers are more linear *[gestures a horizontal line]*, while rhythm is not a layer – it is something like punching, even in slow movements of Beethoven symphonies – *[sings the beginning of Eroica's second movement]*, and at the same time *[sings the rhythmic element]*. In older music, many slow movements have a sort of funeral march like this. The rhythmic part is not only important in fast passages, but even more in something like a Brahms slow movement.

Is there a character coming from this rhythmic element?

Yes, otherwise the piece sounds long, but it does not move us to tears if the rhythmic element is missing. It is like the building we are in – there is a lot of structure beneath us, holding everything up, yet we don't see it in the final product.

You mentioned that phrasing is important, how do we find it?

By singing – a lot of singing. The motion of it – there is a lot of push and pull. Phrasing is very often connected to dynamic markings. A phrase should always feel alive. A good example is *[sings the opening motive of Beethoven's Fifth Symphony in two versions, one with crescendo and the other with diminuendo].*

Is it about finding direction and emphasis?

Like growing – where is the emotional high point? *[sings example phrases]* There are always moments when you need to feel where the music is leading, and as a conductor, you must show these physically. That brings me to an important point – the more you can communicate through your body language and hand gestures, the less players need to pick up their pencils to mark everything in rehearsals. This also gives you much more flexibility in concerts since your interpretation isn't set in stone in their music. When we play the same program in a concert two, three, or even four times, it cannot just be a copy of the first performance.

When reading a score, the conductor creates a sounding image in the mind, a personal interpretation, makes decisions. Upon working with the orchestra, might some of these decisions need to change?

Sometimes, it depends. There is no such thing as simple music, but some music is understood more similarly by everyone. In Mozart symphonies, for instance, there are differences, but in some ways, it is clear. However, when you go to composers like Sibelius, it is not clear at all for those who are not used to his language. There are so many details that should be in the right place before the music starts to sound good, and if you are not aware of them, it sounds very bad. That is why now I have my own orchestral materials for all the symphonies by Sibelius, Nielsen, and Beethoven – to save time. If someone has done it in a completely different way, you use a lot of rehearsal time for erasing and writing down new things. Having your own materials is a practical solution to ensure your ideas are there from the start.

There might be so many details that there wouldn't be enough time to go through all of them during rehearsals?

Exactly, yes.

Going back to the composer's musical language – when reading a score, do you think it is necessary to study other pieces by the composer to get a deeper understanding of their music, or should the focus be only on this one piece at that moment?

If you start now, you are already too late – you don't have time to go anywhere else and must try to survive with that one piece. But yes, of course, the more you know about the musical language of a composer, the better. It doesn't hurt anything, it only helps.

Do you think that score reading and score analysis are actually the same thing, happening at the same time? Or would you say that you first read the score and then come back to analyze it?

Good question. Well, I'm not a scientist, nor am I the theoretical type – for me, they are the same thing. Why analyze a score if the goal is not to perform it? When I was at the conducting class in the [Sibelius] Academy library, I saw a Beethoven score – maybe the *Fifth Symphony* – where someone, whose name I fortunately don't remember, had done some sort of analysis. Every second or third bar had markings, the entire score was covered in *[gestures handwriting]*, with the most knit-picky details being pointed out. I could never read off of a score like that!

Placing the theory layer on top of the music?

Exactly. As I said, it was every second or third bar, and I thought – no, thanks. If I even tried to understand and started to conduct that way, I wouldn't be able to make any music. The comments written there may have been important to someone, but when you read a score, if you are a musical person, you just start to feel how it should go – how the composer wants it to go – and develop your own understanding of it.

Should you always keep in mind that the purpose of reading the score is to serve conducting and performance?

If you go to the world's top restaurant, you don't need to know every ingredient in the recipe the chef used – you can enjoy the final product if it tastes good. But if you are a chef, you must know those details and how to create that experience for the guests. How does this translate to music and the score? The conductor's goal is always to create emotional feelings for the listeners of the concert. At some point in the process, you must feel those emotions yourself to understand: "Okay, this is where we are going." You need to live through the ideas in the score before you can begin to conduct and share your feelings with the orchestra, shape the music and bring it all together for the concert.

There needs to be a feeling of the music. Is it also about picturing?

Yes, some people may picture various things and situations in their minds. We all can recognize the feeling of hopelessness and then recognize the moment when it starts to lose this angsty kind of feeling – when the music starts to move away from that. It reminds me that most Finnish conductors show only Paavo Berglund's angry type of face. Perhaps that is not right, but these days, there are so many smiling conductors – and that is unfortunate.

Are conductors smiling too much on the podium?

You can smile if there is a reason for it, absolutely, but I once experienced a conductor leading Mahler's *Ninth Symphony* while smiling constantly – nothing but smiling – and that is fake. This piece is about death, about facing the fact of dying soon. Mahler himself suffered from heart failure, and then you see a conductor smiling – it was just terrible. I am sure many people criticize my face for being so serious, but I believe that the best way to show feelings is through body language – including facial expressions – that reflect how the music is going. This is something that can be shared with everyone on stage. But happiness is not the only emotion which should come out from music.

After recognizing the musical elements in the score and finding the feeling of the music, how do you balance these aspects, make decisions and bring everything together?

It should all come from the score. This applies not only to the conductor and the orchestra but also to chamber music and even solo performance – you must create something that has logic. There are often lots of connections in the music. You need to find out how what came earlier connects to what we hear now, so they are not two separate, different things.

To find the inner logic in the piece?

Exactly.

How are ideas connected and built into a whole?

One should learn every single section to see the big picture in the end. Once you know those small details, you are more able to put everything together, ensuring that there is a longer musical line.

Some conductors conduct scores by heart. What is your opinion on this, and would you have any advice on how to memorize scores?

I am not particularly good at that. I played as a professional clarinetist for eleven years and had some great experiences with conductors who performed from memory. However, I also had many very bad experiences where it was obvious that the conductor wanted to conduct from memory but didn't know the piece well enough. Instead of leading, they were leaning on the players. In my opinion, it is okay to conduct from memory if you can do it without causing harm to the musicians. When we listen to recordings on the radio, however, do we know whether the conductor has the score in front of them or not?

No, we don't.

As long as the musical experience is great – fine, who cares? Another thing to consider is that conducting is relatively easy when everything goes well, but what if something happens in the concert? Suppose an English horn comes in one bar too early – can you manage it? Do you know the piece so well that when chaos starts, you can notice and react – now, wait, now, go? There are conductors who have the score in front of them but don't open it, or they glance at it sometimes without watching it at all. That is not important, whether conducting is done by memory or not. The goal is to make good music, not to impress the audience. In some countries, many people judge how good a player or conductor is based on just these kinds of things.

Are there any anecdotes you could share about score reading?

If I have heard any anecdotes, I have forgotten them! But speaking from my own experience – conductors, please don't leave your studying process too late. Start earlier. If possible, study the score intensively, then set it aside for at least a few days, if not weeks, before returning to it. Let it rest, and when you return to the same piece later, it will come back to you – that is the key. I've had many experiences where I started studying something far too late, leading to a near-panic reaction in the first rehearsal – and maybe even in the concert. So, don't underestimate the importance of time. The more time you spend with the score – if you use it effectively – the better. However, if you are not focused, just having the score in front of you won't help if your mind is elsewhere.

Have you been using a method of reading scores slowly at first and then in tempo?

For me, that sounds like a method used when practicing an instrument – you start by playing your part slowly, and then you build it up bit by bit until you can play it in tempo. This doesn't work for score reading. You first need to study the score thoroughly to reach the point where you can make decisions based on the various sections. Score reading is not about progressing bar by bar like with an instrument.

Contemporary scores are often so complex that it takes time to understand the composer's language. We can hear a short passage in our mind, but what is the role of it in the whole piece? How do we find the meaning of what is written, and how to play it?

Let's say the first and second violins are playing the melody – you can spend a lot of time with those 16 bars to understand how they should be played. Once you know that, and the passage is repeated somewhere else, perhaps in the woodwinds – you don't need to spend the same amount of time on it. Score reading is not about going from one page to the next in a linear way. There are many connections, and sometimes the character of the music depends on which instrument is playing. When the melody is in the woodwinds, it might require a different character than when played by the strings. If four instruments are playing something similar, should one be slightly louder than the others, or should they all be at the same volume? If a piccolo, oboe, clarinet, and bassoon are playing together, should they sound like one organ register? Often, you make a decision only to realize two days later – oh, that doesn't work at all. The more you read the score, the clearer the big picture becomes. A large piece always comes from hundreds of details, even within a single page. If you focus only on big pictures without building from all of the details, it is not good.

When reading the score, shall we constantly ask ourselves how it should be played?

Always.

Not only how it sounds, but also how to achieve it?

Yes. Perhaps the same idea in other words would be: What is the character of the music? What should come out of it?

Is it dance-like or lyrical? And what is the emotion – is it sorrowful, hopeful, euphoric? Finding these kinds of things from the score?

Yes, absolutely. It is like building something out of Lego – there are many small pieces, but once you put them together, suddenly – oh, it's a rabbit!

Would it be beneficial for conducting students to add layers of knowledge from recordings to their score reading?

Yes. It is like reading by candlelight – we no longer need it. A hundred years ago, you might have needed two candles to read a score. Now, we use electric lights, even the flashlight on our smartphones. So why don't we use all the possibilities we have right now and let them help us make even better music?

The way of reading scores is changing…

Some people are a bit purist about this, saying, "No, I stick to the old ways," and questioning why things should change. But it is beneficial to take advantage of today's tools – listen to many recordings, attend live concerts, and watch performances on YouTube. Use as much available material as possible to make your own interpretation and deepen your understanding of the piece.

When reaching for old textbooks on score reading, we find them full of clef and transposition exercises. This is how score reading was taught a hundred years ago.

Yes, exactly. I have one anecdote for you. When I was quite young, [Paavo] Berglund didn't want to teach, but he allowed people to follow him when he was working. I was in Bournemouth when he had rehearsals and then went on tour, performing the same program several times. Paavo was a serious man – not many smiles, not many jokes – just the essential things. During a lunch break, as a young conductor, I asked him what I now realize was a very stupid question: "How important is it to know all these kinds of forms which are inside the music, like in a Beethoven Symphony?" He replied, "I don't know, I'm not sure. But the only thing that matters is that it should sound good." Whatever your method, the method itself is not what is most important. What truly matters is that when you step on the podium, the music should sound good so that people can enjoy the performance. Berglund studied and read scores over and over again, and I am sure he knew everything. But the most important thing is that it should sound good.

Is that the point of the conductor's work?

Exactly, yes.

I would still like to ask a question about tempo – how do you choose the right tempo for the music so that it is neither too slow nor too fast? When reading the score, from where do we find the tempo?

If the composer wrote metronome markings, start from there. If you want to change them, you need to have a reason why. But don't go too far away – those markings reflect a specific idea the composer had in mind. If there are no metronome markings, you have more freedom to find out for yourself. For example, *Andante* – what does it mean? Sing the phrases, play the rhythmic element – mostly, the rhythmic element might give you the answer to what is the right tempo. Tempo is always connected in some ways to your breathing. I always mark down the tempos I believe are correct in my score, but I find that I often change my opinion when I come back to a piece a second or third time.

In Mahler's symphonies, there are many tempo changes. Do you first read the score with the written metronome markings?

Yes, and often I don't need to change anything. When a composer writes something a certain way, there is a reason for that. But then, there is the eternal question about Beethoven's symphonies.

Beethoven's metronome markings?

Yes, the tempos he marks for the fast movements are often just impossible to play, particularly the *staccato* sections for the wind players – it gets too fast and sounds hysterical. When I recorded the cycle, I took off about ten percent from the tempo markings when needed, but not more than that.

When reading the score, the conductor needs to imagine the orchestral sound. How would you recommend for conducting students to develop orchestral sound imagination?

Hopefully, they play an orchestral instrument and have performed in an orchestra many times. I know there are conductors who haven't – Karajan, for example, was a pianist – but I think it would be much more difficult for someone to do this job without ever having sat in an orchestra.

Playing in an orchestra helps develop orchestral sound imagination.

If you are a conductor and don't have enough experience, go to rehearsals. Orchestras often allow you to sit somewhere on stage – near the percussion, next to the woodwinds, or by the horns. During rehearsals, try to absorb the sound. When you are in the middle of the orchestra, the sound is very different from what the audience hears. This is a good way to learn.

To develop orchestral sound imagination, we need to hear how the orchestra sounds. It is not enough just to read scores.

Yes, that is one thing about Finnish conductors. People keep asking – more often than you can imagine – why so many great conductors come from Finland. Almost all Finnish conductors have worked in an orchestra. Jukka-Pekka was the principal second violinist in the Radio orchestra and Sakari was the concertmaster. Even Esa-Pekka – he was a great horn player, not a regular member, but he played as a substitute in every orchestra in Helsinki. Hannu was a cellist, and Susanna was a cellist as well.

Is the young generation going also this way?

Yes, that is a strength here. Generally speaking, you need to be proficient in at least one orchestral instrument and able to play it at a professional level – or close to it. This greatly benefits your work as a conductor.

The Architectural Metaphor –
Charles Olivieri-Munroe

Interview on 3 August 2024

In a situation where you receive a new orchestral score that you have not conducted or heard before, how do you begin your work of reading it?

Regardless of whether it is a new score or one I already know, the basic approach remains the same. It is a bit like coming into a new city and arriving at one of the city's landmarks – a great building, a cathedral, a parliament, or a castle. First, you take in the general architecture – the overall shape of the building, and then you begin to move into the details. You start to identify, to recognize which epoch the composition belongs to. Now, presumably, you would already know this, but certain details in the building – and in the music – will reinforce what you already know about the composer and when the piece was written. Then you go even deeper – entering the building – and you see how the rooms are divided.

Basically, I start with an overview and then move inward. What does that mean in terms of orchestral music? Well, first I want to understand the duration of the work: is it a 20-minute piece? A 60-minute piece? I want to know the length. Then I want to know whether it is divided into individual movements. I want to know what the orchestration is – and that is usually on the first page. That already gives me an indication of the complexity of the work I am about to study. If it is just a piece for strings, it won't be as complex as a Mahlerian, Straussian, or Stravinskian work, which involves multiple woodwinds, brass, percussion, harp, and so on. I start from the outside and then move in.

The next point – once I know how long the piece is, what the orchestration is, and that it's a three-movement symphony, for instance – I start with the first movement and look at its architecture, recognizing where the climax lies. I divide the movement into periods, trying to identify them within the piece. Then I go into more detail. For me, it is very important to determine where the quietest moment in the piece is, and where the loudest moment is – so that I have those two points in my mind and know where they will take place. Now, specifically regarding your question – if it is a new score – there are, of course, special characteristics of studying a completely new piece, where you can't find it on Spotify, YouTube, or have a CD recording of it. A completely new score – here, too – can be rather simplistic, or very complex. Is it tonal? Atonal? You know, that is part of it. What is the quality of the composer? Is it a well-written work, or is it somehow mediocre?

Then what I do is I take a basic pencil. I usually shame conducting students who bring to masterclasses scores covered in blues and reds; I find it as sacrilege and graffiti on a beautiful building – if we are going to continue using the architectural metaphor. I am going to step aside from the new piece for a moment. Say you are studying Beethoven's *Fifth Symphony*, and students come with all reds for *fortes*, and maybe blues for *pianissimo* or *piano* symbols, with lines and everything – why have they done this? They have done it because they are using these colors as crutches, like walking sticks to assist – that is what they are doing. Then what happens? They are usually young, and maybe they will come to have the opportunity to conduct the symphony once, and then maybe again – every time they conduct it, they will learn it more deeply. I tell them they will end up kicking themselves for having polluted the score with all these colors, because, in time, it will become obvious, they will remember: of course it is a *forte* here, and a *fortissimo* there – I didn't need to circle it with all these colors.

This is what I found in my career: that you actually start removing more and more of what you wrote, and you end up with, in a way, the basic authentic score – and all those writings are in here *[points to his head]*. And that is true score study, that is when you really know a work. Now, there are some genius conductors who have photographic memory – Lorin Maazel was one of them, Zubin Mehta is another – and there are others who could just look at the score and then memorize it. They could actually write it out. That is genius, and it is unusual. For the normal, good, studious conductor, the approach, I believe, should not be to put all these colors. We come back to what I was saying – you take a pencil and what I do is use the pencil to draw the periods, the episodes, and then, diving even deeper into that – is it four-bar phrases or six-bar phrases? I just simply put a little line every four bars, or something like that.

Very important is to identify when is the first time that any instrument plays in the piece. Often you don't have the whole orchestra – everyone – playing in the first bar. Take a symphony again of Beethoven – where do the trombones come in during the *Pastoral Symphony*? They don't play until the fourth movement, *The Storm*, and then again in the fifth movement. This is important, because they are waiting for you – for that cue.

Is this important for the conductor's contact with the orchestra musicians?

Yes, and that you show that you know the score. When the cymbals and triangle play the first time, I sometimes put a little exclamation mark, meaning that this is their first entrance.

What does marking the phrases and periods help with? Is it to understand the structure more and build the piece, or does it help to memorize the music?

All of the above – it is exactly as you said. It helps to memorize; it is a road map in a way. Also, when you are conducting the work, you can see from a distance: four bars, four bars, four bars. It is like driving a car – you are not looking one meter in front of you, right? You are looking further ahead. It is the same with the score. If you have drawn these vertical lines, it is like looking at the score from a distance. You are not going bar by bar – it would just be too much information, too close. I use a pencil for this purpose, and I typically mark *crescendos* with lines meaning getting louder, *diminuendos* with opposite lines, *fortes*, *pianos*, and instrument entrances, using abbreviations.

And no colors – everything just with a basic pencil?

I rarely use colors – I really don't. When I am conducting opera, I sometimes use colors for the vocal lines of the singers – I conducted *Yevgeny Onegin* just a few years ago. But I did when I was younger – definitely. I used reds and blues initially, and I regretted it afterwards. It just looked awful – you can't erase it, but with pencil you always can. By the way, I am not into using iPads for scores.

That is one of the technological changes, and it is interesting to see that it hasn't taken over the world of conducting.

I have met conductors who bring iPads to masterclasses and workshops. They have them right there.

The youngest generation?

But it doesn't necessarily mean it is better. The only advantage of an iPad is that you can have all these scores downloaded onto it, so you don't have to carry the physical scores. But it is so wonderful to have a physical score – on paper. It is like carpentry, like wood, like paint. After all, we are dealing with instruments, some of which were built hundreds of years ago. It just seems to jar: you have an orchestra of violins and cellos and oboes and flutes and horns and trumpets, and then there is an iPad in front of the conductor. It seems so contrary to the arts, contrary to my feeling. Computers, iPhones, iPads – our lives are already so filled with these touch screens. Let us celebrate those moments when we don't need to use them. I love scores. Also, they are handed down to you – I have scores that were given to me by my professor, and there is something special about that, even seeing his markings.

Do you have a personal attachment to your scores?

Absolutely. It is like books – like literature.

You mentioned that you look at the duration of the piece. Where can you find information about how long it is?

For most works, you just go on YouTube and immediately see the length of the video – that is the length of this Mahler symphony, this Beethoven concerto, or whatever it may be.

Do you familiarize yourself with this before getting into the details of studying the score?

Yes, also because I am involved in programming my own concerts, so I know that I want the concert to be roughly a hundred minutes of music, plus the intermission between the first and second halves. Sometimes – look at Mahler's *Third Symphony*, for example – it is the longest symphony ever written. At ninety minutes, that is all you would perform, and you wouldn't put anything else in the program. You have to know the duration in advance.

And how does a conductor create a sounding image of the score in the mind – so that, before going to the orchestra, the conductor hears the score in the imagination? What is your own experience? Do you ever use a piano for this, or some other instrument?

You used the right word – it comes from experience. I can now open any Beethoven symphony and hear it. From experience, from having conducted it, from carrying that soundscape in my head – from years of doing it. I know what a Beethoven symphony should sound like. There is a big distinction between how a Mozart symphony sounds, or a Vivaldi piece, or anything else, depending on the era it was written in – Baroque, Classical, Romantic, or Modern. As the orchestra developed, it grew larger. So a Mahler symphony has a bigger sound – more complex in every way – with all the additional instruments he implemented. The harmonies became more dissonant, the music became longer. The music of Gustav Mahler and Richard Strauss was the apex of European Classical Western music. Then, after the First World War, when economies were destroyed and there was no longer money to support these huge orchestras, you had the neoclassical approach of Stravinsky – he wrote for smaller ensembles again. If I am studying a piece by Stravinsky, one of his neoclassical works from the early 20th century – I already know what it should sound like, in terms of texture.

Does this experience come from listening to orchestras, from your own conducting in concerts and rehearsals – not just from reading scores?

Yes, totally so.

Is it through contact with the orchestra that the imagination of orchestral sound can be developed?

Yes, and it comes to you. You get to a point where you almost don't need to study. I almost don't need to study a Mozart symphony or concerto. I just did a piano concerto this week – I could have literally gone to the rehearsal without studying and just started to conduct it. I immediately go into autopilot; I know what to tell them. Basically, I can look at the score – if it's a Mozart score – and already see all the things that need to be said before they even play a note. And if it is a good orchestra, they will know what to do without me telling them. What am I talking about? In Mozart – in Classical and Romantic music – as soon as the brass are playing a whole-bar sustained note, unless they automatically bring it down instead of just playing what is written, which is *forte fortissimo*, they will cover everybody else. I will automatically show them to attack the *forte*, but then immediately die down, so they don't cover the smaller notes being played by other parts of the orchestra. These are things you just learn from experience – and you hear it. Also, the way the articulation is: short, transparent articulation for Mozart – if we're talking about Mozart – that is basically experience.

Is it also about knowledge of style and the composer's language – as well as about hearing and imagining the sound – how it is supposed to sound when it is this specific composer?

Of course, yes – and also knowing how to balance an orchestra.

While reading the score, does the conductor rely on their imagination and experience?

I don't like the word *imagination*. Imagination, for me, suggests freedom of ideas and so on – but we always have to derive our interpretation based on what the composer has written in the score. I don't want to criticize or talk semantics, it's just that I don't think *imagination* is the right word in this case. You interpret what has been written in order to best represent what the composer himself heard and wanted to be heard by an audience. That is our moral duty as interpreters – whether you are a conductor, a pianist, a violinist, or whatever. It is interesting to see how trends shift, because what I am seeing now is a trend toward a more personal interpretation – which I do not agree with. Almost nothing can be criticized anymore; everything is accepted. But that is not correct. It has to be an educated interpretation. Otherwise, anyone can get up there, just wave their hands, and it is considered a justified interpretation. I think you need to demonstrate that you really know what the composer wanted – and show fidelity to the score. What does that mean? The Classical period, it was more about form and maintaining tempos. Later, in the Romantic period, the rules were broken: tempos were much more varied, and we moved away from strict orchestrations.

What other elements do you focus on when reading a score? Do you analyze the harmony, the chords, or are there any other aspects you could mention?

Well, I also look for consistency in the composer himself. If it is a typical sonata form – where you have exposition, development, recapitulation – I look to see if there are disparities in phrasing and articulation. For example, Dvořák comes to mind – I am speaking to you from Prague. I've conducted a lot of Dvořák's music, and with him you sometimes encounter this problem: the same phrase appears at the beginning of a movement and then again later, but there is slightly different phrasing, a *fp* here but not there, or an accent here but not there. So what is right? Otherwise, the melody is the same. Was he sloppy? Did he do it on purpose? This is where the conductor has to use his or her experience, education, and knowledge of the period to make an informed decision about what is right. And in some cases, it has to be corrected. Sometimes a lot of corrections have to be made.

Or take a situation I always remember: an Italian conductor who is no longer with us, Aldo Ceccato. He conducted in Milan. I met him in Bern, where he was conducting Beethoven's *First Symphony*. In Beethoven's time, the flute had a more limited range than the modern instrument. In the score, you see the flute and violins playing in unison – so when the melody goes up, at a certain point the flute drops out because it couldn't go any higher. The violins continue the melody, come back down, and the flute rejoins. What the conductor did was add the missing notes to the flute, according to the possibilities of the modern player. That is a debate: are you destroying the composer? There will be purists who say, one shouldn't do that, and others – like him – who think it is a completely logical and reasonable thing to do. I myself don't do it, but I understand why and where this idea comes from.

Have you ever changed or added something in a score – and if so, why? What were your reasons?

I have, I am guilty. Again, I would justify what I did based on other music from that same period, where I think it is more effective to do what I did. I can give you some examples of both adding to the score and resisting the tradition of adding. Sometimes, at the end of a symphony – when you have that fanfare building up and the last movement is exciting – and then you reach the last chord, with the timpani playing just one note, just a downbeat – I will add a timpani roll, just to create a fuller body of sound. Now, of course, a purist would not agree with that at all. But I do it very selectively. On the other hand, in the Wagner's *Meistersinger Overture*, conductors like Karajan typically repeat the last bar – it feels more balanced that way – and he also adds a timpani roll. I decided that actually, it is not necessary. If you move the tempo forward, you don't need to pull it back and add a bar. I think I'm one of the few conductors who give a very spirited end to the *Meistersinger Overture*. You can hear it yourself on YouTube – it is with the Moscow Philharmonic Orchestra, from several years ago. I was very pleased with the way they played it, and there, you can hear that I play the original what Wagner wrote.

I'm trying to think of other examples where I have made changes. Actually, I was influenced by [Karol] Szymanowski, the Polish composer of the 20th century. His *Concert Overture* has a very exciting ending – at the very end, there is a brass chord with a timpani roll, and in the next bar, the bass drum joins the orchestra. It creates a very effective ending. I used that idea retroactively in [Bedřich] Smetana's *Má Vlast* – specifically in *Blanik*, the last movement – where I felt the ending was too dry. There is a trumpet fanfare, and then it is – chord, chord, chord. I added the bass drum to the timpani, just to create more exuberance. I would also be careful about where I did that – I might not do it in Prague. I do those kinds of things very sparingly.

Tempo is commonly known as an important concern for conductors. When you study a score, how do you find the tempo that you like? Do you measure or plan the tempo with a metronome and write metronome markings into the score?

I don't like to use the phrase "what I like". What I like is not important – and in fact, one of the first questions I ask students when they get up on the podium on the first day of a workshop or masterclass is: "How did you determine the tempo?" You would be amazed – people say things like, "I feel it that way". I don't care what your feeling is, that comes last in the hierarchy. First: what is the metronome number? Second: what is the Italian or German tempo marking? Three: what is the smallest note that can be played at that speed? Finally, after you have taken all this information into account, that influences and determines your feeling. But I am not interested in your feeling – I am interested in the composer's feeling. This is something I usually tell my students, and they open their eyes and realize. I determine my tempo based on what I just told you. I also take into account the ability of the group in front of me and the acoustical properties of the concert hall. If it is a very resonant hall, in a very fast tempo you will not hear all the notes. But a dry hall favors playing the music a bit faster.

Is it essential to respect the tempo the composer has written?

Of course. It is like being a detective – you look for clues and all the information you can find. And yet, it is so limited in the score. We only have the notes, the pulse, the rests, the metronome markings, the dynamics, the *crescendos* and *diminuendos*. It is not much – just black dots on a page.

When you read a score, do you think about performance issues – what is going to happen in rehearsals and concerts? Do you consider, for example, bowings?

Absolutely – that also comes from experience. You learn to identify things before the rehearsal: "Oh, this is going to be tricky." It might be difficult to get together with the other groups of the orchestra, or it could be challenging from another perspective. I do look at bowings, and that also comes with experience. You learn from working with orchestras, from watching other orchestras, or from string players. I am a pianist by background myself, but you learn which bowings create certain sounds that are appropriate for specific pieces. Repeated downbows in a violin section would probably be too aggressive for Mozart or Vivaldi – even for Beethoven, it is very rare. But in Tchaikovsky – I am thinking of the *Pathétique Symphony* now, the explosion in the development section of the first movement *[sings the music of the Allegro vivo]* – that could almost all be played downbow, and it creates an incredible *marcato*, exciting sound. There are other examples where knowing bowings is important, because it can really change the sound. If you know what sound you want, and you understand bowings, you can shape the sound. You can tell the concertmaster, "Hey, I want this bowing."

Do you prepare orchestral parts and send bowings to orchestras?

There are some pieces of music that are so iconic and particular, and certain works that, outside the country where they were written, are often misunderstood or not played properly – unless the correct bowings are provided. I am thinking now of Smetana's *Má Vlast* (*My Country*), where the third symphonic poem, *Šárka*, can be such a mess – and so much rehearsal time wasted – if you have to start from scratch with bowings. The Czech Philharmonic, and the Czech orchestras in general, have cleaned up the score. They know the best bowings to get the best possible effect. It is like when I conduct [Krzysztof] Penderecki's *Second Symphony* – I conduct it a lot, I love it – and I know from Penderecki himself which bowings he preferred in certain areas of the piece.

Going back to the technique of score reading – everyone would like to read scores fluently, but one of the challenges lies in transpositions. What would be your advice to a conducting student on how to read transpositions in a score? Should they replace them with clefs – for example, D transposition with alto clef, or F transposition with mezzo-soprano clef? Or is it better to think with a transposing interval – for instance, that a clarinet in B-flat sounds a major second lower, and a horn in F a perfect fifth lower? Or do you have any other method of reading transpositions?

I just use the interval – I am used to doing it that way. In terms of fluency, one thing I have noticed is that, as a young conductor, I tended to make things more complicated. I would subdivide more than necessary. As an example: [Gustav] Mahler's *First Symphony*, the *Titan* – there are places where he pulls back the tempo, and in the old days, I would subdivide and really spell it out for the orchestra. And it was together. Later, I discovered how to go for a more flowing line – still pulling back and observing what he wanted, but perhaps not as much. Again, it is a bit like the color-marking scenario, where people write with colors as a kind of crutch. Sometimes conductors want to subdivide too much for that same reason – they feel the security of the beats through their arms, rather than having the security of the sound and the beat inside them. They need to wave their hands in order to feel secure with the beat.

What I've really discovered is that, as you get older and gain more experience, you want things to flow – like in Beethoven's *Fifth Symphony*, you don't have to go *[sings and conducts the opening motive of the first movement]* and cut off, then cut off again, and all that kind of stuff. There are other reasons why one shouldn't cut off – simply because you are adding a bar of music. That is one of the biggest things I've discovered when I look at the arc of my performances, from when I was younger to now: things tend to flow more. I am much more concerned with lines – the line of a phrase, or an episode – and not breaking things up so much.

When reading a score, do you sing some of the lines – do you go through the score by singing?

Yes, sure – and I will go to the piano, too. If it is a new score, I will play it so I hear the harmony and figure it out.

I am very grateful that you are sharing your experience. It is very interesting to hear about the changes you have gone through.

Music is life. Music is a reflection of life – classical music. Pop songs are very two-dimensional – she left me, I love her, I miss her, I would, you did – and it is over in three minutes. It is catchy, and you sing along. But when you listen to an opera or a symphony, there is so much that uplifts the soul; it speaks to so many aspects of life. In one symphony, you can experience humor, tragedy, and the intellectual part of life. If a composer implements a fugue, for instance, it is very mathematical and very intellectual. And yet they are spiritual, and can have so many faces. Put together, it is such a moving experience.

Again, as you get older and experience life, I find it, to be honest, quite extraordinary that a great orchestra would hire a twenty-something-year-old conductor. He may be dazzling, even great with this, but he simply cannot bring to a body of musicians the depth of all the sufferings of life. At that age, you are barely an adult. Have you had a relationship yet? Have you gone through breakups? Have you experienced deaths in your life? Maybe he has – maybe someone does, even at that age. That is why I love interviews with older people, which you can find on YouTube. It may seem a bit silly – people asking a seventy- or eighty-year-old: "What do you regret in your life? What would you tell your younger self?" But there is something in that. I love listening to older people. There is a certain wisdom that comes naturally from simply having lived all those years. And we don't even have to be talking to philosophers or doctors – it could be just a simple man or woman, a farmer. You would be amazed at the depth and philosophical things they could say to you.

Does all of this influence what you see in the score?

Absolutely, of course. I had a short bout of tinnitus once, after having an MRI, and I freaked out. It was the worst thing I could imagine having as a musician – I heard this high-pitched sound. Thankfully, it left me. But then you conduct [Bedřich] Smetana's *From My Life* (*Z mého života*) E minor string quartet – which George Szell orchestrated for full orchestra – where the composer puts into the music the tinnitus. He went deaf and knew that is what he heard: a high-pitched whistling. It is written into the piccolo for that effect. Suddenly, it speaks to you, it is closer to home. Or, God forbid, if you've lost a child, as Mahler did (he lost his daughter before writing his *Ninth Symphony*). I haven't, thank God, lost a child, but I can imagine that if I were to conduct that symphony after such a loss, it would speak to me that much more. I would move the orchestra with that much more conviction, because I could truly relate. It is no longer theoretical or anecdotal – it becomes personal. And the longer you live, the more times you interpret music, in the same works you find that your interpretation changes and adapts according to your place in life. And that is not a bad thing.

When you returned to a piece later in your life, did you find new or different things in the score?

Of course. I remember Claudio Arrau, the great South American pianist – he would study the score until the very last second before going on stage. He used to say that he did this because he would always find something new in the score – just by reading it, not by playing it.

I've met conductors who advised: never listen to recordings – read the score and create your own image of it in your mind. At the same time, we live in a world where recordings are easily accessible. Do you think recordings can, in some way, be useful for score reading?

Of course. The reason older conductors say *don't* listen to recordings is that they want to encourage young conductors to hear the score in their heads, not rely on an already recorded result. I've seen the results of this: some young conductors – you can tell they have been practicing with a recording. And then, when they get up in front of an orchestra, instead of leading the orchestra, they are being led by it. That is because they have trained by following a recording. And you can't conduct a YouTube recording – it plays what it plays. Then they are in front of an orchestra, and they are not leading it.

One of the fascinating, magical things about conducting is that you must anticipate ahead of the beat. When you get used to a certain sound from a recording, it may not even be what the composer wanted. Not all recordings are well balanced. You can be influenced by wrong tempos, by all sorts of things – even wrong notes. As with everything in life today, recordings have to be used responsibly. What do I mean? Take iPhones – we all see it: everyone is on their smartphones all day, every day, even in restaurants. A whole family sits at the table, both the kids and the parents are staring at their smartphones. It is great technology, but it has to be used responsibly. In the case of conducting, recordings should be used responsibly – not as a substitute for sitting by yourself with the score, with no outside influences, and trying to absorb the sounds into your mind.

For conducting students, is it important to read the score before listening to recordings?

Yes, go to the piano and try to play the score on the piano.

What about premieres of contemporary music – have you met any special challenges in reading such scores?

Of course. It has never been performed before – there are no recordings, it is a brand-new piece. In that case, the important thing is that you can really hear the notes and know them well, because if the orchestra plays something incorrectly, you need to be able to recognize it. You don't have the benefit of having heard a recording a hundred times beforehand – you have to be able to identify that in a score.

When you read a score, do you try to memorize it, or does that happen by itself? Or do you not try to memorize it at all, because that is not the point?

I don't think that is the point. It happens by itself. In my case, I do conduct from memory sometimes – but only those pieces which I really own. I know them so well that I can say I own them. I can rehearse them without the score, and I can conduct them in performance without the score. It is simply because I know those works so well; I have conducted them so many times that I find a more organic, natural reason to conduct without a score. But when someone does it just to dazzle the audience – I am not impressed. Often, they are just conducting the melodic line and miss many cues which they should be giving.

Does memorizing scores also happen as a result of experience, then?

It is also a matter of experience. My professor told me, "At forty, you are just beginning to become a conductor."

The Magnifying Glass – *Anna-Maria Helsing*

Interview on 13 July 2024

When you have a score in front of you, how do you begin your work of reading it? What elements do you focus on first, and how do you proceed?

Of course, it very much depends on if I am reading a Tchaikovsky score or contemporary music I have never seen before – it varies a bit. If it is a large opera, I would probably start by reading the text, moving from the libretto to the score. I first try to get an overall picture of the piece by flipping through pages to observe where it starts smaller, where it is growing, and where are the tempo changes. Then, I dig into all the details. As I go through the score, I read every note and try to understand it. I begin with chord analysis, reading vertically to grasp the harmonic structure, especially if there is tonality. This helps me find wrong notes and eliminate lots of mistakes, as I will notice if something is not as it should be. Once I have that base, I easily go through the score again, reading horizontally and working on the phrasing, how many bars connect to each other. With that done, I am already quite far, and I just go back to decide on how I want the interpretation, which tempos to choose, how does this sit. I notice, of course, problematic spots – sections that may be difficult for the orchestra – and I consider how to solve them. Things that stick out you will always notice: *Oh, that is a very long note for a wind player, this passage is trickily virtuosic,* or something similar.

There are two essential steps for me. First, I need to know the piece, I have to learn it. This is why my approach varies depending on if it is a new piece or something I already sort of know. If I have a picture of how it sounds already in my head, I will much sooner go into thinking about how I want it. With contemporary music, it takes quite a lot of time just to absorb the piece and know how it should sound. Sometimes, I will have to go to the piano, especially to hear what the chords sound like. For a long time, I used to play through every piece I conducted, except for maybe Haydn or Mozart – just to make sure I get into it. To sit and read a score is one thing but playing it can reveal a lot. When I play, I feel if some patterns are wrong. It is hard to describe – maybe because if I were just reading the score, I might think, *Yes, this looks fine.* But when I play it, I sense, *No, this is a mistake; it should be the other way around.* When patterns repeat, it is much easier – my fingers go the way it should, and I can see that it does not. There are many methods of getting to know the piece, but after that, there is still work to be done. And that is perhaps not score reading so much, but more score preparing, or preparing for performance.

How do you decide on the phrasing? What makes your decision that here a phrase starts and there a phrase ends, how do you recognize this from the score?

Sometimes it is hard to decide, I must admit, because you can choose this, or another way. It can be a personal or subjective matter.

Do you examine aspects such as instrumentation, texture, or something else?

It can be many things, of course. When you see one instrument playing a line with a bit of accompaniment, followed by a large tutti, it is pretty clear that from here we have a point of change. It can be the instrumentation, but many composers also use this method of melodic things happening – there is one phrase, and then you feel another starting. Sometimes, the instrumentation shifts in the middle of a phrase, it does not have to be that which decides. It depends on what happened earlier and what follows, and sometimes I have to go back and change, because as I progress further into the piece, I realize – *oh, it is not exactly as I thought.* I do not only go phrase by phrase, but I also put them together into larger entities. For example, if I have two four-bar phrases, followed by two five-bars phrases, I might write for myself 8 and 2*5, and those together will build one chunk of something. I have to go through the whole piece to really get those as I think they should be.

Today's conductor works on both contemporary and older music from the 18th and 19th centuries, so on different kinds of scores. When preparing pieces for world premieres, have you met any special challenges in reading the newest scores?

Yes, if the scores are very out of everything and composers just create sounds and lots of playing techniques, they can be quite challenging. Suddenly, you don't have barlines anymore, or they can be even more free. Sometimes, you really have to think why the composer chose to write the score this way. Most of the time, you find the reason – *yes, if traditional barlines had been used, it would not work with this or that.* But usually composers are very reasonable, and they are well aware, that in order to get their music performed, they have to make sense. If we can't understand their scores, we will probably think, *Oh, not for me then.* There are quite a few contemporary composers on the scene today who are very precise in how they mark their scores, with instructions on how to play their techniques. I always give feedback to contemporary composers on this. As soon as it is a little bit unclear, how this technique should be played, questions will arise, taking away time from the rehearsal of their music. A composer should always want as much time as possible into playing and interpretation of their piece, not into an orchestra full of raised hands asking – "Maestro, how should we do this? How should we do that?" – then you lose all the time for that. If composers are strict in how they notate in the parts and scores, it is a win-win for everyone. This has improved quite a lot, because twenty years ago I had far more scores that felt incomplete and left many open questions.

Are those questions about, for example, articulation?

Everything. Articulation you can leave also to the conductor, but the more written down, the better. For example, is an *accelerando* going into the new tempo, or where is it going? And if you see a *più mosso*, does that mean it is now faster, or did the *accelerando* lead into the *più mosso* and you just continue? That is a huge difference. It is much better to get all this information from the score. You will not find that in older music, but you can get it from today's composers.

While studying scores of contemporary music, have you been in contact with the composers before going to the orchestra?

Absolutely. I always send them my errata list with corrections, and they can go through it and say, "Yes, you are right," or "No, here I actually want it like that." I think they will learn from those lists because they will know how we think, and they will notate their next piece even clearer to avoid the same questions.

What about reading scores of older music, such as Mozart or works from the 19th century? Are there any other considerations you need to take into account, or read these scores differently?

Yes, because you don't get as much information from a score, composers did not give so much information back then. Mozart will not make sure that you know how long the quaver should be, or the semiquaver. Composers left much more out for the interpreter, the performer to decide. That means that when I read such a score, I already know I won't look for that information written anywhere in the score, but I will have to decide on those things myself. I will try to find from the score what will make the most sense, what would be logical. Mozart and that kind of music can be terribly boring if you just let the orchestra play through it. Not because it wouldn't be fantastic music, but it has so much in it that you can really lift out. He has put everything in for you to realize: *Oh, here you can do it completely differently; here you can change the atmosphere; here you can get another mood, another color from the strings,* or something. I try to find those subtle points, like a slight difference in the repetition. *Should we bring it out in some way? And if so, how? Should we do it more piano, or more forte, should we change the tempo a little bit?* Reading the score more like Sherlock Holmes with his magnifying glass. You can find a lot, but not at first sight – it is as if you don't see it at first, and then you must dig in a little deeper.

You mentioned the mood and character of the music – are these important in score reading?

Absolutely. Leif Segerstam said that you must always have a vision for every piece you do – what is it about. For example: *they are at sea, and a stormy wind is coming.* It is a good principle to remember that the more pictures you have, the better you can help the orchestra. You might give them one picture and when you play it, you will hear it is not yet the right one. Then it is very good to have more pictures to throw at them and see which one works best for every player. Yes, moods are crucial, because musicians mostly know how to play their parts when they come to the rehearsal, but what you can do is give those images – "That is a very fine solo, how you play it – but what if you were in love? Or had a headache?" Just find something that will bring it out.

There is so much inspiration to be found in the score. You have worked also on opera music and mentioned that first you get to know the libretto, the text. After that, how do you approach the score? Do you focus first on the soloists' parts? Do you work on one number at a time? How do you read an opera score?

Operas are often very complex, but also there I go through the whole score – note for note, really put it down, so I have a sense of how it should sound. I am reading many things at the same time. I don't know how to describe it, but I go through every page, more or less every note, to get a grip on every detail. Then, to really learn the opera, I make time, for instance, to play the choir parts separately, to know how the choir sounds without the orchestra. Solo parts I usually try to sing in some way, depending on the music. If it is contemporary, I make sure I know where from the singer can get the pitch for their entrance. I try to find a good way to identify those and how to do the solfege of every singer part. Otherwise, I will be quite lost when there are no recordings, and I am just reading it slowly. I need to be able to sing those lines to recognize if the singer makes a mistake – otherwise, how could I correct it? However, in traditional operas, I wouldn't attempt to practice something like *Tosca* or try to do those fermatas, because I am not a singer. What I can do myself does not help much, I still wouldn't truly know what they are capable of. For me, singing is more about finding the pitch. I can also explore how the phrase feels and where I might want to breathe. To be prepared to follow a singer, I need to understand how they breathe. I usually consider this in advance, and once I meet the singer, I often realize, *Oh, they're doing much better than I expected and it works well for them* – so I don't interfere. However, it can be helpful in cases where there are doublings in the orchestra, such as when an oboe plays with the singer. The oboist needs to know where the singer will breathe.

How do you use the metronome for score reading? For example, do you use it to read the metronome markings in the score, to check your interpretation, or for other purposes?

In contemporary music, I check the metronome markings written by the composer and tend to trust and rely on them quite a bit, as composers today are very specific about how they want their music to be performed. When they include a metronome marking, it usually means they have carefully considered it and want that exact tempo. I check myself – mostly, I can take a metronome, and whatever it indicates, I am usually very close to it when recalling from memory. However, I use it to confirm that I am spot on, that my 132 is where it should be and my 79 is accurate. This is quite useful because, although I have my own method for finding the right tempi, there are times when I need to make small corrections. So, for me, the metronome is primarily a tool for verification. When the music includes a significant *accelerando* or a particularly tricky tempo transition, I try it in my head. Once I feel I am at the right tempo, I might check it and realize, *Oh, I'm a little too fast, I need to take more time there*. I mostly use it for that. In some extreme cases of highly virtuosic pieces, I might try myself with having the metronome briefly on. For instance, if there are twelve bars where I feel the orchestra is rushing, I will check it to ensure I know exactly how the tempo should go in that section – where to avoid rushing or dragging, and where to maintain a steady pace. I use a metronome to check that I am absolutely in tempo for a specific passage, because sometimes we have a tendency to rush certain patterns, and I might feel that inclination just as a first violinist or a piccolo player would. It is helpful to confirm: *Oh, it's really not faster than that – very good.* So I should remember not to push the orchestra too much, for instance. However, I rarely use it for those situations anymore, mostly just to check and establish the correct tempo.

What about older music where the composer wrote a metronome mark?

Sometimes, I simply don't agree. I think composers might have been influenced by editors who insisted they include a metronome marking, and they thought, "Well, maybe this works." And perhaps that tempo was very good one hundred fifty years ago, but today it would not feel right. In such cases, I make my own decision and choose a tempo that feels natural and comfortable for my interpretation.

When reading the score, do you consider the acoustics of the performance venue and the characteristics of the orchestra you will be working with? Does this affect your score reading?

It can. If I am going to a regular concert hall, I may not know its acoustic properties, especially if I haven't been there before – but most concert halls are generally fine. When performing in church – for instance, in a couple of weeks, we have a new contemporary opera with a massive texture in a church in Finland – I might need to consider the tempi and how to ensure clarity, as I know there will be a significant delay in the church's acoustics. The same applies when considering a singer. If you know in advance that the singer has a fantastic, powerful voice, you can anticipate how to balance the orchestra accordingly. You look at the score and immediately know: *This will work just fine.* Sometimes, you may encounter a different situation, and you will know to take care of it. Of course, in reading operas the range of the singer will decide on the balance of the orchestra. If they are up in a strong, resonant register, you will treat the orchestra differently than when they are in their lowest register, that can't be heard as easily.

Can you predict problems in balance relations already while reading the score? For example, when the strings are in a very high register, do you consider making adjustments to balance them with the voice?

Absolutely. If you have a soprano going down into the low register, around c1 [middle C], you know there will be a problem if a lot is going on in the orchestra.

Nowadays, recordings of music are widely accessible everywhere. How do recordings influence the way you read a score?

Recordings are helpful, and I need to be aware of traditions. It would be foolish not to know how other conductors have approached the same music in the past. However, I first read the score – go through it to form a sounding picture – and I try to not make any exceptions to this rule. Otherwise, I risk skipping over something crucial to my own understanding. After that, I try to listen to a few different recordings. Of course, I am guessing there, but knowing my fellow conductors, I select both older and more recent interpretations. I try not to listen too much to just one recording. With the score in hand, I go through one recording, then another, gradually building a broader perspective. Opera can be tricky because it has so many traditions. When you hear it performed, you can realize why a certain tradition exists – it has to do with the singer, or it will not work very well another way. Traditional operas are among the most challenging ones, you need to really know what you are doing there. I will put quite a lot of time into those scores.

Recordings provide insight into performance traditions and reveal how differently people interpret the score.

I used to love going to other people's rehearsals. Nowadays, this is more difficult because I am never at home. But when I was studying in Helsinki, I liked to do that. If I have a piece coming up that I feel particularly passionate about or have some uncertainties with, I like to break it down to ensure I feel comfortable conducting it for the first time. If I see that this piece is being set up somewhere in Helsinki, for instance, and I happen to be at home – I go to the first rehearsal. I ask for permission to be there because I want to hear how the orchestra sounds when they read it for the first time. I don't want a recording of it, because recordings are already rehearsed, I want to hear where the problematic spots will be – that is very interesting for a conductor. If you have the opportunity as a student, attend as many rehearsals as possible, and go to the first days. The dress rehearsal is too late – everything has already been set. Recordings allow you to hear what you don't want to do and what you might want to do, and both insights are valuable. For example, you might hear a *subito piano* and think, *Oh no, that doesn't feel right* – and now you know. Otherwise, you would have to try these things yourself with the orchestra to be sure.

Observing rehearsals is a valuable and practical way to deepen your understanding of a score. Fluent score reading requires proficiency in reading clefs and decoding transpositions. In the questionnaire, you mentioned that for reading E-flat and E transpositions, you use the clef substitution method of changing to bass clef. Why don't you apply this method to other transpositions?

I simply don't need it in other cases, either they are so close, like B-flat and D is one step, or I know the alto clef from playing the viola, so I recognize it instantly. I think I also admitted that tenor clef is a bit trickier, but I still read it from the C-line. The cello has it so often, that I don't need to think of something else. It is probably the same as with alto clef – I am already used to it.

What about horns in F, do you think a fifth down?

Yes, but those are so common that sometimes, when I have scores in C, it can be even tricky. It is really very comfortable the fifth.

The B-flat and D transpositions are only a second down or second up, does this make it not so difficult to read?

It is not difficult, but I must admit that D transposition is more challenging than B-flat, probably because it is less common. Even though it is just a second, it does not sit as well for me. The most difficult situation is when you have horns in three different transpositions – say, two horns in F, one in D, and one in A. In that case, you can't immediately see the chord. If all four horns are in the same transposition, it is much easier because you can recognize the chord and get it from there. But when they are different, you have to read them differently, and that many brains we do not have.

In situations where there are three or four horns in different transpositions, do you write chord names into the score to avoid having to read them each time?

Absolutely.

Score Internalization and Layout – *Tito Muñoz*

Interview on 13 June 2024

In what ways, and in which musical elements, does playing the violin help you in orchestral score reading?

In a couple of ways. One is that I am not a great pianist, so I use the piano very minimally when hearing things. Having spent a lot of time working as a professional violinist, I feel my sense of sound and pitch is much more attuned to that, my instrument. When I can, or when I feel it is necessary, if I am having a hard time and need to quickly hear something, I usually have my violin right next to me, and I will just play it to hear intervals and certain things. I also use it, of course, for bowings, as string players do – for technical and practical purposes. It is just my instrument – it is what I turn to when I need something. I don't feel like using the piano, so I reach for the violin.

Do you write bowings into the score? What do they mean for you?

It depends. I don't always write bowings in my score unless it is a specific kind of bowing that I know I am going to need to remember and tell an orchestra to do. That rarely happens – usually, when I work with an orchestra, bowings are fine. But once in a while, there might be a certain thing that I have to put in my score. Otherwise, it is my own parts that I do the bowings for. If I send parts to an orchestra for pieces which I have specific preferences, that is when I do it. For some pieces, I have my own set of parts that I send to the orchestra.

Do you use your own set of parts only for older music, or generally?

Both, it depends. I obviously do for the Classical era, and if I ever conduct Baroque (which I don't do that often), then yes, I would probably have my own marked-up parts. For example, for [Handel's] *Messiah*, I have my own marked parts because in America, we perform it every year – it is like a tradition. I have a whole set of parts marked the way I do it, because it is a bit like jazz – where markings are minimal, and you have to add your own. Haydn symphonies – sometimes. It depends on whether it is a symphony that I conduct a lot, like *Drum Roll* or *La Reine* – for those, I have my own set of parts that I use. For [Stravinsky's] *Sacre du Printemps*, I also have a set of parts, so whenever I do that piece, I usually send my own set, because I have a lot of markings, bowings, and all sorts of things in there.

In the questionnaire, you mentioned that you don't write so many things into the score. Does this give you a better vision of the music?

This is how I feel about it – it is just the way I've always been. When I first started learning conducting as a kid, a teenager, I saw my older friends and colleagues who were conducting marking their scores, using colors and all sorts of things. So I thought, *You have to do that – that is like a thing.* Especially since Otto Werner Mueller was a teacher at Juilliard – I knew him as the conducting guru in New York City – he was all about colors. He broke apart scores and had a system of marking things. People who studied under him followed that system of mapping out the structure of a piece, the layers, and so on. I remember, in the beginning, I started doing a bit of that – analyzing, writing in keys – but a lot of it seemed very irrelevant once I actually began performing, working, and rehearsing. I realized that many of the things I was writing down I could already hear, remember, and just see in the score. I didn't need to write them – it felt almost like a waste of time. I was sitting there analyzing and writing all this stuff, but I kept thinking, *why?* So, little by little, I just stopped. Now, I really don't write anything. The only times I do write in my score are when I need to do math – for example, in modern music, where there are tempo modulations and I have to remember the subdivision three bars before I get to something new. Things like that, where I have to practice my beating.

The beating patterns?

Correct. That is usually when I do have to write things. If I am writing things and need to write, then we get into notation – which is a very interesting topic. And not just notation, but engraving – the actual process of creating the score. I do a lot of engraving now. My COVID project was focused on arranging and engraving. There is one piece I re-engraved because I wanted to do it with a youth orchestra, a summer camp orchestra. I had played the piece myself as a kid in youth orchestra, and I wanted to do it with the kids. I purchased a set of parts, and they were in that old Broadway-style handwriting – done for a radio show, so it was a one-and-done situation: write it quickly, play it once, and it is done. Those were the only parts available, and no one had ever created a new engraving. So I said, "Okay, let me do it." In doing so, I learned a lot about how a score is visually laid out – and how much that can affect what you need to write and what you don't. That got me on a kick, especially with new composers. I am always criticizing how they make a score, because a lot of modern composers use Sibelius or Finale. They just write the music, make it to 11x17 paper or some large format, print it, and it is done. But the more time I spend engraving, the more I realize these different details professional engravers know – things that make a score look good. And that affects the way performers and conductors visualize and see a score.

There was one piece I did a couple of months ago in Phoenix where I actually re-engraved the score. I told the composer and showed her: "Look – because of the way you have done it, I have to mark phrases, write in all these things. You have too many measures in one system, too many things in one page, you don't hide empty staves… all sorts of things." Once I redid it, I didn't have to mark anything. It was very easy to read and not a problem. Sometimes that is an issue – if I get a score and it is not clear how many measures are in a system or in a phrase, I might have to draw barlines and phrases. I just did Mahler's *Second Symphony* for the first time, and in the *Scherzo* movement, it helped me visually to mark the four-bar phrases so I could see them very easily and not have to think too much. Otherwise, it was difficult to remember – sometimes it is five, sometimes three, and so on. When I mark my music, it is usually for practical reasons: phrases, conducting patterns in modern music, and instrumental cues, when needed.

The visual layout and engraving of a score significantly affect how a conductor reads it – that is an important message for composers and score editors.

Yes. It is amazing how, back before computers, publishers had to design every single page and then carve it into a metal plate. That meant there was so much attention to detail – how everything was laid out, the spacing, the size of every element. Now, computers do it all for you, and a lot of composers don't know how to engrave. They never learned the art of engraving, and that is lost. Sometimes I get these scores and I am just like, *I can't read this. I have to mark everything. Why? If you just – you know – it doesn't have to be so big. If you just hide certain things…* Now I am much more sensitive to it than before, because I've started doing a lot of these projects myself.

When approaching older music, what do you look at first when reading a score? Is it a specific group of instruments, a musical element, or do you immediately imagine the whole score? How do you begin your work on it?

What is interesting about old music is that it generally follows more patterns than modern, or modern-ish, music. The phrases are usually 4, 8, or 16 bars long. The structure is typically very clear, so oftentimes I don't need to go through and identify it – it is usually pretty self-evident. You know if there is an introduction, where the exposition starts. Generally, I just start by listening to it. I open the score, and I can usually immediately hear it pretty well – I just start listening to it as if I were listening to a piece. I also read chamber music a lot with my friends. Sometimes we will come across old pieces I've never played before, and when you are sight-reading chamber music with friends, you are making an interpretation on the spot. That is usually what I am doing – playing it in my head. When I get to the end of a phrase and think, *Do I want to take time here?* – I make the decision: *Why would I do that? Where is the structure in all of this?* Then I keep going and just listen to it. Once I have a general sense of the piece, I get an idea of the trajectory – where the phrases are, where the development will happen, and what leads into it. I feel like a good composer's music makes sense when you hear it, and then you can just pull an interpretation from it. That is usually how I start with old music – I just listen to it and see where it takes me.

You have also conducted a lot of contemporary music and world premieres. Do you find that reading modern scores is different, and what challenges does it pose?

It is different, just because it's so vast and varied. Modern scores can range from urban, hip-hop type of pieces – which we do a lot in America, to all sorts of new music. It also depends on the vernacular you know as a musician. There is music I grew up with here that I know very well and can identify with pretty easily. Once I see it on paper and do what I just explained – visualizing and kind of listening to it – I am usually like, *Oh, I know what that is. That's pretty straightforward. I've heard this before, or I've played this before. That sounds like the bands I knew when I was a kid.* As an example, I did the premiere of Valerie Coleman's *Fanfare for the Uncommon Times*, which she wrote during COVID as a sort of answer to *Fanfare for the Common Man* by [Aaron] Copland. It is written for the same instrumentation, and she identifies her music as American Black music.

There are rhythmic elements and elements of gospel church – but it is not always evident if you don't really know that tradition, especially because the instrumentation is for brass. It might sound a little bit "modernish", or there might be a phrase that sings – but because it is played by a trombone or trumpet, it doesn't immediately tell you gospel unless you know what you're listening for. I remember going through it and thinking, *Oh, this is church. This is like she's singing at church. This is the choir.* For me, it was immediately evident, but I don't know if it would be for someone who doesn't know that music intimately. I remember when we were rehearsing, she came to the rehearsals and was saying the same thing: "This is like this", or "This is like that". And I was like, *I get it, I understand.* It just really depends.

But when you get into things like Abrahamsen or Ligeti – when you are dealing with complex harmonies and very difficult rhythmic elements – that is the kind of stuff where I just have to figure it out. I am sitting there conducting patterns, singing rhythms, trying to make sense of what to do. There was one piece I did – *Schnee* by Hans Abrahamsen – probably the most difficult piece I've ever conducted. There was one movement, that I opened the score, looked at the first page, sat there and said, *I don't know what to do. I don't know how to conduct this.* I was literally stumped, I didn't know how I was going to beat this music. That was a very disconcerting feeling – I've never had this happen before, where I have a modern piece and don't know what to do. So I went on YouTube, praying I could find a performance. I was about to get on the phone with the composer. And there it was – a performance! The ensemble that premiered this piece recorded it – an amazing recording. I eventually got on the phone with him and asked, "How did they do it?" And he said, "Well, they didn't have a conductor; they just kind of thought of it all in one." And I was like, *But that's impossible – it's so hard!* Eventually, I found a video of a New York ensemble with a percussionist as the conductor. He conducted it in a way I never would have come up with – it wouldn't have been my solution. It is not evident from looking at the score that it should be done that way, but it was actually the best solution. I did the piece with the Mahler Chamber Orchestra, and when we got to that moment, I said, "Okay, I want to try this. I'm going to try this way of doing it. I saw it on a YouTube video – it was…" *[laughs]*. I remember that the meters didn't align with the way I was going to conduct it – it was a 9/8 in two and an 8/8 in three – so the players with 9/8 had to subdivide within my two, and so on. I said, "Trust me, it will work. It should work." And we did it. It was uncomfortable. They were like, "Could we do it the other way?" And I said, "Okay, let's do it the way it looks on your page." We did it that way – and it didn't work.

Was this about the inner subdivisions in measures?

It was very interesting because the inner subdivisions of the way the piece was written, and the way it seemed you would want to conduct it, didn't quite align. It felt better to try to fit those meters into a larger subdivision that wasn't the same, but made more musical sense to them. So, you have music like that, which is very challenging in certain ways. Then you have music that is much more folk-vernacular – like, for example, hip-hop, or rock – which has a lot of those kinds of elements. Bartók used folk music. They all used folk music at some point, for whatever reason. Then you have minimalist music, which depending on the kind, is also very challenging because you have to find the inner drama to make it work. A lot of repetition can't work very well on its own. I listen to it and try to find where the tension is – and it is not evident in the piece. You can't notate that. It is in the way you push an articulation, the way you *crescendo* through a phrase that might not be written, to keep attention going. It depends on how the harmonies are laid out and so on.

For me, modern music is interesting because it is so varied, and every kind of piece requires different sensibilities and different priorities. I am also doing a piece by a composer named Michael Hersch, an American composer I work with a lot. He writes very dissonant music – it is very difficult, not what you would expect an American to write, actually – not at all. He is like the American *Ligeti* or the American *Kurtág*, so he doesn't get performed much in America. But I've done a lot of his music, and it is actually very structured and very musical when it comes to phrasing. Once you get past the language that he uses, you can make very natural music. But the language itself is so dissonant and sometimes so difficult to hear – that it makes it hard. But once I realized what his language was, it actually became easier. And with his music, I treat it similarly to the way I treat old music – I just listen to it, and it kind of tells me where I need to go pretty easily.

Depending on the composer and the piece, do other elements become the focus when you read a score?

I think other or certain elements become more of a priority, at least in the beginning. First go through of the piece – there will be elements that I need to focus on first. For example, even complicated music with tricky meters

– it is not like it isn't music, it still needs to be interpreted, it needs to sing, needs to be all of that, but there are these little barriers that I have to figure out before I get to that part. That is why sometimes I have to just write out the math and figure it out. Once I have that, then I can go back, sing it, and internalize it that way. And then it becomes more comfortable because I understand it.

When you are reading a score, do you also imagine how you will conduct it? Are you working on the beating patterns?

I hesitate to say that it is about conducting. Even with music that is more mathematical and requires me to figure out the math, I still try to think about it as if I were a player in the orchestra – not with my hands. I try to figure it out as if I were sitting there, having to play it. What would I need to think subdivision-wise, in order to understand what the section is. One of the things I still have in my mind from our time at Aspen[94] is something Murry Sidlin told us at one point, and I still hold on to it very strongly: "When you are first going through the piece, sit on your hands and don't conduct." I agree with this very much, because you don't want any deficiencies that you might have as a conductor to influence how you interpret a piece. You want to be able to hear the piece the way the composer hears it in their mind – not based on the way you physically move – because the moment you gesture, that will create a trajectory and time that has nothing to do with anything except that gesture. I don't want to have that at first. Only once I am able to hear it, sing it, and know how I would play it, then I would say, *Okay, gesture-wise, what would that feel like for me to show?*

You mentioned that you sing the score. What does singing give you in getting to know the score?

I think of the score, and I also teach this – especially when I work with youth orchestras, I try to remind them – that the notation, the actual printed music on the page, is in itself an element of music theory. What I mean is that the composer had just thoughts. The notation is a structure for those thoughts. But in the end, it is the thoughts that matter. There are certain things that you can't notate – things the composer might have heard. They might hear this or that and then have to structure it in a way to write it down – similar to how we conduct. I hear what I want to hear, and then I have to structure

---

[94] Tito Muñoz and the author participated in the American Academy of Conducting at the Aspen Festival of Music in 2005.

it physically in a way that I can show it, so that the orchestra can follow me. I especially remind kids: "Look, the music is what it is – the sounds are what they are. It's not 3/4, it's not 4/4, it's not quarter note, half note – none of that. The composer just heard something, sang something, and then had to decide: *Okay, is it in four? Is it a whole note*? And then they wrote it down."

That is why, for me, singing is important. I want to get away from the notation as much as possible so that I can really hear something that is living and breathing. The notation, for me, is just the theory behind it – like: "I heard that, and that's four beats, so we have to write it as 4/4." That is why I think of it this way. Singing is very important to me because that is when you can really make an interpretation and breathe it.

Through singing, do you get to the essence of the music and to what the composer was imagining before they wrote it on the page?

Correct.

Nowadays, almost everyone listens to recordings – that is the possibility we have. You mentioned earlier that you listened to another conductor's recording. So, what role does listening to recordings have in your score reading?

That is very interesting. I know there are some people who are anti-recordings and say they never use them – but I think even those people use recordings too. I am cognizant of a couple of things. One is that you need to know the piece as well as you possibly can before you listen to a recording. But let me backtrack. Let's say you are a kid and you are in a youth orchestra – what are the pieces you know the best? They are all the pieces you did in youth orchestra, when you spent months rehearsing for the concert and were so excited because you played X, Y, and Z for the first time, and you sat in the orchestra. What I remember from those pieces I did in youth orchestra – the things that are ingrained in my body – are mostly the interpretations from that time. Whatever the youth orchestra conductor did, that is what I internalized and remembered, at least as my starting point. When I conducted *Firebird (1919)* or *Enigma Variations* for the very first time, my foundation for those pieces was my experience in youth orchestra. Similarly, when you are an assistant conductor, and you are covering and assisting, you are listening to someone else's performance. You are learning the score, yes – but you are still listening to someone else's interpretation. I don't necessarily think that taking in someone else's interpretation is a bad thing

– I think we naturally do that in life. We hear things, we hear performances, we hear rehearsals – we are always doing that.

It becomes tricky when you listen to a recording and you don't know why decisions were made. You can't ask the conductor, "Why did you take time here? Why did you...?" Also, you don't know what was edited – and that is a big factor. Sometimes recordings are heavily edited, and even the tempos and timings might have been changed. Then you've learned it that way because you listened to that recording, and when you hear the same conductor perform it another time, it is completely different – because it was the editing that shaped it. For me, a recording can be dangerous if you don't know the context around it and if you don't use it in the way that it exists. I personally prefer listening to live recordings. If I use a recording, I try to find a live one – an old live recording with two microphones – that is what it sounded like. No close mics, no editing and mixing. Anytime I can get my hands on an old recording, that is interesting to me. But I try to learn the piece first. Then I use the recording as just: *I wonder what they did. I wonder what this conductor did. I do it this way, but I'm curious to know if anybody else does it the way I learned it – and if not, then why?* And the *why* has also evolved for me, because the more experience I have as a conductor, the more I hear a recording and know why certain things happen. It's because someone forgot to beat this, or forgot to cue that, or didn't breathe with this – and all of a sudden, you have more context for why things are the way they are.

To make this whole thing a little shorter – I use recordings very judiciously. But I have to know the piece well enough before I listen to a recording so that I am comfortable questioning everything about it. Leonard Slatkin told me a similar thing about recordings: "Use recordings – whatever – if you want to use them, okay. But don't use them if you can't know why a decision was made." For example *[sings the third theme from Dvořák's Ninth Symphony, first movement]*, somebody did that *[rubato]* one time and recorded it that way, and then everybody started doing it, and nobody asked why. If you are not questioning why, then you are not using the recording properly.

After reading the score, a conductor can recognize the differences between the interpretation on the recording and what is in the score. What would you say are the biggest challenges in reading scores?

The biggest challenge for me is when it is a new composer that I don't know – figuring out how they are using notation for their music and what their language is. Everyone has their own way of utilizing the concept of notation to create music. For me, that is always trying to figure out how to get past that and hear their voice – what they are singing in their head. That might be the biggest challenge for conductors in general, whether they realize it or not. Maybe it is because some conductors get too stuck in the notation – they get too caught up in saying, "I see quarter notes, I see this, it should be like this, I should conduct it like this." Stop. Just listen. Sing it. Forget that there is anything on the page, and then the music will come to you. It is about trying to get out of the notation, trying to get to the composer – that might be my biggest challenge, and the thing that is of utmost priority when I am learning a new piece or a new composer.

The notes themselves can mean different things for different composers, and the point is to get behind the notes to reach the music. For many conducting students, especially at first, much of the work is just to decode the transpositions and identify the pitches, rhythms, and so on.

Now, this is very interesting. I am fascinated by this aspect because I never had formal training in techniques for reading transpositions – for example, whether you are changing keys or not or using clefs to do it. I won't say that I am terribly good at it, but I am good enough to read scores and figure it out. I've done enough score reading over the last twenty years that it has become my second nature. I think what helps me – and probably helps a cellist with tenor clef, or a pianist with bass and treble clefs – is just having experience. It is like with languages: if you already speak more than one language, then learning others is usually a little bit easier. I think it is the same with transpositions. If you can get past fluently reading more than one thing, then you can usually get past it and see everything the way it needs to be. The layout is also a huge help. For example, when I see a horn line, I know it is in F or G, but I also know where it is visually in the score. If I am reading something, my eye immediately goes to that line, and I hear it in F – it is not even a question.

Do you think about which instrument is playing – and then immediately you know what kind of sound the notes will make?

I am attached to it by where it is on the page – that is an aspect of it as well. Sometimes, when they condense a score, they might hide a lot of staves, and then the horns are at the bottom. All of a sudden, I have to remember, and then I will write "horns" so I know what I am looking at. But if I know where they are, then immediately, when reading, I am visualizing it. One thing I really despise nowadays is when composers give you a score in C. I know they are trying to make it easier for you, but I spend so much time figuring it out. Just keep it the way it is! I want to see what they see – of course, I want to see what the clarinet player sees – but that is not really the issue. It is just that I am so used to transposing where it needs to transpose. It is like, *Don't change it for me.* But I think that can be a problem – Prokofiev's scores, for example, are in C. I'm doing Prokofiev's *Fifth Symphony* with the kids this summer, and that is a score in C. Even though it is easier, it is harder in a sense because I have to really re-transpose back. I see a horn note and I am like, *That's low – oh, that's because it's in C; it's not actually low.* That is where it gets a little bit tricky.

Does it have to do with the instruments, which are going to be transposing anyway, like clarinets will be in B-flat or A, and horns in F? In Prokofiev's scores, the English horn is notated without transposition in alto clef, even though it is a transposing instrument in F.

Exactly.

Conductors get used to reading scores with transpositions. There aren't going to be clarinets in C playing in the orchestra, so this is not a natural way of thinking about it.

And then there's the visual behind it. When I see and hear an English horn line, I see it in the transposition – I don't see it in alto clef. When I see that, it is just so disconcerting, that's what it is.

You have also conducted opera, and you mentioned in the questionnaire that when you read an opera score, you sing the soloists' parts. How is that important for your score reading?

I have to break this into two sections. One is just about having a soloist in general – whether it is an instrumental soloist in a concerto or a vocal soloist in an opera. I always want to have the soloist's music as internalized in my body as humanly possible. That means that the moment they make an *accelerando*, take a breath, slow down, or do anything – it is so ingrained in me that I can immediately react to it. Most of the time, I have to follow them – or I have to make it easy for the orchestra to follow them, which is the real way. But still, being able to do that requires me to know the soloist's part intimately. That is number one. Then, for opera or anything vocal, it is about the text. The text has so much information about how they create a word, how they move from a consonant to a vowel. Consonants are usually pickups to the beat. The way they create words is so important for the ensemble, and it is essential for me to know their timing. I always want to have their words inside my mouth as well – so I know exactly what they are doing and can accompany them without a problem. All of that information gives me a lot to work with, and it is crucial just to make it going and as effortless as possible.

Would you like to add any other aspects, or do you have any anecdotes about score reading?

The biggest thing I mentioned earlier was the actual layout and engraving of the music. I will give you an example. Recently, I did a new oratorio that was written for an orchestra in the US. The composer sent me the score – this big thing – and that was the first page *[shows the score with empty staves and very small notes]*. I got this and thought, *This is impossible,* because it is an hour-long, brand-new piece, and I can barely read anything. He didn't quite understand the concept of proper engraving – he just didn't know it. For example, flute 1, flute 2, and flute 3 were all on separate staves – none of it was condensed. I said to him, "I'll do it. I won't charge you – just send me your files." After he sent them, I made my own score in Sibelius, and now it is a lot easier to read because everything is separated and condensed. It just makes a huge difference *[shows the new score]*. Also, there are less measures per system, and they follow the phrase structure – so you can see the phrases much more easily. With the original layout, I would have to draw a line every four bars just to know what bar I am conducting. That is the thing I can't stress enough to composers, especially: the idea that notation can make reading a score so much easier – if you know how to properly lay it out on the page.

Have you been engraving pieces just for your own conducting, or for other works as well?

No, I've usually only engraved things if it is a modern piece and they can send me the files – because I am not going to sit there and input the whole thing from scratch. Or, if it is a piece that I really like – for example, this piece I did with youth orchestra. It is not performed very often, and it is a piece I am probably going to conduct again. It is by Morton Gould, and it is called the *Latin-American Symphonette*. The score itself is fine, although it has a lot of mistakes. But the parts are handwritten *[shows parts]*. For something like bass clarinet, it is not a big deal because there aren't a lot of notes. But for the violins and flutes, which have chromatic passages and fast notes, it is very hard to read. This bass clarinet part is actually very funny – whoever wrote it out in the 1940s got to the end of the second page and realized they hadn't left enough space for the last staff. So, as you can see at the bottom of the page, it is handwritten just to fit in. This is what you get when you buy it – it is basically impossible. But of course, professional engraving costs a lot of money if they have to hire someone. Now I did it myself, and it makes a huge difference. It can sometimes mean the difference between being able to sight-read a piece or not, between being efficient in rehearsals or not. It is that kind of thing. I find it all very fascinating, and if I have the time, I enjoy doing it.

I've seen old handwritten parts filled with layers of additional markings, and then the orchestra is having a difficult time playing the piece, fighting with the notation. This is a great thing you are doing for the future of these pieces.

Hopefully, yes. I've had some fights with publishers over this kind of thing too, actually. There is one piece by a Mexican composer that I tried to get published because it is copyrighted in the United States, but outside of the U.S. it is in the public domain. It is a really amazing piece – very rhythmic and cool, but written for a huge orchestra. I've done the piece a lot, and it is performed quite a bit here in the States. The parts are even worse than what you just saw. In the U.S., it is published by a major publishing company, and you have to rent it from them. I made a new engraving – a proper critical edition – I got the manuscript, contacted scholars in Mexico, and the publisher sadly wouldn't give me the time of day. They constantly deflected and didn't even bother. So, I put it on IMSLP – for orchestras outside of the U.S. to be able to use it freely. But it's amazing: even when you're working with the best intentions to create this material, there are still politics, money, and all sorts of issues involved – if it is copyrighted. And that can be a struggle too. But you just do the best you can.

It sounds like the story of Stravinsky, who had to write new versions of his own pieces in order to have them performed in America.

There is one very quick anecdote I remember. My first job ever as a conductor was with the Cincinnati Symphony. I was an assistant conductor with Paavo Järvi – he was my boss there. Paavo was the conductor of the symphony, and they also had a big pops season – the Cincinnati Pops. At the time, the director of the pops was a guy named Erich Kunzel. In America, he was very famous for pops, film music, Broadway. He was one of David

Zinman's classmates and had studied with [Pierre] Monteux – but he decided to go in the path of Pops concerts as a career, and he was very good at it. I remember my first week in Cincinnati was a pops week, so it was with Erich. Apparently, he had been tending his garden and had cut his left hand, which was now completely covered in a bandage. He came to conduct in Cincinnati but couldn't turn pages, so my job was to sit in front of the podium, read the scores upside down, and turn pages for him. It was fine – it was pops repertoire, so it was all easy to read. Everything was in four, the phrases were in four-bar groupings – it was pretty straightforward. But I got a chance to look at his scores and see how he marked them. It is all about priorities – what is important for the job you have to do. In his case, pops was his life. That means: one rehearsal, just a run-through, not much rehearsing, no time for nuance. The orchestra plays – and with a great orchestra, they can sight-read a lot of that material with no problem. Part of his conducting job was turning around to talk to the audience between every piece – saying something, keeping the energy up in the room. Oftentimes, when he turned back to conduct after talking, he might not even know what music was on the page. He would just see what the meter was, glance at the metronome marking he'd written in big red ink, and shout, "One-two-three-four!" like a bandleader – and they'd start playing. Only then would he begin reading the music. And I thought: *This is ridiculous!* But it worked. Most of those arrangements were simple blocks – woodwinds come in, then brass, then strings. Very straightforward. And that is how he marked it, big and clear: "woodwinds", "brass", "strings". He beat time with the right energy, cueing who needed to be cued – and it worked. That is what the music and the ensemble required in that situation. It was eye-opening for me. Not because it was bad – it wasn't bad at all. It was exactly what he needed. His job wasn't just conducting; it was also talking to the audience. So if you need to turn around, keep the energy up, and just give a cue – what do you need on the page to do that? He even had a metronome on the stand next to him. What he wanted me to do was read the metronome mark in the score, and while he was talking to the audience, I would set the metronome to that number. Then he'd turn around, look at the light, shout "One-two-three-four!" – and off they went. It was amazing!

The choice of tempo is important.

The tempo is important, but also – when you break it all down – he could for sure sit there and play whatever the harmonies are; he is a trained musician. But that is not the priority in that moment. He doesn't have to do that.

He doesn't need it for the job – it is not necessary. So in the end, I think it is always about thinking what is practical. When you are learning a lot of music and going from week to week with new repertoire, what is actually necessary? What do you want to spend your time doing? What do you want to spend your time learning? That is just the reality – whether it is good or not, or whether one likes it or not, it is just how it is. If you have more time to really learn the piece – that is great. One thing I like about re-engraving is that you learn every note of the piece – because you are literally going through and inputting every single note. That is very helpful, because then you really know the piece inside and out. But it is all priorities.

The Daily Routine of Score Reading – *Philippe Bach*

Interview on 12 August 2024

Could you describe your score reading experience, share how you read scores?

Actually, I have not changed in this since I started conducting, but I am getting faster and faster, because the more scores you study, the faster you get at it. For example, if you study your first Wagner opera, it takes a long, long time, but I really love doing it. For me it is like an instrumentalist's practice of the instrument, a daily routine. My daily routine is studying scores – new ones, or also scores I have already conducted. Sometimes if I have time, I buy a new score of a Beethoven symphony, or something, to go with a fresh and another mind. Then it is always the same – I study the structure, the harmonies, the phrases, the "Takt-Gruppen", as we say in German.

What really changed in the last fifteen years is that you can listen to everything on YouTube, to twenty different recordings, but I think this is bad for young conductors, because I find that some young people just listen to great recordings and want to copy them. It is important that you make up your own mind as a conductor. It is, of course, great to listen to recordings – especially when conducting Italian opera, because there are so many traditions. It is very comfortable these days that you can listen to old performances, but it is still better to study the score first and then listen, so you can decide about the traditions – if you like them or not. If you then discuss with the singer, you know about them. It is important to know about these traditions and in this way we live in great times that you can listen to many great conductors. But still, studying the score is very important, and not just listening to performances from other conductors.

I am not a pianist, but sometimes if there are difficult passages, I play them very slowly on the piano to get it into my ear. I am lucky that I was a horn player, so I am quite fast with transposing. As a horn player it is really an advantage, we are very quick, it does not matter which transpositions or songs, we can read very quickly and easily. That is the way, and I love it. I also really like to conduct new pieces – new music, but also unknown pieces, because I think we have a fantastic profession, and I really love to study scores.

When you read scores, do you study several works at the same time, or do you focus only on one score?

It always depends. When you are very busy, sometimes there is no way around it – you have to study in parallel. But when I can choose, I prefer to work on one piece after another. When you are under pressure – I once read a book about George Solti, and he said that if he had two weeks and there were two hundred pages, he would read twenty pages every day – sometimes I think that is the only way to get rid of the stress. And sometimes, we have stress. If I have ten days and I need to know three hundred pages, then I read thirty pages per day, or something like that – it is a bit like practicing.

Do you go through a score multiple times, focusing first on some specific element, or do you read everything at once?

I read everything at the same time, but of course, I come back to it later. I don't read the harmony first and then the rhythm – no, I do everything at once. It is different when you are conducting concert repertoire or opera. When you are conducting a concert in the professional world, there is usually very little time, and you really need to know what you want. If you are doing a full stage production of an opera, there is much more time – six or eight weeks – and the first four weeks are only with the singers. I like that, because it also allows you to develop your interpretation. In rehearsals, you see which tempo suits which singer, and also the staging. What I love about opera is that you can build an interpretation during the rehearsals, before you go to the orchestra. Those are two different concepts.

Is it like adding dimensions to the score through this work with singers?

Yes, you are flexible with the tempo – when it goes a bit far, you know about the *rubati* and all those things. It comes in the rehearsals.

The art of the conductor is very complex. It starts with the score, continues with the musicians in rehearsals, and in opera, also with the stage director.

Absolutely. It is the same when you are conducting a very famous piece that the orchestra has played a hundred times – you may know how you would like the oboe solo to sound, but you might have a very experienced oboe player who has performed it forty times. In that case, it is not easy to persuade them to do something completely different. That is our life: we always need to be flexible and react to what we hear. But I still think the most important thing for a conductor is to have an idea, because the musicians expect that. If you don't have an idea, you should not be a conductor. I am not saying you can't change it, but you should have a very strong interpretation in your mind – know what you like – because that is why we are conductors.

When you read a score, do you predict where there might be moments of flexibility in the interpretation, or does that emerge at rehearsals?

More the latter. It depends on the music – especially in opera, with all the *rubati*. It is instinct, and it is not only about what you feel, but also about what happens together with the singer.

You have conducted a lot of opera – how important do you think it is for a conductor, when reading the score, to know the text and the language?

That is very different in opera, because everything comes from the text. In opera, the first thing I do is translate the text word by word. It is much easier with languages you speak – I still find it very difficult to conduct a Russian or Czech opera. I prefer to conduct in German, Italian, English, or French – the languages I speak – because most musical decisions should come out of the words, from the meaning of the text. That is very different in vocal music compared to symphonic music.

Therefore, when reading an opera score, is it most important to start with the text?

It is the most important part, because sometimes the orchestra reacts to what the singer has sung before, but sometimes it is the opposite – the orchestra introduces the new mood of the situation before the singer. It is important that you know what is what and have a word-by-word translation – not just a general sense – so you know exactly: this word needs an accent, this one should be soft, or this moment needs to be tender before she says that, or something like that. There are composers who write everything into the score, and others who write very little. In opera, for example, Puccini writes very precisely, but Wagner writes much less. It changes from composer to composer. But again – the more you conduct from a composer the easier it is. If I were young again, I would study much more, because I used to study only the things I conducted. The problem is always that we do not have enough time. But it is important for a conductor to explore other pieces by a composer: what they were writing in this period, chamber music, piano music. That is also a very nice part of our profession – getting to know so much great music.

Thinking of score reading not only as reading notes, but as reading the music – do you think this so-called "seeing behind the notes" comes from experience?

And also from the historical context of a piece – in which period the composer lived, what was happening around him, and how it influenced him. Sometimes we say, "It is a copy, it sounds like blah-blah," but that is common in art. When you are young, you have your idols, and you want to try to imitate them. The greatest composers also imitated others – Beethoven loved Mozart, and Schubert loved Beethoven. It is the same in painting or architecture; it exists in every art.

The historical context deepens our understanding of a composer's work. You mentioned transpositions earlier – reading them from the score can be a challenge. In the horn section, for example, there are often changes of transposition, or multiple transpositions – sometimes even four different ones at the same time – creating quite complex score reading situations. Could you please share in what kind of way do you read transpositions? Do you use one method for all kinds of music (tonal, atonal, chromatic, and so on), or does it change depending on the music?

I transpose very quickly in my head. I know some people do it using old clefs, like soprano clef, but because I was used to transposing as a child, it is really not a problem for me. However, if you are a violinist and have never done it before, I imagine it can be very difficult. I have a very good friend – a composer, a violinist, a great musician – and I asked him to do a version of a wind orchestra piece for symphony orchestra. It was very challenging for him, even though he has perfect pitch. He said he needed a lot of time, because in wind orchestra there are so many different transpositions. When you are starting, if you are young, it is worth doing exercises – just write it down. For example, in [Verdi's] *Don Carlos* there are four horns in four different keys. It is very hard, so just do an arrangement to learn it and see it in C.

Do you think and hear in your mind that the notes sound an interval lower or higher than written?

Yes, absolutely.

As a horn player, are you used to thinking with the transposing interval?

Yes. In Switzerland, when I was studying, we learned the DO-RE-MI method from [Zoltán] Kodály, where you change the DO – that is also a possibility in tonal music to learn it quickly.

In this method, DO is the first degree of a key and is moveable to different pitches. Do you think this helps in reading transpositions?

Absolutely, yes.

How can we achieve fluency in score reading? Do you think it comes with practice and experience?

Absolutely. What I still do in tonal music is write every harmony into the score. That is the way I learn it – then I hear it. I have always loved harmonies and different chords. When I was younger, I wrote much more – this is the tonic, this is the fifth, this is the third – because sometimes, under stress in front of an orchestra, the mind is not very quick, and you can get blocked. When it is written down, you don't need to transpose again – you really see it. I don't need this anymore, but I did when I was young. It is about intonation – you have to listen to every note. You need to learn it, and you can only learn it by doing it. Many conductors say, "The orchestra musicians look after that themselves," but no – you need to help them: which note is the octave, which is the fifth. It is important to work on intonation, because the musicians expect that. In youth orchestras, an important part of our job is teaching young players how to listen.

From reading the score and analyzing the harmony, conductors can see where the thirds, sevenths, and other components of the chords are. Musicians in the orchestra have only their own parts, while conductors can see all the orchestral parts together in the score. So, from the score, conductors can determine the basis for intonation and how it is going to work.

Absolutely.

You mentioned earlier that you sometimes read complex passages of the score on the piano. Is that to find out the harmony?

Yes, sometimes the harmony, but sometimes also the melodic lines, when it is very atonal. I have perfect pitch with horn because I played it so much – the horn I can anchor – but not with other instruments. So if something is very difficult, it is worth for me to play or also sing it. If you have a contemporary opera, play it slowly that it gets into your ear. If you are not a pianist, it does not make sense to try to play the score on the piano in tempo while leaving things out – that is a waste of time. When I play the score on the piano, it is something that makes my ears improve.

When you read a score, do you imagine the sound of the orchestra?

Absolutely, yes.

Do you go through the score in your mind, trying out different tempos?

Yes.

What about contemporary music – do you remember any special challenges you encountered when reading these kinds of scores? Was there anything different or surprising?

These days, there are so many different ways to notate music that it can be a huge challenge. Sometimes, especially when conducting the first performance of a piece, it is worth listening to a computer-generated audio just to get an idea and to train the ear. It has nothing to do with what will happen afterwards, but it can help you imagine the harmony or the melodic lines. Most composers these days also do it themselves, they compose on the computer, so they have an audio file of the piece.

Can this technology help in score reading?

Also, if you have very complex tempo changes with relationships between them – it helps get it into your body and hear it. The metronome can sometimes also help. As a conductor, it is important to train in metronomes – to know tempos like 108, 80, or 120 – and be rather precise, good in that. Sometimes, you go through a score in your head with the metronome, just to internalize it. Thankfully, music these days is much more flexible again than it was when we were in Aspen[95]. At that time, everybody tried to do the exact metronomes of Beethoven, but I think that has changed.

---

[95] Philippe Bach and the author participated in the American Academy of Conducting at the Aspen Music Festival and School in 2005.

I remember the recordings of all the Beethoven symphonies by David Zinman, our teacher at Aspen, in which he follows the written metronome markings[96].

I think music is not a beat, it is like a pulse, like your heart. Every human being has a heartbeat – when you are excited, it is faster; when you are relaxed, it is slower – and it is the same with music. When a composer writes a tempo, it is never exactly the same all the time.

Is it true that when you read a score, you create your own idea and vision of the music, but during the performance, various elements can influence it, so the result may not be exactly as you had imagined?

Absolutely. Of course, every concert hall can also slightly change your tempo. If you play in a very dry acoustic, it is different than if you play in a church. But still, it is important as a conductor to be very good in tempi – to know them and be more or less reliable. Musicians hate if you do the same music one day, let's say in tempo 80, and the next day 120 – it does not look professional.

When you read a score, do you use a metronome?

Not at first. Later, when I go through the score, I try to imagine what I think it should be and then control it with the metronome – it is my idea.

First you get to know the music, you imagine it, and then you check your own vision and feeling with the metronome?

Yes. Some composers are very good at writing tempos, others not – it is not sacrosanct. A composer friend once told me that often what he had written was too fast. For me, it is sometimes the same with Bartók, and also with Ligeti.

Bartók even measured the duration of individual phrases...

Yes, Bartók was obsessed with calculating and timing – with *Zahlen*, figures. His *Second Piano Concerto* is nearly impossible to realize in his tempi.

Do you sometimes sing the score to get a feeling of a phrase?

Absolutely.

---

[96] David Zinman recorded the cycle of Beethoven's symphonies with the Tonhalle-Orchester Zürich in the 1990s.

How does singing help you in score reading?

One thing is to train the ear – that is clear – but much more important, it is about the phrasing: where the music goes, and also about small *rubati* and all those things.

Is it also helpful in rhythmical music, like Stravinsky's pieces? Do you read modern pieces differently compared to older music?

When you do Stravinsky, you don't need to sing the pitches, because the rhythmical element is there. But like a percussion player, it is good to speak the rhythm so that it gets into your body. What is written is important, but even more important is the feeling you have. You can find great people who are fantastic at mathematics but terrible at rhythm. It is more about getting it into your body, not into your head. Maybe you know it in your head – but if you don't feel it…

During score reading, is it good to physically execute the rhythm in some way?

By using your body, so that the rhythm is in your body – yes, absolutely. Also in transitions, because that is the hard thing in opera – you have so many transitions that need to work, and often you don't have many rehearsals. In opera, you have less time during orchestral rehearsals because there is more music than in symphonic concerts. In transitions, you really need to be sure about the relationship between the tempos. These relationships are very important, especially in opera repertoire. For example, when professional conductors did not exist in Mozart's time, every tempo change in opera was related to another tempo. That is also a very important part of studying scores, especially in opera – to think about the relationships between the tempos.

Do you think this is also very important in later, Romantic operas by Wagner?

Yes, I always look for it. Sometimes composers want there to be no relationship, but in most music – and especially with good composers – there is some kind of relationship.

Have you ever found, when reading a score, that you needed to add or change something in the score?

I try first to do what is written, but sometimes I see that it will not work, especially in balancing. There are composers who are like holy gods, as

Mozart – you don't have to change one note. When I was studying, I was very lucky: we had chamber music lessons with Siegfried Palm, the famous cellist. Many composers wrote for him – Penderecki, Lutosławski, Ligeti – all the great concertos. He taught new chamber music, and he was very free with the text: he listened, and then he decided whether it sounded good or not. I think we, as conductors, need to help the composers – we need to do what we think is best so that the music sounds good. If a composer wrote his first piece, maybe he did not yet know everything – Rachmaninoff's *First Symphony* is not as good as his *Symphonic Dances*, of course. In such cases, you might need to change things so that it is the best for the piece.

Is score reading a creative process in which the conductor uses imagination to help the composer, so that the piece can have its best possible performance?

Yes. There are many famous stories. When we were young, it was the time when urtext editions came in, and you really needed to do them. But I think we got too much into this, because composers in their own time were all very free with everything. This is a story about Toscanini when he was very young, playing *Aida* for Verdi. He asked the composer, "Maestro, why didn't you write *ritenuto* here?" Verdi replied, "Every good musician feels it – I don't need to write it".

When you are reading a score, do you think of the audience – how they will hear and experience the piece?

Not really, no. When I try to interpret a piece, like a Verdi opera, I never think, "Oh, in Puccini's time they would have done it like this" – I don't like that. I always try to perform a piece as it would have been in the time of the composer. Not exactly, but with the traditions of the time – phrasing, *rubatos*.

Nowadays, conductors have access to much more knowledge about performance practices from the time of the composer. It is possible to take into account the performance traditions of the composer's surroundings; for example, we know that Brahms expected the use of portamento, and we can hear it on recordings by Joseph Joachim. However, on some recordings, musicians take interpretive freedoms with the score, and some of these have become new performing tendencies. In opera, there are quite a few of these. How do you deal with this variety and huge number of different performing traditions and fashions?

You need to know about them, and then find and decide your way. These days, because nobody buys CDs anymore, there actually aren't as many recordings being made by orchestras as there used to be. But it is nice to have them, especially for opera. All those Carlos Kleiber recordings – he did very few, but every one of them is really a historical musical document that will last forever because it is so perfect: *La Traviata*, *Der Freischütz*, and *Der Rosenkavalier*. It is a bit of a shame that we don't make these kinds of recordings anymore; now there are far more live performances being recorded and sold. I really love these perfect recordings of Kleiber – it is very nice to listen to them.

Because you have studied the scores, are you able to recognize Kleiber's additions while listening to the recordings?

Yes, and his ideas are perfect in the recordings because he could do it twenty times. He was such a perfectionist.

In the past, conductors had many more rehearsals when preparing a recording or a performance. The lack of time is one of the challenges of our times.

Absolutely.

Do you prepare your own orchestral materials for operas, including bowings and nuances?

As I am not a string player, I always need some help with bowings. When I conduct a piece at a famous opera house, I ask for a copy of the first violins' part, just for my interest. When I conduct a piece with my orchestra here in Switzerland – since they don't perform a lot of opera – I use materials from some of the pieces I assisted on, just the set of string parts, and I give them to my leader. He can then decide if they are good or not. It is also a question of time, because sometimes there is very little. It is much faster if a conductor has their own material prepared with all the phrasings, of course.

Could you share any kind of anecdote related to score reading?

I remember a conducting lesson with Peter Eötvös; it was a complex score of his. I will never forget how he stood beside me and really took the time to teach me how to listen. He said to me, "Can you hear here? Listen there." He was such a genius and had perfect pitch. The earlier you start studying many, many scores as a conductor, the better.

Was this during a rehearsal with an orchestra?

It was a chamber ensemble, about ten musicians. That is another thing I didn't mention – when you are standing there as a conductor, you are under stress, but if you are listening to a colleague conducting, from the audience or from behind – you can hear much better. Sometimes, when we are conducting, it becomes harder to hear. There is a famous story about Karajan, who said that only when he was sixty years old were his ears good. It is sometimes hard for a young conductor to accept, but this is how it is. If you conduct your first Wagner opera, it is very hard, but if you have done seven or eight Wagner operas, it gets easier.

To develop orchestral sound imagination, it is helpful to listen to orchestras and compare the sound with the score. Do you have any other ideas about how this could be done?

Naturally, a German orchestra, when playing Wagner, really has it in their blood, and it is the same with Italian music for Italian or Spanish orchestras – it sounds different. These days, orchestras are much more international, and we Swiss are especially privileged, because we usually grow up with three cultures. Also in the music world, we are very international, and that is a nice thing. Of course, you still need to find your own way, but there is a Wagner sound – how Wagner is played by the Dresdner Staatskapelle or the Gewandhaus Orchestra, or also Brahms – you need to know about that. And how the orchestras of Milan, Bologna, or Rome play Verdi. It is authentic; the people have it in their blood. With modern technology, we know much more about the international world, but still, composers have very much to do with the character of the people they lived among.

It is a big advantage in today's world that conductors can travel and listen in different countries to how musicians perform their national and local music. This can be very helpful in understanding the score and in getting to know how the composer imagined their music would sound. We live in a global world, but music keeps its individuality – styles are important.

Yes, absolutely.

Would you like to add anything further about score reading?

I really think it is the same as with conducting – you need to find your own way to study as a conductor, but the more information you have, the better. You can try different things, and everyone should find their own way to do it. Studying scores is really important for a conductor – it is our work. I actually think it is even more important than conducting itself. I didn't mention it earlier, but when I study a piece, I never start by conducting it. First comes studying, and only later do the movements come for me.

The conductor's work with the score is often unknown, even to orchestra musicians.

I completely agree with you. It is much harder for us to conduct a Haydn symphony than a Stravinsky piece. A Haydn symphony requires much more thinking…

So much in the score is not…

Written.

Open Sound Image and Leadership –
Maria Badstue

Interview on 14 July 2024

When you open a score of a new piece that you have never heard before, how do you begin reading it?

It depends very much on your main instrument and how well you play the piano. I am not a pianist – of course, I can play a little – but not to the level where I can feel the music flowing. I can get impressions of the chords and some small details. If it is a Brahms symphony, I already remember more or less what is happening as I knew the music for many years. But with a newly written piece, I first mark the periods – *do I think in eight bars or four bars before something new happens?* Those overall groups of happenings are, you could say, like organizing the score, so I know what and who is important, when and where – very basically. Especially when I was younger, I also focused on direction. With new scores, there can be very different instruments – strange or unfamiliar settings – and so I have to know: *Okay, this one is placed here?* Very practically, I go over these aspects, mark the periods, and then start to play the score, either on the piano or my instrument, the trumpet. I still do this because my first conducting teacher in Denmark told me, "If you don't play the piano very well, you have to play all the lines, all the parts, on your instrument." When I was very young, I did that – every time I got a score, I played everything on the trumpet. This way, of course, you do not get the harmonic picture, but you do get clarity. Whatever instrument you play at a professional level, you can really feel where to breathe, where the music is going, and it helps you understand the musician who plays it in another way. Then of course, if you play the trumpet, as I did, which does not have such a big ambitus – your octave sometimes sounds crazy. But often, you still get a very clear idea, and you transpose a lot. I am sure there are not that many conductors who do it this way. Nowadays, I do it less and less – first of all because I do not need it as much, but also because I don't play so often. Either I don't have time, or I don't have my trumpet with me.

Does playing parts of the score on the trumpet help you feel the phrasing and how to shape the music?

Exactly. Basically, you could also be singing – but still, it is with the instrument. If I were a singer, I would have sung it, of course. But you can read it on an instrument on which you feel like a musician.

In what sense, then, is the piano useful for your score reading? What does it help you with?

It is useful, for example, for playing the bass and the melody. Contemporary music – true, I do play it sometimes – that could be very high or big intervals, or something like that. Then I play it to clarify what is actually written. Sometimes I will play two or three of the parts in a slow tempo, like cross-playing them.

This year, you conducted The Rite of Spring *by Stravinsky – a very difficult score, with many layers and instruments playing different things at the same time. What steps did you take to read this score? Did you read each instrument or group of instruments separately before imagining the score as a whole?*

First of all, that was a piece I already knew, because we did it in the academy. It is actually a bit the same process as described above – maybe I am simplifying too much – but you know: *okay, now the horns are the important ones, now it is the trumpets, and then someone else is accompanying.* A lot of *The Rite of Spring* is built on rhythm, so I tried to make it easy in a way, especially the ending, which is so well known for being difficult because it is rhythmically complex. I just took it step by step. And yes, I did read the instruments separately, because at the beginning there are so many different wind parts, and they are really in and all over each other.

It is not really possible to play this score on just one piano…

I have felt for many years that, because I don't play the piano well enough, it is frustrating in this sense – you feel you have to be a good pianist to be a conductor. It is an advantage in many ways in this process of studying. But actually, in the beginning, I played all the parts of *The Rite of Spring* on either the piano or the trumpet. It takes a lot of time, because it means playing through the piece about twelve times or more. But once I've done that, I feel a better sense of preparation. I did that very much when I was young, so I felt I knew all the parts and was more secure with everything. When you have played it many times, you start to also remember – or feel – the harmony in a way. Over time, there is more and more you do not need to do, because you already know how it sounds – especially in the old repertoire. New written repertoire is, of course, more difficult in this regard.

After reading the parts separately, do you imagine how the instruments sound together?

Yes.

In the questionnaire, you mentioned that when you read a score, you think about where to lead and where to give space to the musicians. In what kinds of situations does this occur in the score?

I am just sitting and preparing [Richard Strauss's] *Ein Heldenleben* right now, and there is a very big violin solo – look, here it is! *[shows the score]*

This piece is one of the most challenging scores for a conductor to read...

I am doing it in India – Zubin Mehta is conducting there – and I am taking four rehearsals for him of *Ein Heldenleben*. I have never done it before – and true – not an easy piece. We are also doing *Don Juan*. There is a big violin solo in the middle, where sometimes you can leave the violinist very much. It is like with singers or soloists – sometimes you can really leave them, give them space to play, like in a cadenza. It depends so much on the player and their personality. That also applies when it is an orchestral musician who has a solo in the score. Some like you to inspire them or be with them, and some prefer that you stay away. Maybe some of them are even on trial and very nervous – so we have to very quickly feel what kind of personality and situation we are dealing with.

Some of these situations you can predict from the score, but when you meet the musicians, you might have to change your thinking.

Exactly. I don't plan that too much. More and more, I try to just go there and feel what is happening from the musicians, because it varies so much – some of them really don't want any interference. There is also this extra layer: our job is not only to give someone space to play whatever they want – we also need to maintain the overall responsibility. If you give them all the space, you are just like a traffic semaphore – now it is you, and now it is you. But on the other hand, that feeling of freedom for the musicians – could be nice. I am doing a research project in Odense about this: how and when to interfere. If I do a lot – what happens to the overall performance? And if I don't do much – what changes? How does it affect everyone if I am very much on them, or if I step back a little?

When reading a score, do you see different possibilities for how you could perform the piece?

Yes, and I do experiment with that during rehearsals. I might even try not to interfere during one part of the rehearsal, and in the second part, I will try to move it more – and then we would see. Of course, that is also within the limits. You can't do too many different things, because then people get confused – *Who are you? What do you want to do in the concert?*

So, there is not just one way to imagine a score – you can have a variety of possibilities and an openness to how the music from the score will sound?

And it depends very much on the kind of orchestra. If they have a lot of their own initiative it's a slightly different approach. If you give them something, they just fire away – then it is more about holding it a little. But if they don't have that energy themselves, you have to give more. It also depends very much who the leaders are – the *Stimmführer*, the concertmaster, of course – what kind of people they are. It is all very interesting.

Today's conductor travels a lot, and there is not always a piano available – but recordings are widely accessible. Does listening to recordings play a role in your score reading? If so, what does it add or change?

I think it is funny, because when I started with Jorma [Panula] – I know him very well – it was really like, "Don't listen to recordings." That was the big mantra. And everyone around us was saying, "Oh, we don't listen to recordings, no, no, no." But everybody knew that everyone listened to some extent – of course we do. I try not to listen at first. First, I try to play it myself. Then I listen, and especially if it is with singers, I always listen to ten different recordings to know the possible traditions. Singers have so many traditions of all kinds – staying on a high note, and so on – even if it is right or wrong in relation to the score. You have to know it, because sometimes there is not enough time to argue; you just have to make it work with whoever singer comes in. Then, for example, with *Ein Heldenleben* – now that I've gotten through the score reading – I have listened a couple of times, because it can be done very differently, especially in the tempi and phrasing. This is also to get ideas of how, because with [Richard] Strauss there are so many notes. If it is too fast, it doesn't work – it is too difficult. But if it is too slow, it also doesn't work, because you lose the character. That is something you can actually hear very well. And it is not only because of the quality of the players – sometimes I just feel, *Oh, that was a really good tempo for them, for this music or moment.*

When you listen to recordings, do you compare different tempos and observe which one makes the music sound best?

Yes, and sometimes I feel – *okay, here is a tempo that makes sense.* Then, when you listen to recordings with video, you also get ideas about body language. Of course, you cannot imitate or copy exactly, but you can still get ideas. Earlier on, I watched a lot; nowadays, I listen much more.

Do you use recordings to check the balance of the orchestra or search for technical difficulties in the piece?

Balance is always difficult in recordings because it is never real – it is not like being in the hall. A producer has fixed a lot of things, or the balance is very bad. I don't judge balance. I just check if I can hear the melodies or the important elements – the motifs and themes. If I can't, then I know, *okay, they had trouble in this recording, so maybe I will have the same issues.* You get ideas of where balance problems could be, because if they didn't manage it in the recording, it might be the same in real life.

You mentioned that you play the trumpet, which is a transposing instrument. Transpositions can be a challenge in score reading – how has your experience been with reading them? Are some transpositions easier for you than others? And if so, why?

It is only about training. Of course, F transposition is easier because we do it all the time. It is more difficult with E or E-flat, just because we don't have them as often. If we play in E-flat, it is only four tones or a minor third up, depending on whether you are playing the B-flat or C trumpet. Transposing in D from a B-flat trumpet is a major third up, which is almost like playing in bass clef. Everyone develops their own kind of strange little routine for that. Mostly trumpet players play on a B-flat trumpet, so they transpose up a whole tone when reading something for a C trumpet. But when you switch to F, it depends on which trumpet you are playing.

When you read transpositions in a score, is it similar to how you play on the trumpet – by thinking of the transposing interval and counting tones?

Yes. As you get older and read more and more music, you get better at guessing what is happening. You can see that the horns have a similar line, and then you notice – it is maybe a third up or down compared to the melody, or it is the same. Then you don't have to read all the notes.

Reading the score is an important part of a conductor's work – a process in which they strive to understand the music, the composer's language, and consider performance issues. This goes far beyond reading the notes or playing the score on an instrument.

Score playing is so much dependent on your level at the piano – simply your technique. Can you play quick scales? Can you do all the things? If you really can't do that, then you will never be a good score player. But that doesn't mean you are not a good score reader.

When reading the score, the conductor creates a sounding image of the music in their mind. What you described earlier was very interesting – that through score reading you don't hear just one fixed version of the piece, but instead create an open, flexible version, full of possibilities that will concretize during rehearsals with the orchestra.

I believe perhaps there are two kinds of conductors. Some are very good because they can really push through their own ideas so clearly. Their presence and will are so strong that people just do whatever they show or say – maybe [Daniel] Barenboim is a bit like that, or [Zubin] Mehta. This requires a very special type of personality, and some very good solo players are also like that – they just go, and then everyone else, the whole group, follows. Sometimes you can feel it – okay, here is someone everyone listens to and follows. Then you just go with that person, and everything is fixed. But maybe the truly great conductors can do both. And Barenboim and Mehta, for sure, can do both.

What is the second type of conductor?

That is when you have this ongoing dialogue that you prepared or intuitively know. Let's say two instruments have a phrase together – maybe they just have a very good way of phrasing together, and then you don't need to interfere much. But maybe they don't want to play together, or they don't like each other – then you have a problem, and you have to lead, because they won't agree. And maybe they actually run it by themselves but still look for inspiration – that is the nicest way. They basically do it themselves, and you give some suggestions here and there.

Would you say that the conductor is making music together with the musicians in the orchestra?

Yes, it is really fun when it turns out that way – then it truly is, of course, a fantastic job.

Have you been adding markings to the score – for example, bowings?

The bowings, of course, are done by the concertmaster, but I sometimes have some ideas. Sometimes the dynamics have to be changed from the conductor's side, especially if singers are involved, and it is not always enough just to show them. I remember when I was assistant at Wiener Staatsoper – it was such a big opera by [Paul] Hindemith, and they only had two rehearsals. If I hadn't written *piano* here, *mezzopiano* there, and this and that into all of the parts, it would have taken the conductor too much time to explain everything, and the musicians wouldn't have gotten it. The conductor asked me, "Could you please write this, this, and this into the parts?" It was quicker for me to do it during the break than for it to go through the library and archives. I could just do those things in the break. But sometimes, if you don't do that – if there is very little time and the conductor doesn't have time to do it – then it doesn't happen. In that sense, yes.

Today's conductors often work on a wide range of repertoire – from world premieres of new music to older works, such as pieces from the 18th and 19th centuries. When reading older music – let's say, a piece by Mozart – is there anything different for you in the way you read a score, compared to reading a contemporary one?

Yes, because you can guess much more of it. The cellos and basses always play more or less the same, so you don't have to be too concerned with this. The violins are mostly in thirds, octaves or something similar, and the horns as well – maybe in sixths. In that way, you can more easily guess the actual tones and harmonies. For example, *okay, if the bass goes that way, then the rest is going this way,* because I know the harmonies.

Is this something that comes with experience, after reading several of Mozart's pieces?

Yes, exactly.

When you work on a piece, do you begin by reading the score, or do you first explore the composer, the traditions, and the context around it?

I always start with the score first – always. For example, *Ein Heldenleben* – I only got it last week or so. I've never done it before, and I know, *Okay, I have a month, and then I have to do it really well.* You can almost never start too early with a score, so it is better to have it read. If you have read it, or played it, or listened to it – or felt it somehow in your body – then it is already digesting or melting into your body somehow. Then afterwards, you can read all the cultural and historical background – all the context.

Do you think that, in order to understand the score and know it more deeply, it is important to let some time pass and then return to it?

Absolutely.

You mentioned earlier that you sometimes read the score twelve times – does this help it "settle in", so that you get to know the music better?

Yes – and also much more than 12 times! And especially if you've had the chance to conduct it, and then some years go by and you return to the score. I did *Sacre* [*The Rite of Spring*] again after two years, and it was easier. But I also just did Beethoven's *Fourth Symphony* – I've done it three or four times – but it still feels like I am only scratching the surface, in a way. And it the same with *The Rite of Spring*, because there are so many new things to notice in these masterworks. I really love conducting Beethoven, because you feel like it brings you to a new place each time you go with it.

When you return to the score after conducting the piece, do you discover new things in it?

Of course, yes. New ideas about tempo, new everything. And that is very good – that is how it should be. But for example, having only one month to learn *Ein Heldenleben* – I could, of course, have started when I was twenty. I think I should have.

Due to the variety of musical styles and the fast pace of today's life, a conductor has to be very efficient in score reading, with advanced skills and knowledge in order to read and hear the notes – and then create an interpretation. Are there any other things that help you with score reading? Do you have any anecdotes – something that surprised you while reading a score?

Maybe I am surprised that it becomes easier, because I thought it was so very difficult in the beginning. For example, in Strauss – now I can see that some places are only cadenzas, or the harmonies are actually relatively simple. Then he adds all kinds of *[sings fast notes]*, and you get very confused – but it is actually simple.

In Strauss, there are a lot of figurations – has experience helped you recognize the melodic lines and harmonies better?

Yes, I see these more quickly or more easily, whereas when I was younger, I would have been more stressed about all the *[sings fast notes]*. Luckily, it becomes easier – but it is not easy to conduct.

In Ein Heldenleben, there are sections with complex polyphonic writing and syncopated harmonies that are challenging to read.

True, and it is also very difficult to play.

As you read the score, do you also imagine how you will conduct it?

Yes.

Do you think about the gestures and the beat patterns as well?

Not so much the beating and gestures anymore, but I did think about that a lot when I was younger, because I felt insecure and needed to get used to who is sitting where. I used to get stressed sometimes if they moved the horns to the other side or something like that. Now, that doesn't affect me very much. Or if they moved the violins, I would be very stressed – *Oh, I have to look this or that way!* – but now, it doesn't matter so much. I luckily just don't get so affected by those things anymore – also because of the pacing of the time we have. When I have the score, I think: *Okay, what is needed?* They need to have one or two rehearsals with me so they can present it in the best way to Zubin Mehta, so he has the chance to conduct it at his best level. So my job is to fix it and put it together.

Do you try to imagine how it is going to be with the orchestra and predict what kinds of situations you might face?

Yes, sometimes I try to imagine – *Okay, here are three or five possible outcomes of this situation. Maybe it goes this way: they play very fast, they run, they are out of tune.* You can sometimes almost see the issues beforehand.

Context and the Dramatic Arc –
Tomas Djupsjöbacka

Interview on 13 June 2024

In answering the questionnaire, you mentioned that you generally do not use the piano for reading scores, so I would like to ask how you work on the score – do you continuously imagine the sound while reading?

I have to start by saying that the piano thing is partly due to very practical reasons – we don't have a piano at home, and I often work on scores whenever I can. Maybe it's on an airplane, maybe in a hotel room – you know how it is. There isn't always a piano available, and anyway, I'm a very bad pianist. Of course, I can play chords and things, but I'm not the kind of conductor who can take a score and start reading it as if playing properly on the piano. I don't have that skill – or if I do, it's too slow to be helpful.

Your instrument is the cello, and you are also an active cellist. Does it happen that you read the score on the cello?

I don't think I've done it more than a couple of times, but I definitely think in terms of how I would phrase on a cello – how it feels on a string instrument – and I use that a lot. I don't necessarily do it concretely, as in picking up the cello and actually playing, but I imagine a lot there. I also very often do the bowings myself, because I really think that, for a string player, it helps to form an idea of the phrase – how you would shape it. I don't always give the bowings to the orchestra, because with deadlines here and there, it can sometimes, in practice, cause more trouble than help. Sometimes it can sound a bit silly – *should it be an up-bow or a down-bow?* It is not really about that. It is about how the phrase comes alive, and that, for me, is very helpful to use.

Is phrasing something you particularly focus on when reading the score?

It is one of the things, yes. I have to say, one piece of advice that was very helpful for me came from Jukka-Pekka Saraste. I don't follow it two hundred percent, but it was very interesting. He said that with a score, you need six rounds – you focus on different things each time, and after six rounds, you should know the piece. I'm not sure I can do it in six rounds, but what I really like about that advice is the idea that you read and focus on different aspects of the score, rather than imagining you can read everything at once. You focus on certain elements – different ones in each round – and then trust that your brain slowly puts this process together.

Do you have a specific order in which you read the elements of the score?

This has changed – it is a process. Over the past few months, I've been looking at things in a different order than I did a year ago. At the moment, I move much faster and place greater priority on the general form – proportions, length of phrases, and how things fit together on a larger scale. I try to reach that element more quickly, to get the overall structure of the piece. The amount of detail you can get caught up in is often infinite, so you have to be a bit careful not to get stuck there. I also try to do more harmonic analysis and look at the structure of the general movement. From there, I usually spend quite a bit of time on doublings – how they're constructed, unisons between instruments – which then relate to color. I do that, of course, much more with the winds than with the strings. As a string player, I feel I need to put more effort into that kind of work with the winds, because I can't just read it. String texture, since I'm more used to it, I can read faster. But with the winds, I have to put in greater effort to understand it. I'd say structure and harmonic analysis go pretty much hand in hand. After that: doublings, instrumentation, color, phrasing – and somewhere in there come bowings and things like that.

Nowadays, with recordings widely accessible, what role does listening to them play in your score reading?

There are three things that are important to me. First, when I was younger, I was very idealistic – I believed I should never listen to recordings and should form my own opinions. Now, I'm much more practical. Sometimes there is simply the issue of time – if you need to learn something really fast, you just have to do what needs to be done. But the third aspect related to recordings is actually the most important: what they can really help with is connecting to the tradition of the piece. By that I mean, if you can listen to recordings either by a conductor who was close to – or maybe even the composer themselves – you can really try to connect with the source, with the tradition of how the music should sound. For instance, an easy example is Richard Strauss – either conducting himself or through conductors he worked with. Or Bruno Walter with Gustav Mahler. You can also listen to

Hungarian music with Béla Bartók at the piano, or his *Divertimento* conducted by Sándor Végh.

By listening to this kind of recording, can you get closer to the composer's aesthetic and the performance practices of that time?

Performance practice is a topic I find a little more delicate. If there is a connection to the composer's world, it is quite difficult to define exactly what that is. But if we take Hungarian music – which sounds so connected to the language, to how people speak – you hear that firsthand. And then, of course, you go back to the score and make corrections and form new associations. Language is one thing. With earlier repertoire, where there are no recordings of the composer – for example, Beethoven – I often turn to historically informed performance practice to get a more x-ray feeling for the score, rather than something embedded in the romantic, egoistic tradition.

So, can notes mean different things in different times?

That is very well put – saying that notes can mean different things. Not just in the sense that similar music can mean one thing in one time period and something else later in life, but also, when you take, for instance, Berlioz's *Symphonie fantastique*, which I am studying again – the more you know about Berlioz as a person, about his life, the time in which this piece was written, the context – the more you can know what lies behind a single note, one phrase, a whole movement, or even the entire piece. The more you know, the more the music means to you. Then we are on a completely different level from a practical execution of how to conduct a score technically. You need all of that, of course – the hard part is that time is limited. But I am fascinated by how much it influences your interpretation when you know the context of the composer. That is the beauty of it: the more you know about the person, the more you understand what they mean when they say something. It is quite simple, actually – but it takes a lot of effort to get there.

You mentioned that the structure of the piece and its proportions are very important to you – could you say a bit more about that?

I am not interested in structure as a kind of mathematical exercise in proportions. I find that fascinating, but it is not the real aim. The real aim is to understand the dramatic story – the dramatic arc of how the movement or the piece unfolds. That can influence things like how to build a climax, whether you want to take time somewhere because it is a particularly emotionally important moment in the drama – those sorts of things. It might be written in the score, or it might not. And what is definitely never written is exactly how much time you need to take – it is usually some sort of approximate Italian word. In order to judge the proportions of how much, you need to have a full picture of the structure. That also influences tempo choices in the end. Because again, you might have a metronome marking – in which case, of course, you save a bit of time – but you might also have just a character marking. Then the question becomes: how to arrive at the speed where the dramatic elements make sense? For that, you need to know the whole text. You can't just think, *Okay, this little patch of eight measures sounds good in this tempo.* Of course, this is different in opera compared to symphonic repertoire – but the overall dramatic arc is the same.

How much do you use the metronome for score reading? Is it to follow the composer's markings, or do you also use it to time your interpretation?

If the composer put in the metronome marking, then you start from that point. But for me, it is also a lot about finding the affect of the phrase – a character, maybe the character of the movement in general. Actually, I use the metronome more at specific points. The metronome is a tool you can use to try out: at what speed does this character work, and where is the limit – the point at which it no longer works and you need to adjust?

Do you imagine, play in your mind the score in different tempos?

Yes. For instance, a concrete example – I was conducting Sibelius's *Fourth Symphony* with FiBO[97] on period instruments a few weeks ago. I had bought the new Urtext edition – the one with the blue hardcover – which includes much more information and comments from Sibelius himself, notated by Jussi Jalas, who was a relative. In it are Sibelius's comments on the tempos for the fourth movement, though he did not publish any metronome numbers. There are letters from when the first recording of this piece was made in London in 1927 – they had contacted Sibelius two years earlier to collaborate and asked for his feedback. Back then, in the days without internet, they sent him pre-tapes; he listened, made comments, sent letters with markings, and then they did the final recording later. In the same edition, you also find his comments on tempo markings for other conductors and performances of the same piece – and they are completely different. In the second

---

[97] Finnish Baroque Orchestra.

movement, for example, there is a forty-notch difference between two comments on tempo by Sibelius. So which one is it then? Forty clicks is a huge difference in character.

Do you think the composer changed his mind?

Probably he changed his mind – or maybe, under some circumstances, it didn't work. Another similar example of the metronome markings is with Brahms's *Ein deutsches Requiem*, which I conducted a few months ago. In one edition, I found Brahms's metronome markings for every movement – which are not published in the normal score – and they were really very slow. Then someone pointed out to me: "Ah yes, the premiere of this piece was in Bremen, in a church with enormous reverb." Probably Brahms was a practical man and thought, "Okay, it has to be taken slowly – with so much reverb, you won't hear the fugues unless they are slower." So that was mostly because of the acoustics. The metronome number is never the final truth, but a means of getting to the character and affect of the piece. That is what I am looking for when I use the metronome: the affect of a phrase – what it feels like, what it sounds like.

After creating a sounding image of the score in your mind, when you go to conduct the orchestra, how strongly do you stay with that image, and what kinds of things do you need to adjust?

That depends on the level of preparation, honestly. The stronger my preparation is – the more levels I have in my toolbox – the more I can insist on whatever I have come up with in the end. You never go unprepared, of course, but with a bit less preparation, it is easier to adjust – or easier to fall into a spot where you have to adjust. It also depends on how strong the orchestra's wish of the piece is – every orchestra has a different history with any given piece. Sometimes it is very helpful to inform yourself about that culture before going to conduct. If an orchestra has a very strong culture of the piece, I am more likely to listen to that and adjust. It is difficult to draw a final line – you solve it give or take.

Do you make any changes to the score – add markings or do retouching?

That depends. I will give you one example where I did: I conducted Louise Farrenc's *Second Symphony* a month ago. Although she is quite in fashion at the moment, compared to composers of her time, she is rarely played – so there is not a strong tradition of how to play Farrenc. I spent a lot of time with this score, examining articulation markings, thinking about character, and making quite a few – I wouldn't call them improvements, but clarifications. There were often inconsistencies, and when two instruments are doing the same phrase, the same melodic line – the same material – you can clearly see that they should probably do it the same way.

The more classical in time we are, the clearer, in fact, we should be. Later in history, there may have been a tendency for composers to deliberately do a bit of mixing things together, but in the early 19th century, that wasn't really the aesthetic yet. In this case, I spent a lot of time thinking mostly about articulation, and I do think that is a service to the composer. I also know, just from reading history, that women, for instance, did not have the same opportunities to have their works performed. In some cases, their music might have been played by amateur musicians, but not by professionals – and tradition is shaped by professional musicians playing a piece over and over again, and then maybe doing articulations here and there.

If you think of Beethoven – how many times has his music been played? In that sense, sometimes a composer simply did not have access to the kind of professional colleagues needed to work out those details. And in her case, being a pianist – perhaps pianists sometimes think differently about articulation, which is totally fine. But here, I did a lot of articulation work with the score, which I then sent in advance. In this case, I took particular steps to make sure the orchestra received the material weeks ahead of time, because I know from experience that if you have to spend rehearsal time on these kinds of things, you lose so much – it is a terrible waste of everyone's time. I specifically asked: please make sure that not just the string players get the bowings – which is normal – but that the wind players also receive and apply the articulation changes.

What kind of articulation changes were these? For the wind instruments, was it about breathing, types of staccato? And for the string instruments – bowings and bowing techniques like détaché, martelé, spiccato?

I like to talk about articulation, and that doesn't mean whether a note is short or long – it is more about shape. A simple example would be a phrase that is a descending chromatic scale – a kind of sigh, an old affect. If you don't have a slur on a figure like that, it sounds very different from when it is slurred – it creates a very different affect. These kinds of details were missing, or they varied between instruments. What I try to do is unify the musical affect. Sometimes that involves decisions on the level of note length – short or long – but more often the slurs tell you how a phrase is shaped: where the important notes are, where the breath comes. Often you can breathe a little at the end of a slur. But if the slurs are different, you can't shape the phrase the same way. Shape and affect – these are kind of my *credo* of things.

Understanding and using bowings not as a technical means, but as a means of musical expression?

Absolutely, yes – because on a purely technical level, it should not matter at all whether we play up-bow or down-bow. People today are trained to be able to do it either way. But articulation is a system for creating hierarchy – what is more important and what is less important – because not everything is equally important. If everything is equally important, you end up with dead notes, or a series of same expressions – and that is not very interesting. I always use the medical example of a hospital room, where they monitor the heart – the EKG, the heartbeat – and you know what the heart says when the line goes like this *[shows a flat horizontal line]*: it is dead. So, you need to create shapes. Every musical line has some sort of shape, and articulation is one of the means of achieving that.

When you conduct contemporary pieces, do you also work on articulation?

It depends, because this is not equally important for every composer. For instance, I conducted [Kaija] Saariaho last week, and in her music, articulation is generally not the most important parameter – sound color, blend, and similar tonal qualities are much more important than whether it is played down-bow or up-bow. This is part of Saariaho's system. What I am talking about applies much more to music from 1772 to 1915 – a long period, of course. The more classical the piece, the more of these kinds of articulation considerations. Later, in modern music, as I said, the composer may not be as interested in articulation – they might be focused on another musical element. It could be rhythm, for example – and then it is not the same. You just need to be sensitive to recognize what is important for that particular composer.

Nowadays, conductors work on both contemporary music and music of the past, so what you are saying about finding the world of the composer and identifying what is important to them is essential. Does your approach to reading the score change depending on the composer?

Absolutely, totally – this goes into the box of style. You need to be sensitive to style: what works for which period, and even more specifically, for which composer. Everyone, as a human being, has their own set of aesthetics, beliefs, and interests – the things that are important to them. If they compose a piece, you need to familiarize yourself with those things in order to understand what they are saying. It is like a language – you really need to study the language before you can speak a sentence, and before you can interpret one. And that is different for every composer.

From the technical side of score reading, do you begin with a specific group of instruments – for example, the strings – or do you read the whole orchestra?

It also depends a bit on the score, but in general, I first prioritize a horizontal feeling of the score – meaning I don't focus so much on instrument sections or bits of that, but more on the phrasing line.

Does that mean you focus on melodies?

Melodies, and also the bass line – because I'm a cellist, that is very important to me. Maybe in the first rounds I don't separate anything, but in the later rounds I definitely might focus on the woodwinds only, or whatever section. If you have time, the really great thing for the brain is to read every single instrument separately – you read through the double bass part and notice where their *pizzicato* is, how it feels from the double bass's point of view. I have to confess, I've rarely had the time to do that, but ideally, that would be the thing.

The horizontal feeling?

The horizontal feeling first, and then the more vertical feeling follows – so yes, of course, I separate. I also spend a lot of time on the brass, sometimes even more than on the woodwinds, because especially in classical or early Romantic music, the way the brass and timpani phrase things controls the whole orchestra. If you don't pay attention to that, it doesn't matter what the others are doing – the timpani will decide everything. You need to be able to communicate that very clearly to them. That is why I sometimes spend a disproportionate amount of time on the trumpet and horn parts, to understand their function very clearly – and on the timpani, which in this style goes very well together. It is a totally different case with Debussy – this is style-dependent. I have conducted a lot of early 19th-century repertoire where this aspect is very important. I know it is a bit philosophical, but I like to see it as if you have a sentence in any language: if you place the comma after a different word, the meaning changes. It is very simple, actually – but musically, it has huge consequences. It is the same with articulation: what is important, what isn't, what you bring out, and what you choose not to bring out but place in the background. This creates a multidimensional feeling of the music, which is what I operate with – because for me, that is very interesting. Someone else will see different things, of course, but it can have a huge effect on how the musicians execute the music.

I remember, when reading Baroque scores, noticing that sometimes the same melodic line has different articulation markings for the winds and the strings. When you meet such situations, do you try to unify them to express the same idea, or do you look for reasons behind this variety?

That is a dramatic question you need to ask yourself. Should one person imitate the other in a discussion, or should they have a different opinion – or say the same thing differently? It totally depends on the context. It is very dangerous to unify everything – that is a natural instinct, but if you always do that, you risk taking out all the contrasts. Sometimes a composer might think that it is a fun gag to do it slightly differently. If you try to take all of that out, you lose the whole human point. This is a dramatic decision – you have to look at the context in order to make it.

So, in a way, is the conductor like a dramaturg?

Yes – a director, a film director, exactly. I do think there are dangers, because it is not your music – someone else wrote it – so you don't own it. But at the same time, it is your responsibility to make it the best it can possibly be. I like to think of it as a drama or some kind of story (it can also be a comic one), and it really helps to try to imagine that – and think about what would work. It is subjective, that is clear. Then you just have to judge how much of that you can bring in before it starts to feel like you are violating what someone else is trying to say. But in my experience as a musician and performer, most composers like having input from players suggesting things – so why shouldn't it be the same for the conductor? You just have to be sensitive to the degree – how much can we do this? What is helpful, and what is harmful?

The score – is it a starting point, and can we think of it as a script that the conductor works from?

We can, but I want to stress the responsibility – because I can easily see how this might be interpreted as someone just taking the score and doing whatever they want, which is not what I'm trying to say.

Conductors shouldn't make cuts to the score, for example?

No, they shouldn't – nor should they reorchestrate. That's not what I mean. What I mean is: try to find ways to make it alive, make it conversational, make it something that everyone can relate to – musicians, but also the public. Make it into a story, or a picture of some kind. But I want to stress the importance of the responsibility – you really have to weigh how much you can do, and how much you cannot. I see that as a question of respect – and one must never forget that.

When returning to the same score, have you found new things in it – discovered more meaning for yourself, or a different story?

The honest answer is that I am still in the phase of my life where I am doing most things for maybe the first five times. There aren't pieces I've conducted twenty times yet, because I am just not that experienced. I think that will come, but maybe from the first to the third time there is not such a big difference, as you haven't had enough time to live with the piece. Maybe that will happen later – like with string quartets. For instance, I've played Sibelius's string quartet about two hundred times, and with that piece I can say – yes, things have changed. I look at it differently from the first ten times to times 121 through 131. I expect the same will happen with the pieces I conduct, but I am just not there yet.

Could you share any anecdotes about score reading – something that surprised you, or a moment when you discovered something new?

I have two very concrete examples – both from pieces I've recently studied. One is a kind of classic: Berlioz's *Symphonie fantastique*. In the slower middle movement, the tune in the violins and flute – Berlioz borrowed it from a mass he composed when he was twenty-one years old, so there is a text associated with that melody. When you realize that a melody originally had a text, it immediately gives you its feeling – the emotion, the affect. The melody is totally unaltered; it is the same. But what he does with it later is much more elaborate. The initial idea is that he copies from himself – taking something he had written earlier and turning it into something different. And the fact that you know it comes from a Latin mass text informs your decision of how the melody of the phrase should work and how to play it.

That is one simple example. The other comes from a very interesting process we had with the Sibelius's *Fourth Symphony*. In the slow movement, near the beginning, there is a horn chorale passage that is traditionally always played open. But in the Urtext edition, there is a note from Sibelius indicating that it should be played *con sordino*.

It is a big decision – it changes the character.

It is a pretty big decision. Then you have to think: *okay, why does everyone play it open if Sibelius wrote* con sordino, *and that is how they play it on that recording?* If you listen to it, anyone who knows the piece will say, "But what? It sounds quite strange," because obviously, it is a huge difference. Then you have to start weighing the decisions: *Why did everyone change this? Why don't we do what Sibelius wrote?* In this commentary – which is not in the score – *did he change his mind? Did it sound bad with mutes, con sordino? Or did he just mean, okay, it is difficult to play?* Instruments back then were different from those we use today. When I did it with FiBO on original instruments – we had Viennese horns, which were in use at the time – I discussed it with the horn player and had a sectional rehearsal with the horn section. We tried mutes, hand-stopping, various stopping techniques – things they are much more familiar with – and also the open version. The variety of sound possibilities is massive, and then you have to weigh all of that and make a decision: *What sort of image are we going for? What can we make? What can we decide to play that sounds convincing, sounds good – and creates the wanted effect?* We decided on a compromise: hand-stopping, with two horn players using mutes. We created a sound that resembled a quartet of Wagner tubas – but it didn't sound the same as a modern F horn, played open as it is done today. These two examples are both about finding context and connecting to the composer. It is not so much about technical slurs here and there, but I find this fascinating.

Yes, it is! Would you like to add any other thoughts you have on score reading?

Well, the old example of the onion that you peel – that works very well for me alongside the six-round advice. The more rounds you read, the more complete the picture becomes. I like that idea, because when I started to conduct, I was terrified by this romantic image that a conductor just looks at the score and immediately hears everything in their head. I thought, *What is that?* Yes, maybe it is like that once you've done all the work – maybe then you can have it. But I like to remind myself that it is really about the discipline of working through all these layers, so that you might eventually arrive at that point. It is not some magic trick where you wave a wand and everything suddenly makes sense – it doesn't work like that.

Is going back to the score important in order to keep discovering more and more about the music?

I used to think about that a lot – what does it mean to go back to a score? I think you need to focus on something specific when you return to it. I like the idea of intentionally shifting your focus. If you just go back and open it, you'll probably read it the same way you did last time.

To go deeper into the score, do you need to focus on a specific element?

Yes, and then you don't know – maybe you won't find anything, but maybe you will. My point is that if you just go back to the score without having set yourself some kind of parameter, then you don't get anything new. Now, the parameter doesn't have to be score related – it can also come from outside, like the Berlioz example: reading about the composer's background in order to find out more.

Does this add a layer to the score?

It adds many layers.

Teaching Score Reading – *Ilona Dobszay-Meskó*

Interview on 26 July 2024

Could you share your experience in teaching score reading?

I teach score reading and mix it with sight-reading and transposition. For example, I use the first book of Bartók's *Mikrokosmos*, which contains very simple piano pieces. I tell my students to play a passage a second or a fifth lower, and then we move on to another section.

This reflects what happens in a conductor's mind when reading transpositions – decoding the written notes. Playing a fifth lower, is it like…?

English horn.

Do you ask your students to imagine and play every note a fifth lower, or do you have them approach it by changing the clef?

That is why I use Bartók's *Mikrokosmos* rather than a Haydn-period piece – because we don't change the key; instead, we focus on counting the fifths. I also use the first book of *The Russian School of Piano Playing* every week. It includes very simple folk songs and short, eight-bar pieces by Mozart. I give the same instructions – play it a second, third, or fifth lower – and then we change the key. I mix different approaches rather than sticking to just one. Sometimes, I give an exercise where I play a short and simple Wiener Klassik period piece on one of the two pianos in the room and say, "Please play it in another key, starting from this note, without looking at the score." With every lesson, there are more exercises.

When looking through old textbooks on score reading, one finds them filled with exercises in various clefs – soprano, mezzosoprano, baritone, and others.

That is so unnecessary.

Do you think that when music is chromatic or atonal, reading transpositions with the interval of transposition is easier than substituting clefs?

Yes. For choral music or Palestrina, reading with mezzosoprano and other old clefs is fine, but for orchestral conductors, it is not important. If you practice these exercises regularly every week and analyze how your brain processes them, everyone can find their own best way of reading transpositions and clefs.

When you have a score with cellos notated in tenor clef, how do you read it? Does your approach depend on the type of music? Do you compare the notes to other clefs, or do you just read from the middle of the clef, which is c1 [middle C]?

I apply the second approach.

Do you think a piano is useful for reading scores?

Absolutely. Although, when you sent me the questionnaire, my answer was that I don't use the piano. It is an interesting question; I can read a score playing it immediately on the piano, but as a conductor, I don't use the piano when studying a piece. Like Maestro [Yuri] Simonov[98], I prefer using colored pencils.

Do you hear the score in your imagination?

Yes, I do hear the music while reading it.

Do you find the piano useful in the process of teaching score reading to students?

Of course – always. But when I study by myself, I don't use it.

What kinds of things do you mark in the score when studying it?

I mark the entries of instruments after a longer rest. I also mark the part of the soloist – always in yellow. Recently, I've changed how I indicate dynamics. Maestro Simonov taught us to mark piano and forte by writing p and f or drawing a circle around them. However, I find it simpler to color the piano bars blue because, when I turn the page, I might forget the dynamic marking. For example, if the bars have a slight blue color, I immediately see that the sforzatos are within a piano passage, which is helpful.

Do you draw a blue line to mark it?

---

[98] Ilona Dobszay-Meskó and the author both participated in Professor Yuri Simonov's masterclasses in Hungary in the early 2000s.

Not a line – I color the whole bars. This is new for me this year. Sometimes, it distracts me to see circled *sforzatos* and *marcatos* and I forget that the entire passage is in *piano*. So, this coloring method has been helpful.

You associate blue with piano – what color do you use for forte?

In case of *forte* passages, I mark the starting barline in red to see that from here it has to be played *forte*. However, if there is a *crescendo* leading to *forte*, I do not use a red barline – that serves only for *subito forte*. So, for terraced dynamics, I color the barline red for *forte* and blue for *piano*. But if there is a *crescendo* or a *diminuendo*, I just mark the respective sign in red or blue.

Does coloring the score help you when conducting from it?

Yes, it makes it much easier. I feel really stressed when I see a blank page with no signs or markings.

Besides entries of instruments, singers, and dynamics, do you mark anything else in the score?

A lot. For example, I always add metronome markings. If I see *Allegro*, I imagine the right tempo and write down the corresponding number, for example, a quarter = 116.

So, while reading the score, you plan the performance tempo and write it into the score as metronome markings, is that correct?

Yes, that is helpful for me.

Do you follow these metronome indications when conducting?

I know metronome markings very well. When I teach conducting, we do exercises to memorize them and control the tempo.

Have you ever had a situation with an orchestra when you needed to change the metronome numbers, or are you usually able to keep them as planned?

If there is too much reverb, for example, in a church, I change the tempo. However, I don't erase and rewrite the metronome numbers – I just know that everything has to be slightly slower.

You conduct based on your work with the score, and your markings are an integral part of your conducting. Are there any other methods a conductor can apply?

For example, my husband, who is also a conductor, writes the entire form analysis into the score.

Does this refer to phrases?

Phrases and structural elements, such as in a sonata form the introduction, exposition, and everything else. I never do that.

If you conduct the same piece again with a different orchestra, do you use the same score with your earlier markings?

Yes.

In the questionnaire, you mentioned that you often sing while reading a score. How does singing help you with score reading?

One of my conducting teachers said that it is very beneficial to be able to sing through the piece. It doesn't matter which part – the flute, cello, or any other – but don't interrupt; just sing the piece.

From beginning to end? Changing instruments, but singing the whole piece?

Yes, just sing and conduct.

Do you do this with hand movements?

Of course. Those also need to be practiced.

When studying with Maestro Simonov, I remember he recommended using colors to mark different groups of instruments in the score – woodwinds in blue, brass in red, strings in green, and percussion in brown. Do you use this color-coding system?

No, but I use colors for different singers, which is very important. I always mark the soprano part in rose and the baritone in green – this is very useful for me. I also use strong colors for significant melodies. For example, if everyone is playing *mezzoforte*, but there is something important in the horns *[sings a fanfare]*, I highlight it with a strong color, like green – not just red for *forte* – because otherwise, I might overlook it. I use special colors, but only rarely, because if I use them too often, I stop noticing them.

Do you change colors to make certain elements stand out in the score?

Yes, just to create an "attack" on the brain. It is good to use the same color, notation, and markings for the same things, but if everything always looks the same when conducting a long piece, you might forget something – like a bass drum beat. That is why you sometimes need to use a strange, one-off color. For example, if I keep seeing the same markings for more than 15 minutes, I start tuning them out – unless I see a different color or sign. So, I am not always consistent with my markings because if everything is always marked the same way, it loses my attention. I know I need some variation in the score. For instance, if I use red for *forte* and blue for *piano* throughout the score, and there are standard signs for instruments, I might, in a certain spot and only once, draw a circle, use green, or add a sign to attract attention – to highlight the important part. However, I do this only in long pieces. In a short overture of five or six minutes, I don't need it.

Do you prepare and send your version of orchestral parts to the orchestra?

Usually I don't – only when the orchestra orders the parts of the edition I request the score to ensure we use the same edition, for example, Universal.

When you receive a contemporary music score that you have never heard before, how do you begin reading it? Do you first listen to a recording, play it on the piano, imagine it, or start marking it?

Nowadays, every composer has a MIDI version of their piece, for example, from a program like Sibelius. There is always some kind of recording available.

Do you listen to that first?

Yes, of course. You cannot hear a contemporary piece just by reading the score. I often serve as part of a jury, I have a good ear and I am a composer myself, but honestly, you cannot say anything about the piece without listening to it.

Do you ask composers for a MIDI file when conducting their pieces?

Always. Ten years ago, some of my colleagues used to say, "Oh, we don't need the MIDI because we can read the score."

Why has this changed? Is it because conductors have less time, or has notation become more graphic and complex?

If instruments are used in a non-traditional way, that can't be heard in the MIDI file – you have to imagine it. What you hear by these MIDI programs is not an accurate result, but it helps in getting an idea of what happens in the piece. I always ask for a MIDI file.

What kind of information can a MIDI give about the music?

Not everyone is able to abstract from the MIDI. Some people listen to it and say, "Oh, this sounds strange, it's not good, it's not music," because they can't abstract – they just believe what they hear. MIDI is just a ground, a basis, and you have to imagine the rest.

Can recordings be helpful for reading scores?

They are helpful, but after that, you still have to create your own concept of the piece.

Is it a good idea to practice conducting with recordings?

That is not so important.

What about reading the score while listening to a recording?

That's a useful method.

When reading the score of an older, well-known piece, do you only listen to your favorite recording, or do you explore several ones?

I am interested in many recordings, and after listening to them, I form my own idea. These days, recordings are often uploaded to YouTube along with the score, which is very useful. Being able to see and hear the music simultaneously is not enough, but it helps when practicing score reading.

Do you only use printed books for teaching score reading or do you add electronic technology?

I use only books, but some of my students use iPads. I believe this is the future.

Are there any particular challenges in score reading – something especially difficult?

Yes, when your ten fingers are not enough. The biggest challenge in score reading is deciding what to skip. For example, you may want to play the harmonies and the melody, but there are some very interesting eighth notes in there, too *[sings fast figures]*. This is difficult for me because I want to play everything but also stay in tempo. The biggest challenge is making that decision.

What do you do when playing everything is not possible?

I always tell my students: "Make a decision." The problem is deciding which part to skip while playing and I would never expect my students to play everything by themselves. Score reading lessons always have two students; we use two pianos, and we take turns playing different things. The result is important – everything must be there, but one person doesn't need to play it all.

Do you use piano reductions in teaching score reading? Are they helpful for reading orchestral scores?

Yes, they are very useful. First, we play the four-hand piano reduction of a piece, such as a Beethoven symphony, once through. After that, we move to the full score with two students switching instruments.

What do you do when you have a student who doesn't play the piano?

I teach only composers and conductors, so they have to be able to play the piano. They may not have advanced technique, but that is okay – rather than focusing on the smaller voices, they should prioritize the harmonies and the pivotal elements of the score. They may also need to play a bit slower.

Do they have to imagine the technically difficult parts without playing them?

Yes, because those who don't play the piano can still play the harmonies. Everyone can play the harmonies and the music theory they know – one voice in the left hand and three voices in the right hand, or combine chords and melody. There is always something they can play, and I am very patient. Everyone should keep working on their skills and improve gradually.

Do you have any tips on how to achieve fluency in score reading?

Fluency comes from the same idea I mentioned earlier – just sing the piece. Sometimes, I recommend this exercise: here is the piece, now sing one line in tempo. It doesn't matter whether it is the flute, violin, cello, or bass part – just go *[claps a tempo]* and keep it simple. It is liberating. You are not expected to play the whole score – just focus on one part, like the timpani or another instrument – but keep going.

Does this help with feeling the flow of the music?

Yes, it does. When there are four students, and you tell the non-pianist, "Okay, just play the double bass or the timpani part," it is okay. If you say, "Go slowly through the score, and you can jump between parts with your eyes," that is also very useful because you can imagine the rest. This is also beneficial because it forces you to decide what to play and what is most important to you.

Earlier you mentioned harmony, the chords...

We do exercises where you have to play all parts of a six-bar section, including transposing instruments' parts, but slowly. Being able to play everything slowly is important, but it is also necessary to be able to stay in tempo and play just one voice *[whistles]*. I always switch between these approaches because sometimes you need one, and sometimes the other. When working with an orchestra, you must be able to identify mistakes in the score – you might find a wrong note or two. To recognize the problem, you have to read all the details in the score. For example, in the cello part, a clef change might be missing – instead of tenor clef, it remains the bass clef. You always have to read the entire score and identify any problems.

Is there anything you would like to add on score reading?

One thing I forgot to mention is the importance of enjoying the process. In an instrumental lesson, whether it's cello or piano, you play, of course, nice pieces, you are an artist, and you feel good about it. But in score reading, you cannot get complacent – there is always something missing: the tempo, certain parts, or details. You somehow still have to find the fun in it. Confidence is very important. Never stand up from the piano thinking, "I practiced, but it is not quite good." That is why it is helpful to set smaller goals. For example, tell yourself to just "play these four bars with everything," or "I want to hear which notes are in this chord," or "I will just whistle the piece," or "I will play something with one finger." Define your goal – "this is what I want to achieve today with the piece." If you just sit at the piano and try to play something, you will never be satisfied, and you will come to hate the project. Change it up after 15 minutes, otherwise you will get tired and frustrated, feeling that you are not good enough. When that happens, try another exercise.

Polyphonic Voices and Moving Clefs –
James Sherlock

Interview on 19 July 2024

Your background is in piano and organ, have you been using a piano to read orchestral scores?

Yes, definitely in the beginning, not so much now perhaps, because I have developed a mental piano in my head. Though I still find reading a score and "playing" it on the table, physically feeling the spacing of the chords. If I had a lovely piano at home, I would probably still use it more!

When you were studying conducting, did you use the piano in a greater extent for reading scores?

Yes, the way I learned score reading was through a specific organ scholar system. Cambridge and Oxford universities each have 25 to 30 colleges, and nearly all of them have chapels. Each chapel has two organ scholars at any one time. The traditional tests for these scholarships involve reading four-part Renaissance polyphony exercises in the style of Palestrina, in different clefs – G, F, C – placed in various positions on the staff. The exercises began with simple designs using two and three lines, then four lines. That was what I learned first – long before I learned to read orchestral scores.

This particularly Anglican (even though Elgar was a Catholic) way of doing things was the way in which Walton, Vaughan Williams, and Stanford would have been trained. If I had a young student now who was ten years old, I would have them practice moving clefs around too – that seems to me a lost art form. When you read Bach's handwritten manuscripts, you notice that he simply moves the G clef up and down, which convinces me that the brain is capable of making that shift – it is just that we don't exercise that shift these days!

Almost everyone who has come through that organ scholar system becomes reasonably fluent at this. My own particular teacher, Richard Marlow, made our entire university read Sweelinck 8-part motets in G and F clefs – again, through exposure, it just becomes more natural.

When I began to read orchestral scores more earnestly, I found that I was able to transfer these skills. I didn't have any clever systems (I had to learn those later) – they probably would have sped me up a bit – but still I find that the old training allows me to keep track of a significant number of polyphonic voices.

Another useful skill was learning figured bass, as an organist and continuo player – as well as Bach chorales, of course. Having that absolutely foundational training in harmony is still everything to me as a musician.

After I graduated from Cambridge, I stayed on for a year and taught keyboard skills along with other subjects. I would give students Schubert's and Brahms's songs – just the bass line and melody – and say, "Okay, go fill out the rest." Even now, as long as the music is in a traditional harmonic, my eye instinctively goes down to the bass line, scanning for the melodic movement and then the rest. You are not really reading it; it's in some ways guesswork, and as you keep going guesses are confirmed or unconfirmed – you understand the habits of certain composers or periods.

Honestly, if I had a really talented young student, I would start with these kinds of exercises. I truly believe they have given a good foundation – one that is more general than orchestral score reading. Is it perhaps a bit like learning Latin, if you want to really master several of the Romance languages?

When reading orchestral music, do you also look at the bass line and then melody?

Yes, but not because I was taught that way – it is what happens when you spend enough hours doing it, and you begin to take in more information. I remember the last score reading exercise I was given at the Sibelius Academy – it was a [Richard] Strauss tone poem. You're looking at thick blocks of lines, and you can't even figure out what half the instruments are, but you can see, *okay, there are three trombones – and they aren't transposing, so that's easy – and there's the double bass, and I know how to transpose horns...* Then you read the violins or the flutes, whoever has the melody, and then you begin to fill in the gaps.

When you speak of old clefs, do you mean they are movable and start on different lines?

Yes, exactly. We were given old editions of German music – my choir professor was a big fan of Schütz, Scheidt, Schein, and Sweelinck – and many of those editions have what we would call a treble clef (a G clef) that's been moved, usually only a third higher or lower than what you are used to, but still, that is a big thing. If you read the facsimiles of Bach's *48 Preludes and Fugues* on IMSLP, you will again see that he just moves the clefs. The method for learning these Palestrinian-type exercises is that they normally begin with a scale, followed by a drop of a third, fourth, or fifth – unless it is a second.

Do you mean the melodic development of the line?

The lines almost never drop or rise by a sixth or a seventh; normally, the maximum interval is a fifth unless it is an octave. You can visually see what the things are, and in that sense, it is simple yet provides a good foundation. As for the alto clef, I am still not very proficient with it when it's off the staff!

Are notes on ledger lines more difficult to read?

Still for me, yes! But I know what a bottom C looks like on a viola. It is not the most scientific approach, but it is practical from experience.

When you often read in a specific clef, does it become easier?

Yes. I still find tenor clef a nuisance – I know there are tricks, but I have to look at it and think, "Oh, yes, it's that, isn't it?" or transpose it from an alto clef – which, of course, is not efficient. But we find tenor clefs quite rarely, and normally the context of them makes it clear, particularly if it's a solo cello part or similar.

Have you been in a situation where you needed to play a choral in treble and bass clefs in a different key – for example, in D major instead of the written C major?

Yes, and I actually taught myself to do that when I was eight – I was obsessed with playing everything in all twelve keys. That has been extremely useful, because I know how the chords feel, and the pianist's hand does not have to think – it just moves.

Do you think of moving everything by a transposing interval, or with degrees of a scale instead?

No, and so my facility only functions fluently in tonal music. But I did loads of it growing up, playing all the chorales and hymns I could find across all the 12 keys. The Cambridge organ scholar training teaches you to do it too, so I got more and more extreme, taking the Bach trio sonatas on the organ up a tone, up a fourth! I just kept doing it, so of course I became proficient! And then, of course, Schubert's songs – I became very popular with singers, because I could just raise or lower them at will. But then someone brought me some Schoenberg and asked, "Oh, can you do this?" It was still fairly tonal, early Schoenberg, but once the chords get denser and the old harmonic rules begin to shift, then of course one has to really know the music (already how it sounds) to be able to transpose it "at sight". Even Bach, when he does his rich harmonic shifts, poses wonderful challenges to the transposer!

Have you also been using Kodály's DO-RE-MI method with the movable DO?

In England, the traditional teachings don't use solfege. (Now of course Colourstrings, amongst other methods, have become very popular). I've never learned it, and now I find it somewhat irritating! We all learn, of course, the song from the *Sound of Music* – "*Do, a Deer*". I learned the names of notes through studying French, but I still have to think about it. We really don't use that system at all in the UK. I'm still not convinced by solfege!

One of the books I used for practicing was the *Preparatory Exercises in Score Reading* by Morrison-Ferguson, published by Oxford University Press. I used it to brush up before my Sibelius Academy audition, and it was great. I remember it had a wonderful exercise toward the end – was it Mendelssohn? – there is a trio in one of the scherzos for the horns *[sings]*...

Yes, the "Italian", Fourth Symphony, third movement.

And that was written in unbelievably strange clefs, so of course it was very useful.

When you have a clarinet in A in the score, how do you read it? What mental process do you do?

I always just transpose a third because I've practiced that so much. But if it's not tonal music then of course takes longer. I am not pretending it's easier to sight-read *Electra* – then I really have to sit down and do the math. I remember that Sibelius's *First Symphony* is a good exercise because of the opening clarinet solo – I think the clarinet is in A – and the melody full of semitones and tones. I recall looking at that early on in my schooling days, and I found that if you learn that solo, you very quickly get better at doing thirds.

Reading notes is a fundamental skill a conductor has to have when opening a score. On what other aspects do you focus when reading the score? What do you consider the most important? Can you think of any particular challenges you have met in score reading?

I mentioned Electra – it is the density on the page. It looks like tonal music, but it is not, or at least it is not constructed in a traditional way. There are too many different processes happening at once. Even if some are perhaps old tonal processes, they are all stacked on top of each other. In some ways, later Schoenberg is much easier to transpose compared to this incredible density. Also, Strauss has so much coloring – it is very impure music!

How do you approach a score like Electra? Do you try to read all the instruments at the same time, or do you first read groups of instruments or individual instruments separately?

This is why I mentioned the trombones earlier – I love when the three of them are written on the same staff. If the parts are well written, even if the third trombone is not playing the bass line, you just add that from contrabassi. So that gives you the foundation in a thick scoring, probably 85% of the time in tonal music… for an organist, that is the left hand and pedals. If it is a good composer, the trombones and horns will be well spaced to give the chord a nice coloring. Horns tend to be sustained instruments as well, so in a thick passage they underpin everything while all other elements are in motion. I also really don't mind "cheating", when learning big works – during the four years of COVID, I bought piano transcriptions of all the Mahler symphonies by a skilled transcriber, Iain Farrington (they are all available to buy online) and played through them on the piano. These are wonderful arrangements, with all the counterpoint clear. I also played through Electra and some other pieces – the piano reductions are also "cheating", then! But when you use them as an aid to learning the score, you know which harmonies you're searching for in the full score, thus speeding up the process.

So much of this sort of sight-reading scores or piano reductions is about prediction and knowing what is going to come next, by developed instinct. That is why there is a kind of limit on this process… up until *Electra* or Schoenberg's opus 11. The other day, I sat down to score-read *Verklärte Nacht* – even though it is just six lines, it is a lot for the brain to take in the first time around and requires significant processing power!

Do you sight-read scores page by page?

Yes, absolutely. I really don't like scores in C, though I know I'm in the minority here. I've come to trust that instinct – when you read transposed scores, you know approximately in which register an instrument is. But nowadays, almost everyone writes in C and will continue to do so because conductors won't conduct your scores unless they are written in C.

But horn players still play on F horns…

Yes, exactly. So C scores feel artificial, when you have such a degree of transposition – a written C4 for the horn is played as a G4… already a pretty high note.

Does thinking about the type of instrument help you get used to reading it with the transposition?

Yes. Though I must admit that when I'm composing in Sibelius software, I do actually compose in C (although with a strong awareness of instrumental tessitura).

These days, there is wide access to recordings. What would you say is the role of recordings in your score reading? Does it affect how you read the score?

Yes, of course, I use them. A lot of people say, "Don't listen to recordings". Don't listen to them all the time, of course, but they are an incredible historical resource, and one would be foolish not to listen to different traditions, styles. As long as you are not trying to copy the recording. I am someone who loves opera, so why wouldn't I want to hear every great singer who has tackled the role? Analyzing performances of the classics – Mozart, Haydn, Beethoven, Schubert – is particularly interesting, because what you are listening to is the product of a many different processes, bowing, phrasing, breathing. You can't superficially "copy" what you hear of course, and you absolutely shouldn't! Anyway, I belong to the YouTube generation I suppose, and it's an incredible resource.

Can listening to a recording add knowledge to the score in the sense that we learn from it – for example, the physical aspects of how it could sound and the technical limitations of specific instruments?

Yes, and also in developing taste – liking some things and disliking others. One of the things I've observed in recent months is that in so many great recordings, the musicians are not always even together (whereas today we prefer perfection). It's more about the spirit. This is especially true in opera, where many recordings are live, or where orchestras, due to physical complications, cannot hear in an acoustical space the way a symphonic orchestra would.

Has the speed of making recordings increased so much that there is not enough time for rehearsing?

Yes, definitely, but that is also life.

Do recordings give you information about where the difficult sections in the score are?

They provide information about how scores are built and the practicalities of performing them. That is something you do not always get from score reading – you need to develop an instinct for what the practical difficulties will be in the piece. And yes, of course, if it doesn't sound great, it's probably difficult!

You mentioned that you have sung in a choir. Have you been using singing for score reading?

Yes, I've started doing it more and more recently, mainly because it helps with getting both the sound and the gesture. But I don't think I would use it to improve my comprehension of the score. I do it more to get the feeling of the music in my breath.

For phrasing?

Yes, exactly.

And feeling the music inside?

Feeling the music more. It is very hard to say because I have only been working with professional groups for four years at this point. With some groups, I find that I have to basically control the bass line. I remember someone once told me that German conducting focuses on the bass line, Italian conducting on the melody, and French conducting on the harmony. It is a broad generalization, but in recent months, I have found myself thinking more about it and observing that different ensembles need help with different things. Singing has helped a bit more when working with an orchestra where I had to take care of the violins. Here, where I am at the moment[99], I really have to take care of the bass section. So I suppose singing can be useful – it gives you melodic wings.

---

[99] Savonlinna Opera Festival, Finland.

Have you been using any modern tools for reading scores?

No, not really – except piano reductions, where they exist. Next year, I will conduct [Mahler's] *Das Lied von der Erde* – it is just so complicated. I am a pianist, so why wouldn't I learn the piece on the piano? It is simply the easiest way to get the music inside. Of course, piano reductions have always existed, but now they are available for everything – all the Mahler symphonies have been done, all the Bruckner symphonies have been around for a long time, and so have the Brahms symphonies (though those may not be quite as useful). It is all there now, and that wasn't always the case. So, in that sense, I suppose it is a modern solution. I have them all on my iPad. I am not sure how helpful that is if you are not a pianist – simply looking at a piano reduction won't help. It does not give you the information about chord spacing that you need; but in terms of getting the sweep of a piece, it is very useful.

It can be challenging to make your own piano reduction from the score if the piece is thickly written.

Yes, exactly. None of us has any time these days – even if you start learning something a year in advance, it is little pockets of time here and there. I basically know how all the Mahler symphonies go from playing them on the piano, and when I study them, it is just adding to that layer of information. I have probably played them all about five to eight times over the last four years, and now, each time I look at the score, I am simply adding to that base layer of knowledge – which is incredibly useful.

When you are reading the score, do you think of conducting gestures that you will use?

Later, yes – but not at the beginning. It needs to come from a real inner feeling, and I trust those more once I feel that I know the work.

Do you think that conductors develop with experience a better sense of what is most important and what to bring out from the score?

Yes, absolutely. We all learn by doing, or by making mistakes. Composers and conductors are all craftsmen, and we understand more about our craft every day. As conductors, we develop a deeper understanding of the craftsmanship of those composers we perform, and how better to realize that work.

In Mahler's polyphony, have you been able to include all the counterpoints and layers?

It sort of is possible to hold them all in your mind.

But what about reading these scores on the piano?

Then it is tricky, but you have the same challenge with any composer, even Palestrina. These are useful exercises: how do you prioritize and build on that. The last Mahler piece I tried to score-read was the second movement of the *Third Symphony* – "What the Flowers in the Meadow Tell Me." It is an absolutely wonderful score reading exercise. It starts like a Schubert minuet – basically all Schubert – but then builds into different kinds of things, and lots of twists and turns. Yet it remains completely tonal, just with plenty of surprises.

Is your handling of polyphony in older music similar?

Yes, and that is why I would still teach younger students Palestrina and Bach chorales. I would have them harmonize their own Bach chorales – from bass and treble, just from treble, or even by inventing from the bass – like building blocks. It is such a gift to be able to grasp the harmonies physically.

When you read from the bass, does it give you a perspective for the harmony?

Yes. Right now I am working on *Nabucco*. The way it was composed, Verdi sent only the bass line and the melody line to the opera house, and the pianists were used to playing cembalo parts.

Did they fill in the harmony by themselves?

Yes! And for many years music functioned in this way – even Brahms songs (and he was a most wonderful polyphonist) still have a bassline and melody as their foundation.

What about Wagner?

Wagner, like Brahms, an incredible polyphonist.

You mentioned that you pay attention to the spacing of chords…

That matters to me – I think it truly matters in music. One person I haven't mentioned is Ravel, whom I hope everyone studies, particularly composers. His work is just so immaculate.

Do you mean the instrumentation?

Instrumentation, chord spacing, and the resulting coloring – everything is just perfect. That is how you space chords! He's the greatest for this!

With a piece by a contemporary composer, you discover a new language and a new set of priorities in music. When you read a score again, do you gain a deeper understanding of it?

Yes, definitely. Today we have some modern-day classics that orchestras perform multiple times, so like great literature or works for the theatre, our collective understanding and appreciation develops. It's another reason I love working in opera – because you are preparing towards six, ten, or more performances, even (hopefully) with modern works. It creates even more opportunities for taking risks in performance and exploring new possibilities.

To try it a bit differently?

Yes. One thing I tell composers is that if their scores are laid out beautifully, with clear instructions, conductors will take their work much more seriously – and they will perform it. For both practical and artistic reasons, music is aesthetics, and aesthetics can be found even in the layout of a score. Look at Ravel!

A Flexible Sound Image – *Chloé Dufresne*

Interview on 12 August 2024

Could you please share your approach to a new score? How do you begin reading it?

It depends, of course, on the style – and if I know the composer, it is always easier. First, I just go through the piece, mostly reading the strings – probably the first violins. I try to follow mainly the theme and a bit of the bass – basically two or three lines, going like this *[shows a horizontal line]*. The second round would include a bit more of the accompaniment, strings, and then I add the winds and the percussion. Before I start to imagine the accompaniments, I really focus on the rhythm and notes of the theme. The first time, I read without singing it in my head – just a bit approximative, let's say – to get the big picture. Then I start forcing my brain to hear the pitches and almost sing exactly what is there, along with the bass in my head. After that, I just add things and check: *okay, this is the third, this goes with the sixth.* When it is a third or fifth, I hear it more as a color than just the notes. If I see that it goes in thirds, I hear the theme in a slightly stronger way, I am not going note by note.

Do you hear the theme as thicker when it goes in parallel thirds – for example, in Brahms's scores?

Exactly. I kind of switch all the time between perfect pitch and colors. That is basically how I build things in my head. If it is very complicated, I can play it on the piano – but I usually don't, because I don't have one with me.

Nowadays, conductors often travel a lot – and you can't really bring a piano on an airplane, can you?

Some people do, actually – they have a small piano, or they use their phone. But I don't, and I usually don't check the tempi either. Usually, I read the score slower than the music and start searching for the tempo a bit later in the process. There is a tempo when I read, of course, but sometimes I just don't care about what is written, I just take it as an approximate idea of speed

– the real tempo comes a bit later. It is not the first thing I do. I know some people start with that, but it is not how I do it.

Many instrumentalists first read pieces at a slower tempo, and then gradually at a faster one – is this a similar way of reading music?

Yes, exactly – that is how I do it. There are a few steps: first, I read the score (a lot); then I listen, to strengthen my mind and my image of it; and then, when I start making decisions about interpretation and all of that, I stop listening. Sometimes I do listen when I get stressed before rehearsals, but that is usually a bad idea – it just makes me overthink even more. I feel that it will help, but it doesn't.

Do you listen to specific recordings, or to as many different recordings as possible?

If it is a piece that has been recorded a lot, then I will listen to many options – I will search for a variety of different recordings. If it hasn't been recorded a lot, and there are only one or two recordings, I will listen to them, but not too much. I try not to stick with just one recording – basically, that is my rule. But I do listen to as many recordings as I can; it gives me ideas. If I have time, I will do it. If I don't, I will just focus on my own.

You mentioned going through the score several times – how many rounds would you say you usually need to do?

I do a lot of them, and I also write the chords. When I start to have the bass and the theme well in my head, I begin reading more of the accompaniment and what is in between. At this point, I really write the chords into the score – even if it is super easy, even if I know it is D major, G major, D major – I will still do it, if I have time. Sometimes I only do it for specific passages, but usually, when I have worked a lot on a piece, the whole thing is done – so I can just go to the piano and play the chords. But this only works if it is a tonal piece. If it is not, it becomes a bit more complicated, and I will write down in my score who is playing what together. I actually write a lot – I will note things like *fifth*, *sixth*, or *this is unisono* – and I organize it in a way that helps my brain read it faster when I come back to the score.

Do you look at the relationships between instruments – which ones are playing together and in what intervals?

Yes. If the theme is in the first oboe and then in the flute, I will link them with a small pencil mark, and I will also write down everyone who is playing together. I might also color the theme – I do many things. Sometimes my score looks a bit like a painting.

What is the reason for your markings in the score – is it score analysis, or do these markings also help you when conducting?

Both. Some of the writing is too small to see while I am conducting – for example, if I write a *third*. But when working on a *passaggio*, I can actually read those kinds of markings; they help as reminders, even if I already hear it. Basically, marking the score helps with both analysis and conducting, because I also write in the entrances of instruments and all that. The colors make a kind of smaller score to read while conducting.

The colors that you use – do you have a system for indicating instrumentation, dynamics, what is important, or something else?

I use blue for the strings, green for the woodwinds, red for the brass, and usually purple for the percussion – those are my colors. For dynamics, *forte* is red and *piano* is blue, basically. Sometimes, when it is complicated and there is a theme and a countertheme, I use a strong green and a lighter green to see who is doing what. When something is important – a theme or something in the accompaniment I want to bring out – I use the color of the instrument and just highlight it or circle it.

You mentioned that when you read a score, you sing a theme or a melody – do you mean that you "sing" it in your head, or out loud?

Both. I hear it in my head, but when I start singing, it is harder – because I feel it is not exactly the same, or it is not really singable. Sometimes I notice that when I really start singing, it changes a bit how I feel the theme. So yes, I sing a lot when I read – that is my instrument.

Does singing help you find the feeling of the music?

Exactly – and it also helps with phrasing. As I said, it is my instrument, so I feel better singing something than playing it on the piano. When I play the piano, I just make too many wrong notes, and that disturbs me. With singing, I have more control – and I use my tuning fork.

Do you use a traditional tuning fork, or a digital tuner on your phone?

I have the old one – I have three or four of them. Sometimes, when it is complicated or if I don't have my tuning fork, I will use the piano on my phone, but I really hate it. I think it is so much relaxing to just use a tuning fork and find my way from it. For me, if I open my phone while reading a score, it is not the right thing.

You mentioned that you sometimes read scores on the piano – is that to hear the harmonies, play through the piece, or for another purpose?

It is to hear the harmonies and how things change. Basically, I read the score on the piano when the harmonies are very complicated, or when there are things I am not sure how they feel – like a wrong note in the transposition, or something like that.

To check the pitches?

Yes – and how they relate, also octaves and things like that. But I usually don't use the piano; it is very rare. The last time I used it was probably a year ago.

Do you read transpositions by exchanging them to old clefs?

Yes, I use clefs – that is much easier for me. I do not transpose. I can transpose when it is just one step, like a second, but otherwise I mostly use clefs. I know that if it is in F, I use the second C clef.

When there is a clarinet in B-flat in the score, do you read it by changing the transposition to tenor clef?

For clarinet, it depends – because it is only one step, so sometimes I do, and sometimes I don't. If there are a lot of accidentals, then I will transpose, but if there aren't any, I will just read it in tenor clef.

Do you use the clef exchange method in tonal music, but prefer to read by the transposing interval when there are many accidentals or the music is atonal?

Yes, and sometimes I do it just to be sure. Even if it is a big jump or an A clarinet, I use intervals to be certain with the alteration, because this technique only works if the music is tonal. If it is not, then it becomes complicated to read in another clef.

When dealing with accidentals, do you think in terms of degrees in the key of the transposition – where the sharps and flats are?

Yes, when it is tonal, I do. For the F horn, if the piece is in C major, I see it in F major – so I know there is a B-flat. Somehow, it is easy. Sometimes, though, the clarinet in A is written in flats while the rest of the orchestra is in sharps – then it becomes very complicated to use the clef, because we get lost. In those cases, I use intervals. Basically, I go with what is easiest for me, depending on the music.

It is interesting that you switch between these two different methods of reading transpositions.

I was taught to use the clefs – that is how it is done in France. And I am a viola player, so the viola clef is just normal for me, which means it is one less clef to learn compared to others. Now I am using intervals more and more. Finding a good balance is best.

Does your choice of method depend on the type of music or the situation in the piece?

Yes, exactly. If it is Mozart, I will for sure use the clef. It mostly depends on the style. But when we get to [Richard] Strauss or atonal music – or the enharmony I mentioned with the clarinets – it is different.

Like in the second movement of Liszt's Faust Symphony?

Yes, that is very annoying.

Transpositions are a challenge in score reading, and everyone would like to achieve fluency in them.

Especially when the horns are changing all the time. Sometimes it is not indicated at the beginning of the line, so I always write which horn is being used.

Do you write the type of transposition in the score?

Yes, exactly – also for clarinet. I don't want to be in a rehearsal trying to read the notes from the score without knowing which transposition it is. I am careful about that – I will write it down.

Since you have played the viola, do you also work on bowings as a conductor – preparing and sending them to orchestras?

Not yet. First, I don't have much time for it. I am doing it more and more – sometimes I think about it – but most of the time, I let the concertmaster deal with it. If there is something specific I want, I will say it, or if he or she proposes two options, I will choose one. I am not too much into that yet, but I think it is something I should develop a bit more as I go deeper into things. That is probably the next step for me. But I still have a lot to learn, so it is not my priority.

We haven't talked about phrasing, but I do write it sometimes. I might draw a kind of arrow going to the points of a phrase, or write something if I want it to be sustained. If I want something short, I write it down too – and I might also indicate a character.

When you read a score, how do you find the right tempo for the music?

Most of the time, I find it while singing – I try different tempi. At first, I kind of sight-read, so it is slow. While trying to find the phrasing, I get to a certain tempo, and only at the very end I check what tempos are written – sometimes that is a bit too late, but that is usually how I do it. To be honest, I don't really need to have the tempo, it depends. In June, I did a very interesting exercise – I was conducting the orchestration exam at the CNSM[100], where I had seven different orchestrations of the same piece. The students did the orchestrations in a room without access to any recording, or references, and there was no tempo marking written. They all thought about the music independently, and in the end, even they did not write the tempo. When you listen to the piano version of this piece, it is usually played very fast. Some of the orchestrations could be performed at that tempo, but others had to be twice slower. It was very interesting to see how much the orchestration impacted the tempo – it wasn't just about my reading, but also about how thick the texture was. Sometimes I also find the tempo in front of the orchestra – realizing, *okay, this won't sound the way I want at this tempo*. I am usually not very strong about the tempo I want – except in Mozart, where I will know a bit more what I want. It depends on the composer.

Is it that you listen to the orchestra and look for the best sound, the right expressiveness – and then find the tempo together with the ensemble?

Yes, exactly – and very often, it also depends on the hall. But with Beethoven and Mozart, I still try to get the tempo they intended, especially with Beethoven. But I don't have that many opportunities to conduct his music.

---

[100] Paris Conservatory.

Beethoven wrote metronome markings – do you begin reading his scores according to them, or do you first read more slowly, find your own feeling of the music, and then check the tempo with the metronome?

It goes both ways. Sometimes I just try to get the right tempo, and sometimes I will say, "Let's start a bit slower," and then see if I can push the tempo toward Beethoven's marking. It depends a lot on the orchestra, its ability, and how they play Beethoven – some are very sticky on the bow, while others play in a more historically informed style. All of that affects the tempo, and it takes time to find the right one. Singers, for example, usually say I am very stable with tempo – that is the feedback I get. So I guess with singers, I tend to take almost the same tempo each time. But I know that in rehearsal, I might take a very fast tempo the first day, and then slow it down on the second – I learn from my mistakes. Usually, I don't change the tempo during a rehearsal, but between rehearsals, it might shift a bit, also because of my own emotional state.

During rehearsals, are you looking for the tempo that feels best with that group of musicians? And what about the best tempo for the singers? That is not something you can predict just from reading the score, is it?

Yes, exactly – but my emotional state also affects it. Sometimes, in the first rehearsal, I am a bit more stressed than in the second, so I very often take the first rehearsal faster. On the second day, I am a bit more focused, I listen more closely, so it will be a bit slower. Then on the third day, I will think, *well, that was a bit too slow – now I need to take it back*. Somehow, it also depends on how I am listening and what I want to work on. I never bring my metronome with me, we are human and it is a good thing to try, to change our mind and variate a bit.

When reading the score, do you imagine different tempo possibilities and keep an open mind about how you will perform the piece?

Yes, exactly. And usually, before the first rehearsal, I am like, *well, now I should decide*. Sometimes, I make the decision very late.

When you conduct the same piece again, do you change anything in how you interpret the score?

It hasn't happened much, because nowadays I usually work with new repertoire. Basically, I take the same tempi, maybe adjusting a bit for the hall. In opera, I change more often, because the soloists change – and that can affect a lot. But with symphonic music, I tend to stay quite stable. Sometimes, the first time, I want to try it fast, and then I might write a note to myself: "Next time, try it slower." I don't stick to it like the rock, but once I have made a decision, I usually keep doing approximately the same, and I guess for some pieces, there is a natural tempo that stays in my body. It is also easier and takes less time than constantly changing everything – especially now that I have a lot of music to learn. When I have already learned a piece, I try to trust that work – but sometimes, I still find myself thinking about the same questions and struggling, night and day, with how I should do it.

When you conduct the same piece with a different orchestra, do you use the same score you've already marked?

Yes, I do use the same score. It is very annoying for me to change scores because I have a really photographic memory, and I write a lot in my scores. It is especially frustrating when the edition is different, or when I feel I need to write everything down again. Changing scores takes a lot more time for me, and I hate having a clean score. Sometimes it happens – because you forget your score or have a different version – so you have to use the orchestra's score, which is annoying.

Does a photographic memory mean that you remember exactly how the page looks?

Yes, but I usually don't conduct by heart. If I did, maybe it would be less disturbing to change the score – but I really never do it, especially these days. During my student time, I did it sometimes, and maybe I should try to start again. Now I am doing [Bizet's] *Carmen*, and I have a different edition than the one I used before – there are many changes, and it takes more time from me.

When you are working on a long piece such as an opera, do you create a structural plan for it? Do you write out your own outline of the piece?

Of course, yes. For opera, I definitely do it. For symphonic pieces, I usually write the form in the first corner, and also inside the score. Sometimes, I will even note developments in the corner of each page to see where I am in the piece – for example, the exposition's theme A for ten pages, and then theme B. For each number in an opera, I write the tempo, meter, and key. I usually also note the tempo changes and what is being said – the story, the first sentence, and what is happening in that moment. I use this approach a lot in opera. It takes time, but I do it on my computer and then print it out. I also write down the characters – who is singing, and so on. For me, it is easier to see things that way – like, *okay, this character has two arias and six ensembles, and it is always in F major and in the same tempo, so maybe that means something.* I do this if I have the time. Sometimes you start doing it and then you never finish – you get through the first act and the time goes.

What about contemporary music? You have conducted premieres of many new pieces – what kinds of challenges in score reading have you encountered that are different from reading older music?

With new music, I use the metronome much more – and my tuning fork much less. Contemporary music today is often more rhythmic than melodic, while in the past, it was more melodic than rhythmic. I feel that, in general, the ratio is a bit like that. I usually go through contemporary pieces much more in tempo and try to find some kind of inspiration. If it is a symphonic piece, I somehow feel the phrasing, and I don't need to have a story inside it or go too deeply into that aspect. But with contemporary music, I sometimes really need to call the composer to get an idea of the colors, the characters, and the sounds – so that I can be inspired and inspiring in front of the orchestra.

How much do you work with the composer on the score?

Not too much. I like working closely with the composer during rehearsals, and before that, I send some questions. I am usually quite late in my work, so I don't want to be in contact too early. I want to know the piece very well to be sure of my questions – and to have only one meeting before the first rehearsal.

When reading the score, do you conduct it with your hands, or do you go through it just in your mind?

It is a bit of both. Usually, it is in my mind, but if it is difficult – like one-two, one-two-three [changing meters] – then I will actually do it. I won't stand in front of my mirror, though probably I should. Basically, I do it with my score, using just small gestures to get into the pulse and keep the tempo. Yes, it definitely helps.

Do you feel the music with your body movements?

Yes.

How do you read an opera score when the text is in a foreign language?

I haven't done much Mozart opera, but I assisted at the Opéra de Paris in *Cosi fan tutte*, and there was someone there to help with the text. When I conduct French opera, I really know how I want the French to be pronounced – because I was a singer and all that – but when it comes to Italian and other languages, I've noticed how valuable it is to work with someone who knows the language very well. I plan to ask more and more often to have someone with me in rehearsals for that – also to better understand the libretto, the jokes, and how the words sound together. I think it affects a lot the phrasing. This is something I really want to develop, because not many people do it, but I think it is extremely important.

Do you mean working with a language advisor?

Yes, exactly.

Have you been using any modern technology for score reading – for example, an iPad?

No, I like books – I am very old-fashioned. I just don't trust the technology and because I write so much in my scores. I think books also help to know the form. If there are a lot of pages on your right, it means you are still at the beginning; and as you come closer to the end, you feel it just by turning the pages. Yes, I love my scores as objects. But it has happened – for example, at the Malko competition – I remember there was a piece with a lot of changing tempi, so I created a kind of metronome track for the piece: four bars at 60, three bars at 80, and so on. A kind of "tape" of the tempo changes. I remember doing that, but it took so much time that I don't do it anymore. It was really helpful for the competition, though.

Was the "tape" you made for practicing the tempo changes?

Yes, exactly – and to get used to them in my body, especially because at Malko we had just one reading of the piece with the orchestra. You couldn't make a mistake in a transition – you really had to know it. That was my way of getting it right from the beginning. But I don't usually do that. I don't use technology, except for listening to the piece.

Do you watch videos of performances – and if so, is it before you read the score, while you're reading it, or afterward?

I never watch videos – which is probably a bad thing. When I do, it is because I have a hesitation on something – how should I beat a passage for it to work. If I have a hesitation, I will check on YouTube to see how another conductor does it and what the solutions are. Somehow, I feel that this is something I could do more, because now I have my own gestures and my own way of doing things. Sometimes I find colors by watching people, even more than just listening to them – but I don't do that much. Maybe in ten years, if you ask again, I will tell you I have discovered something good about videos. Among my colleagues, I am one of the conductors that has watched the least videos. I usually work with a closed computer, a closed phone – just my tuning fork and metronome.

The work of a conductor is very complex. First, you read the score, get to know the music in detail, and build your own idea or concept of how to perform it. Then comes the entire stage of transferring that to the orchestra and the audience – which involves manual technique and communication with people. Is score reading the first step of your conducting work?

I have noticed that there are also different steps of knowing a score. There is the basic knowledge you should always have, and then there is a much deeper level of knowing that you have to reach. But being somewhere in between feels bad. Sometimes, it is better to stay open to what happens and just adjust to everything – because if you haven't reached the next step yet, it is uncomfortable. Somehow, when I really know the score – when I have reached that next step – I become a slightly different conductor, let's say. I might be a bit less open to what happens and a bit stronger. I've noticed that this shift of attitude can be accepted differently by the orchestra. Sometimes, when I am a bit less ready with the score, the rehearsal feels better because I am more flexible. Other times, when I have studied so much, I am a bit less good at getting what I want – I get more frustrated, and the result is not as good. The orchestra has a lot of impact on the results, as does the way we transmit our emotions to them – on a very human level. Sometimes, it is better to feel good than to know the score well.

A conductor builds an image of the score in their mind while reading it, but to achieve the best result with the orchestra, it may be beneficial for the conductor to remain flexible in this image – open to the musicians' ideas and making music together with the orchestra.

That is true.

Have you considered conducting scores by heart?

I feel super stressed when I conduct by heart. I feel much more secure when I have the score, and this is how I present myself emotionally to the orchestra. If I am stressed, I focus on myself instead of them – I am too afraid of forgetting something. But some people are different; they are much more open when they conduct by heart, so it depends. That was something I dealt with a lot at school. I just don't want to conduct by heart – it creates too much tension for me, and then my brain stops working. It took me a long time to understand that I can't learn everything by heart – that it is not my way. But many people will tell you, "If you know it by heart, you know the music better and you will be freer." I've never experienced that – at least not yet. There are so many parameters: score reading and learning, but also emotional and leadership aspects that are a big part of how the conductor presents the music to the orchestra and the audience. It is life!

Would you like to add anything about score reading, or do you remember any anecdotes on this subject?

The form and writing down of the big structure of the piece, I do at the end. I usually start reading the piece in detail from the beginning, it takes time, and I have a global idea only very late in the process which is a bit dangerous, but that is how I do it. I have met other people who work that way, too. I have struggled with the idea that we are taught to learn the piece globally first, because for me, it is really the opposite.

After working on the details, do you then look at the big picture of the piece?

Yes, sometimes I just start from the beginning, writing the chords – even without knowing what happens at the end. I am just reading everything note by note before I realize that it is the second theme, or something like that. Once I have gone through the score in detail, then I'm like, *oh, this is the first theme, this is the development.* It is easier for me to make the big picture after having done the small one.

These days, conductors read scores by composers from different eras, styles and musical languages – which requires much knowledge. We now have access to resources such as historical treatises, composers' letters, and recordings. It is a challenge for conductors to work with such a wide range of repertoire and materials.

Yes, there is a risk that we have too many options – and then we somehow get lost in our own work. What concerns recordings – it is good to listen to them to get ideas from others, but sometimes there are just too many recordings. If you have to listen to ten recordings of *Madame Butterfly*, which is three hours long, how much time does that take? It is better to use that time to just learn the piece yourself. That is how I feel.

Transpositions and Score Reading – *Vlad Vizireanu*

Interview on 11 June 2024

What do you focus on most when reading an orchestral score? Do you read the score through multiple times? If so, what are the elements that you look at first, and what are the ones that you look at later?

The first thing I try to get a hold of is which transpositions I'm dealing with (ideally, the fewer, the better). I read transpositions in different clefs and adjust whichever accidentals I need to, so it is helpful to figure that out first. Then, tempo is my next consideration. I don't really restrict my final tempo to how fast I can play it on the piano, because it wasn't intended for the piano. Then I just start grinding through the piece and breaking it up into as many large and small sections as is necessary to create a structure out of it. I usually use recordings to listen to the entire product and score reading to focus on individual parts or smaller combinations, so I can hear details better in my mind.

How do you memorize an orchestral score? Do you visualize it in your mind, or write out a plan on paper, or does listening to recordings help? Or do you use some other method?

While I have steadily improved throughout the years, I've actually always been a very slow sight-reader. It has been my weakness ever since I started as a pianist. On the other hand, I always had a very solid memory. I was able to memorize scores relatively quickly, if I had properly marked them beforehand and had enough time to put in the work (of course, recordings are very useful as well). I try my best to always have every score relatively memorized (if not absolutely). The more concerts I have now, the less time I have to perfectly memorize scores, but I've figured out how to learn a score effectively enough by now, that I'm able to reach that level with consistency. While memorization is impressive and effective with an orchestra, the most important thing is to establish your interpretation in detail, so you know what you are listening for. Whether you've memorized the score or not, that's what counts in rehearsal most.

Are there any anecdotes that you could share from your score reading experience, for example considering a specific composer or piece?

Honestly, I really can't think of a specific anecdote about score reading. Like I said, while I use it to solidify my understanding of musical details, it's never been my *forte* as a musician. In a modern world of recordings, score reading is much less emphasized in music programs, which I think should definitely be changed.

Do you use clef substitution for reading transpositions also when there are a lot of accidentals, as for example in music by Igor Stravinsky? If the instruments are in different transpositions, do you think simultaneously of different keys of the transposing instruments, for example clarinet in B-flat (B-flat major), horn in F (F major)?

As a pianist, I read clefs my entire life. When I started reading scores, clefs were my natural go-to as well. It's easier for me to just think of concert pitch directly rather than doing intervallic calculations in my head for every transposed part. In all honesty, I think transposing parts are completely pointless in a conductor's score. While each transposing instrument has its own color and sound quality, which should be recognized, there is nothing musically meaningful in notating each instrument's transposition in the score (especially when all scores can easily be changed to concert pitch at the click of a button with modern software).

Is there any advice that you could give to a conducting student on how to learn to read orchestral scores fluently?

Start as early as possible and practice daily. This is basically advice I never got. I was expected to just know these things without any real guidance in school. Score reading should be taught every semester with gradually increased difficulty. It should be a requirement for conductors, along with sight-singing, rehearsal techniques, and orchestration. These basics are not addressed in modern academic programs as they should be. Conductors are expected to pick them up as they go, which is not helpful in the end. It would be much more helpful if conducting were available as an undergraduate major (in the USA), instead of beginning at the Master's level. I could have used four years of college to heavily drill these basics. Instead, I essentially started learning everything in my Master's, which is too much to cram in too short a program.

Zooming into the Score – *Eero Lehtimäki*

Interview on 17 June 2024

When you open the score of a piece you haven't heard before, how do you begin reading it?

Before opening the score, I want to know who wrote it – just a bit; I don't go into details at this point. Then, when I open the score, I try to read through it as quickly as possible without stopping – that is my method. The things that I do stop for are usually this "zoom-in method" I have. I check how many movements we've got, the tempo descriptions for each movement, and whether it goes in three, four, five, etc. While reading through as quickly as possible, I look for tempo changes: are there big structural blocks, like an introduction and allegro, for example, or do we stay in one tempo throughout the movement? Later, I zoom into the sections within those blocks. Once I've read through a movement and noted the tempo changes, I read through all the movements this way. Then I go back to the first one and see whether we have key changes and similar elements – and from there, I go deeper and deeper.

After going through the score for the first time, noting the tempos and overall structure, what kinds of details do you look for when you return to it – dynamics, articulation, or something else?

My order of things would be first having the tempo changes, then the changing meters – if they're not constant. If the meter is changing all the time, I assume this variation actually becomes constant, and checking through it becomes a detail. When we have the music going in 4/4, and then comes a section in 3/4, I want to know that and take it apart, so to speak. Otherwise, I begin to look for the dynamic max and min – the high and low points – and then, step by step, I zoom in from this fuzzy landscape to seeing the trees in the forest.

Does this method allow you to read scores more efficiently and faster?

Yes, that's right. Technically, you can keep zooming in as long as you have time – but if the concert is tomorrow, you can still use the same method. I don't have to change my approach depending on whether it is a "jump in" or something coming up in half a year.

What kinds of tools do you use for score reading? Do you use a piano, a tuning fork, a metronome – or do you sing, for example?

I've never used a tuning fork – or even had one. I'm not primarily a singer, which might have something to do with that, nor am I a choir conductor. But the piano is an important tool for me. I try to use it as much as possible – though not as much as you might imagine – because I'm not a pianist anymore. I used to be a pianist, then I became a clarinet player. Still, I use the piano to find the harmonies. Once you already know what's happening, it becomes a great tool for finding phrasing and everything else.

What else do you use the piano for, besides figuring out the harmony and phrasing?

For finding wrong notes. One thing about it is that you are really forcing yourself to read all the notes, instead of just scanning through and seeing the harmonies. When you're really playing it, you notice how it is supposed to be – that you have a C-sharp and a C-natural at the same time, and things like that. It is easier to spot those details when you have to read much more slowly. And with my piano playing especially, I really have to go slowly, so it helps me be more patient with the reading. It must be only a few times when I've used my main instrument, the clarinet, for score reading – and that has been when I was conducting a clarinet concerto.

Did you use the clarinet then for checking the phrasing and breathing?

Not exactly. I used it to get a sense of how the soloist might play it – trying to leave that decision to the performer – but just to have an idea, as a plan B to offer if needed. I also have very basic skills in viola, and that has been very useful for thinking about bowings. I don't do bowings for the material; with my knowledge, I think it is better to leave that to those who really handle it. But still, it helps to have an idea and to check layers, accentuation, and harmonics – which, I have to say, can be really challenging.

To clarify how the harmonics sound and how to play them?

Yes – and whether they sound at all, because some – especially contemporary composers – use harmonics that don't always work that well.

Have you been in a situation where you had to fix or change a harmonic?

Yes. There was a situation – it happened twice – where the double bass section argued that a harmonic doesn't exist. But it does, it makes sense, and it comes from the composer. I think it was one by Ravel.

The Mother Goose Suite? There are a few difficult harmonics in that score.

Yes – those minor third harmonics that people usually think don't exist, but they actually do.

As a conductor, did you need to help the musicians in the orchestra and explain to them what kind of harmonic it is and how they should play it?

Yes, and also what note it should be, because they usually think it is a mistake. It was correct in the first place, but they changed it to something else, and then you have to find what it should be. It is easier with a living composer – you can ask who's right and get confirmation.

Reading harmonics can be tricky.

For that, it is fantastic to have the instrument – and also for double stops, to check whether they are possible or not.

You have worked on contemporary pieces. Have you found differences in reading contemporary music scores compared to traditional ones?

Yes – and even within the different genres of contemporary music. For example, what does it mean when, let us say, eighth notes have no articulation marking? For some composers, that means "shortish", while others assume that if nothing is written, the notes should be held to their full value. That is one of those cases where, when you ask the composer, the answer is usually – "of course it's long", or "broad", or "short".

This information is missing in the score, isn't it?

Yes, and it might be "always" for a specific composer – but completely different for others. In the older style – all those Classical Viennese pieces – it is usually quite clear what was meant. But the off-string and on-string matter is always something that bugs me. This eighth-note issue is one of the most problematic, and the use of the *tenuto* line is another. I've noticed that many contemporary composers assume that if nothing is written, the note should already be played at full value. In that case, the *tenuto* line can actually separate the notes and give a certain kind of accent – and then you have to argue how to read the note. An accent: is it long or short, if nothing else is added to define it? These are the articulation issues.

Are you used to working closely with composers on their scores to clarify such issues?

Yes, I always try to contact them. I also think it's a good, subtle hint to them that these things can actually be understood in different ways – and that in the future, they might want to be more specific.

When you read the score, do you mark it in some way?

Very little – only when something is really unclear, such as these articulation marks. Usually, I just write in corrections. And then we have those scores that are meant to be B2 size but are printed on A4 – in those cases, you can't see the tempo markings, not even with a magnifying glass. So I write them in, just to be able to see them in the first place. Earlier, I trusted that I had learned it and that it was there, so I thought – *why write it?* But as more and more programs kept coming and the schedule became tighter, I realized I wasn't winning anything by not writing. One idea I've taken on is that if I lose my score and get handed a blank one before the performance, I should still be able to conduct from it. Now I have actually started making more markings.

There is a story about Leonard Bernstein – that each time he performed the same piece, he would use a different score in order to have a new and fresh approach.

That is brilliant. I also know a conductor who, for some pieces, has three or four scores – each with a different set of markings.

That is very interesting.

I have also used the score for marking how different conductors have done things in rehearsals, just to have an idea of how it could be done. It is really nice to see that in some Beethoven scores I bought twenty years ago, there are marks from three different conductors. Then, when I look at a specific place, I can see – *okay, like this* – and decide how I want to do it.

Nowadays we are surrounded by recordings. What is the role of recordings in your score reading?

I usually try not to listen to any recordings before I have read the score myself, to have fresh ears for it. I've noticed that sometimes my first impression and interpretation can be very different from what others are offering. That might be due to editions or performance traditions, but I am so happy to find my own idea first, without having it polluted by other people's versions. But then, I do listen eventually – just to know the tempi, if there is a tradition or something accepted. If nobody is playing it as fast as I imagined, I have the alarm bell ringing – *maybe it is not playable.* I check whether I am within the max and min range, and if I am outside that, then I have to know why and be prepared to answer the questions: *Why is this faster? Why is this slower?* It is all about traditions, especially when working with older music, where so much wasn't written in the score. In Finland, we don't have this continuous link they have in Vienna or Paris.

Today's conductor has to navigate all kinds of musical styles, and the meaning of notation has been changing.

Yes, exactly.

Where can the conductor learn about the styles from? You mentioned that you want to know about the composer. Do you read composers' letters or other sources for this purpose?

I am a bit of a nerd when it comes to the Classical period. I play five- and twelve-key clarinets myself, so I have some specialized knowledge in that field. Letters – yes, a bit. It is very interesting to see, for example, what Mozart writes about the tempo of a menuetto. He once attended a performance and remarked that the tempo was very fast. We can't know exactly what he was comparing it to, but at least we know it was faster there than elsewhere. Even nowadays, people still say, "This is the menuetto tempo" – yes, maybe for the dance – but even in Mozart's time, there wasn't one universal menuetto tempo, and we know that from these letters. I've also tried to read all the basic sources, like Leopold Mozart and Quantz.

Do you mean the music treatises?

Yes, they've been important. And also Clive Brown's *Classical and Romantic Performing Practice*, Charles Rosen's *The Classical Style*, and books on historical performance practice.

Has studying these influenced your score reading?

They are important, but I have a more recent approach of my own. Of course, it is a continuous inner debate about what the style should be and when. My key message at the moment is this idea of changing fashion. I think it's really important and interesting to know how things were originally done. We can't know that with complete certainty, but to some extent, it doesn't even matter – it is like asking how tight the leg should be in jeans compared to the original style. We can find out – but it has changed.

Fashions of performing have been changing.

Yes, exactly. The fact is, what we're doing – which we easily forget – is performing the music today, not two hundred years ago. Something that must have been really nice, cool, and appreciated back then just makes no sense to us now. And the way we perform it today might not make any sense fifty – or certainly a hundred – years from now.

When you read the score, do you think about whom you will perform the piece for? Do you think of the audience?

Yes, to some extent. After all, we're performing it for them. Of course, it is important to respect the composer – but they are often long gone, so why try to please them by doing something that is no longer in fashion?

Do you feel a need to connect with the audience?

Absolutely. Should we play this trill one way or another – it is important and nice to know how it was originally done. But that was the *bon goût*[101] Leopold Mozart wrote about. And that sense of *bon goût* is changing all the time. I think that is actually the key point – like the use of *vibrato* or the choice of tempi. We are now performing pieces in Musiikkitalo's[102] large concert hall that were once played at garden parties, and we are still thinking about what the original tempo was – but we are not at a garden party anymore. In many cases, we are using one analogy while forgetting that everything else around it has changed.

Should we take into account where we are performing the piece?

Absolutely – we need to take it into account. If we are playing in a church versus a very dry space, we already have to adjust the tempo in score reading. That is why you have to know the place where you are performing in

---

[101] bon goût – *[Fr.]* "good taste."
[102] Helsinki Music Centre.

advance. If it is a huge stone church, you cannot take the tempos as fast as they look on paper or sound in a MIDI file.

Instruments have been changing over the years. Because of that, do you need to make retouches to scores of older music, or is it something you do in rehearsals?

It is usually something I do in rehearsals. Old brass instruments, for example, didn't cut through everything the way modern trombones and trumpets do – you could play loudly and still get that brassy sound without covering everything. When you try to go brassy today, it is hard to achieve without being at triple *forte* all the time. I already look at that while reading the score.

Do you prepare your own set of orchestral parts?

No, I never have. I've been thinking about it – especially with some pieces I've worked on and done some really deep research on – it would be really nice to have my own set. What I did do was build a "backstage" section on my website, which I share with the musicians. It includes errata and a database of pieces. I send the librarian a link, and it is very easy for me to say in rehearsal, "Just go to the link and check your errata."

What kinds of things do you list there?

It is usually just wrong notes, changes in dynamics, repetitions, and things like that – but the interpretational stuff I do myself during rehearsal. Having a prepared set of parts would be faster and easier. What is good about the technological approach is that I used to have a single list with all the corrections, but now there is a separate list for each instrument. You just click on your instrument name and get the corrections. It is impossible to miss – if you just open the link. Of course, that can still be hard for some musicians…

Have you met any special challenges in score reading?

I come back again to the size of the score. I don't like transporting huge scores – I prefer them in A4, so they fit in my bag. Recently, I've conducted two concerts from a small iPad. It was contemporary music, available in a notation software file, so I rewrote the score myself – removed all the empty staves and changed the font to make it larger. That is also a score reading issue, which I solved by adjusting the score itself.

Does the layout of the score affect the effectiveness of the conductor's score reading?

Yes, absolutely. Even the fonts can make quite a difference.

How was your experience conducting from the iPad?

There were pros and cons. One of the issues is that, since we conduct standing up, you have to balance on one leg while trying to find the pedal for the iPad with the other. It is much easier when seated – when I was playing chamber music, it wasn't a problem.

Turning to the technical side of reading scores, how do you read transpositions? Do you move each note by a transposing interval, or do you exchange the transposition for another clef?

I use clef substitution. I had never done it before taking the score playing class at the Sibelius Academy. It was such a eureka moment, and I started reading that way right away – I find it really brilliant. As a clarinet player, I've always used interval transposition, since I often had to play from C parts – but not anymore. I also use clefs for clarinet, although I notice that, having done so much with intervals, I still oscillate between the two methods. For horns in E-flat or F, for example, it is easy to go straight with the clef, whereas with the clarinet, I still switch between the two methods, and it is not entirely consistent.

When the notes have many accidentals, or the music is atonal, do you still continue reading transpositions with the clefs?

I do. There are some additional problems with accidentals. I have to add that it is much easier with transpositions you are used to. But then – especially horn parts in bass clef – you have to double-think: first put in the extra effort to figure out which clef it is, because you don't use it that often. But the good thing is, for example, when you have a pair like bassoon in tenor clef and clarinet in B-flat written on neighboring staves – instead of reading two different clefs and two different transpositions, it becomes one. I think that is the best thing about it.

Let's take Stravinsky's The Rite of Spring. In some movements, clarinets are in B-flat without a key signature, and the music doesn't sound tonal – when reading these clarinets, do you think in B-flat major, which is the key of the clarinet, or do you think of the two flats from the transposition?

I just think of the two flats – keeping it very technical and trying to get rid of all that stuff.

So, you're not imagining different keys simultaneously?

Exactly. One of the most challenging things is when some composers actually write instruments in different keys. These are not common moments, fortunately, but for example, when the clarinets continue in the same key even though the others change – that is problematic for me. It is also confusing because you usually check quickly – *okay, we have two more sharps, so it's clear that it is now in B-flat.* Especially when instruments change quickly – in A, in C, in B-flat again – you would like to see and know instantly which clarinets are being used, just by calculating the key signature. But if the key change doesn't affect the clarinet player and they keep playing in the old key, then you see – *okay, according to the key signature, this is not a B-flat clarinet, even though it actually is* – and those are really confusing moments.

***I remember there is such a place in Brahms's* First Serenade.**

Then it means that even though you do the clef replacement, the clarinetists have instruments playing in a different key. I think those are nasty surprises.

That must be difficult to read for everyone.

Yes, they are not nice. But I have to say, on this exact point – when we have these pops concerts where arrangers write the full score in C, I usually request a transposed score. I'm so used to reading transposed scores that they tell me more. For example, with horns – if it is super high, I can see it right away in a transposed score, but in a C score, it's much harder to tell, especially with music that hasn't been tried or performed a million times before. It is much easier to see from the transposed score whether we are below the limits – for example, if the clarinet is written too low, I recognize it right away. When the clarinets are written in C, the part is actually played on a clarinet in A or B-flat, so you always have to triple-check whether it is not too low – does it work? If the score is transposed, it is much easier to just scan through it.

That is a message to composers and arrangers – please use the traditional notation with transpositions in the scores…

Yes, and usually with modern notation software, it is super fast and easy. When we start a project, I just tell the people writing the arrangements: please send me the versions in transposed notation.

Does the transposed notation help you better understand the players' situation?

Yes, exactly – you see more information from the players' point of view. It also makes sense, because sometimes, especially with accidentals, the notation can look much more complicated in the transposed part, and vice versa. When you have the C score, you just don't understand what the person playing a transposing instrument is doing and why. But then, when you see the transposed score – *okay, they have a double sharp here and double flats all the time* – that is why they are playing a bit funky.

Would you like to have the same notes the musicians have?

Yes – then it is so much easier to understand why something is happening in a certain way. The worst thing is if the score doesn't one hundred percent match the parts – when you see a wrong note in the score, it doesn't mean that it is wrong in the part, and vice versa. It is so much harder to fix, especially in advance.

Some conductors request from the publisher the exact same set of parts they worked with before.

Yes, I understand why – that is a good point.

When you read a score, do you pay attention to memorizing it, so that when you go to the orchestra you can conduct from memory?

At the moment, that is not my plan. There was one point when I actually did try to memorize, and it is very nice to conduct a concert – or even rehearsals – when you can be very free about it. There was one interview with Sir Simon Rattle, and I really loved his approach – he starts conducting from memory when he notices he hasn't been turning the pages. It is not the point; it is just a side product. That is my approach – letting it happen if it happens.

Do you have any other personal method or preferred way of reading a score that you haven't mentioned yet?

For reading scores, I quite often use this "Memento method" from the film by Christopher Nolan. The technique just happens to match the structure of that film. The idea of *Memento* is that it starts from the last scene. It is about a man who has problems with short-term memory, so he can't remember what happened a while ago. He's dropped into a situation and doesn't remember who is who, and then the scene proceeds normally, chronologically, to the end. After that, we have the second-to-last scene, where again he doesn't know where he is and who the people are, and it ends where the previous scene began. Then we continue in reverse order. I read scores like this – starting from the last rehearsal mark to the end, then going from the second-to-last rehearsal mark to the last one, and so on.

This way, do you read the score from the end toward the beginning, by sections?

Yes, exactly – by sections – and I always end the section I'm reading with the one I just previously read. Through this, I know where I should be taking the music. We usually use this method in normal rehearsals when preparing a concert: "Okay, this is the tempo we should have," and then we do the *accelerando* before. I apply the same method to score reading. It's also psychologically brilliant – you are all the time "coming home", so to speak – arriving at something you already know. That is what we are needed for: leading the way, rather than just being in the moment with everyone else and then being surprised ourselves – *Ah, okay, now we're here*. Somehow, for me, it is like broadening the perspective – making the vision of the horizon much clearer. Because then, when I conduct, I know I'm taking it there and helping the orchestra move into that section.

Do you go through the score in your mind both from the end to the beginning by sections, and from the beginning to the end?

Yes, exactly. I do that when something needs to be well prepared. For the mind, it is easier to spend more time with the piece when you have different kinds of methods to use.

Does this help you better understand the piece?

Yes, absolutely – especially in terms of structure, to have that long line, the big architecture. It really helps, and I use it. When you mentioned tools – I use the metronome a lot. I often read scores with the metronome ticking in the background the whole time. I keep it on continuously for some pieces when I'm reading the score – to really pump it into the system, and also for tempo in general. It is really good to just have the 80 bpm smashing there all the time – it also helps build tempo memory.

The choice of tempo affects so many elements.

Yes, exactly. Sometimes the music gives a different impression – it looks faster or slower than the actual tempo. Then you can already adjust to the idea in advance. Another aspect we haven't talked about yet is the different editions, which I also try to compare sometimes, especially with Mozart. Orchestras usually use the Breitkopf material, and then I have the Bärenreiter and the manuscript – I compare them. Whenever possible, I want to have the manuscript available and check it. Often there are things – like in Mozart – that people play all the time, but they're clearly a misreading of the manuscript. It's the same with *Pelléas et Mélisande* – the current edition is full of them. I'm happy they're doing a new one for the works of Jean Sibelius.

What kinds of things did the editor change compared to the manuscript?

As an example – *diminuendos* become accents. It is sloppily read – things like: *Why does the flute have an accent or sforzato here in the middle of the phrase?* And then people play it that way just because it's in the score. But when you look at the manuscript, you see it right away – *okay, it's not for the flute; it's actually for the double bass, in the place where everybody has a sforzato*. Then, in the edition, where everyone has a *sforzato*, it's missing from the double bass, and a couple of bars later, it's written for the flute. You can't guess that from the score, but when you see it in the manuscript – they're on top of each other – it is very clear.

By working with the manuscript, do you better discover the composer's intentions?

Yes, and there are really important things – like tempo changes. For example, in the last movement of *Pelléas et Mélisande*, at the death of Mélisande – this *largamente* passage – Sibelius very clearly writes it on the half-bar, but in the edition, it's placed on the first beat. People want to follow what Sibelius wrote, but they are not doing that – they are following what the editor wrote. Mozart is an even better example, because there are so many different editions available today.

Is your favorite starting point for score reading the urtext edition?

I love the Bärenreiter for Mozart, but it is different with other composers.

What about Beethoven?

I usually like the Bärenreiter as a starting point, but they have this issue with the *Keil*, or *staccato* – which is, again, one of those ridiculous things. I write with ink all the time myself, so I know how hard it is to make a clear dot – you usually need a bit of horizontal or vertical movement. The big problem with Bärenreiter is that in the preface, they cite Beethoven in a specific case where he writes a slur and *staccato*, without acknowledging that elsewhere they don't actually make a difference between *staccato* and *Keil*. They just change all the *staccato* markings to *Keil*, which makes no sense. It is as if they've acknowledged that there was a discussion – and then changed everything, instead of making any distinction between the two. And then people are like, "Okay, here's a *Keil* – so what do we do? How should we play it?"

When reading a score of a Classical period piece, do you think about issues of articulation and how to achieve them with the orchestra?

Yes, that is why I try to find the manuscript – to see what kinds of markings the composer used. Often, with Schubert, Mozart, Beethoven, and others who wrote with ink, the process was generally quite quick. They were in a hurry. The concert was about to start any minute – the next piece was coming. It is very common that even in the same place, some marks look like clear dots in the same *unisono* passage. You just have to think: *is there a reason why this is staccato and that is portato?* With *da capo* passages that have different articulation – they didn't have copy-paste – *is there a message in playing it differently?* One of my new approaches to fashion is that I generally don't want to perform something I don't understand. If I see that the first time there's a *staccato* and the second time there isn't, and I don't see a reason why the composer did it, then I can't present it as a different kind of story. If I don't see a reason why it should be different, I try to make it the same – just like copying. Seeing that this "godly" text from the composer states it like that doesn't, by itself, give me permission to present it in a way that makes no sense to me.

In our reality, what would you say is the best way to access manuscripts?

That's the best thing – many of them are already digitally available. When I go somewhere to do Mozart, for example, I usually have two scores with me and the manuscript available on my computer. Then I can compare them if something seems strange. Sometimes you need to write the bar numbers or rehearsal marks yourself. I want to have the same ones the orchestra has, because otherwise it gets complicated. Orchestras sometimes use Luck's or Eulenburg materials, which are often very bad. I don't want to use them, especially if I already have my markings and corrections in the new edition, so I just copy the important stuff – bar numbers, rehearsal marks – and then I can use my own score.

Some orchestras are used to playing from their own parts and don't want to change them.

Yes, exactly – that is really true. I understand that in many cases, the bowings are already prepared, and trying to bring my own set could cause some extra backfire in that sense. It is also a money issue. When I was a student, I bought Dover scores, and now updating the whole library would be quite costly. So I just write the needed corrections into my score – like for Debussy's *Prélude à l'après-midi d'un faune*. My score is full of corrections according to the manuscript. When I see in an orchestra rehearsal that something is wrong in the part, even though it is correct in the score, I usually write it down so I know for the next occasion that it could be wrong.

Could you share any anecdotes, something that happened or surprised you when you were reading a score?

That brings to my mind a very short anecdote about traditions. When I was performing with one orchestra and talking about doing the *da capo* repeat in the *Menuetto*, one of the musicians said, "Come on, we've played it without the repetition for a hundred years." But why play two-hundred-year-old music the way it was done one hundred years ago? There is a direct quote from one of the original books – I think it was from 1805 – saying that if nothing else is written, then you do the repetitions. Therefore, if you're performing music from 1799, you can almost rely one hundred percent on this idea. My reply to the musician was: "If we really want to respect the composer from two hundred years ago, we shouldn't follow the rules from one hundred years ago."

The position of the conductor is to be on the side of the composer.

Yes, exactly. Often, the problem with tradition is that we are not following the tradition of the piece, but rather some kind of "semi-modern" tradition from fifty years ago.

3 Results of the Score Reading Questionnaire

The Score Reading Questionnaire was designed by the author and conducted online between May and August 2024. A total of forty professional conductors, aged 30-60, from around the world took part[103]. The results of the Questionnaire are presented in a series of figures (1-18) and accompanying comments below[104].

The author would like to express deepest gratitude to all conductors who participated in the Questionnaire for the valuable contribution to the study of orchestral score reading and for sharing their outstanding artistry, knowledge, and experience.

Do you use any musical instrument or tool for reading orchestral scores?

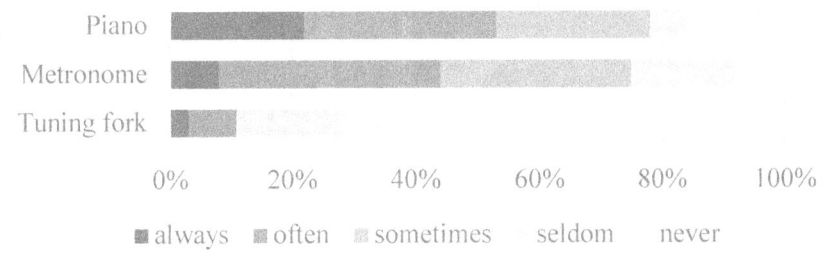

Fig. 1. (n=36)

The answers revealed that eighty-three percent of conductors use a piano, ninety-two percent a metronome, and twenty-eight percent a tuning fork for orchestral score reading. Additionally, seven out of forty conductors reported using other instruments for this purpose, including clarinet, trumpet, viola (2 conductors), violin (2 conductors), voice, and also music notation software. One conductor expressed the view that scores can only be read on keyboard instruments, while another emphasized that one must "hear" the orchestra inwardly while reading the score, rather than playing it on an instrument.

---

[103] List of conductors: Geoffrey Álvarez, Philippe Bach, Maria Badstue, Quentin Clare, David Danzmayr, Ilona Dobszay-Meskó, Chloé Dufresne, Cyril Englebert, Maria Gardolińska, Ayyub Guliyev, David Hattner, Anna-Maria Helsing, Alberto Hold-Garrido, Leo Hussain, Kaapo Ijas, Masayuki Inagaki, Vivian Wing Wun Ip, George Jackson, Johannes Klumpp, Tomasz Labuń, Marcelo Lehniger, Eero Lehtimäki, Edmon Levon, Igor Manasherov, Kornilios Michailidis, Donka Miteva, Tito Muñoz, Mikk Murdvee, Giancarlo Rizzi, Mattia Rondelli, Christian Schumann, Heikki Seppänen, James Sherlock, Ewa Strusińska, Eugene Tzigane, Vlad Vizireanu, 4 anonymous.
[104] Percentage values are rounded to whole numbers.

Do you sing instrumental parts when reading orchestral scores?

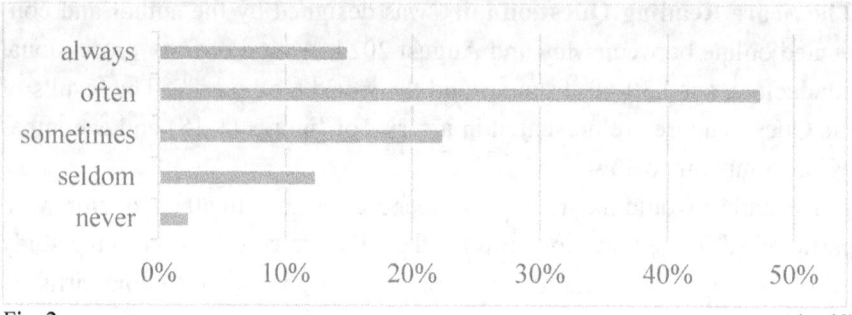

Fig. 2. (n=40)

Almost all conductors (ninety-seven percent) sing instrumental parts while reading the score, with sixty-three percent doing so often or always.

Do you listen to recordings of the piece for reading orchestral scores?

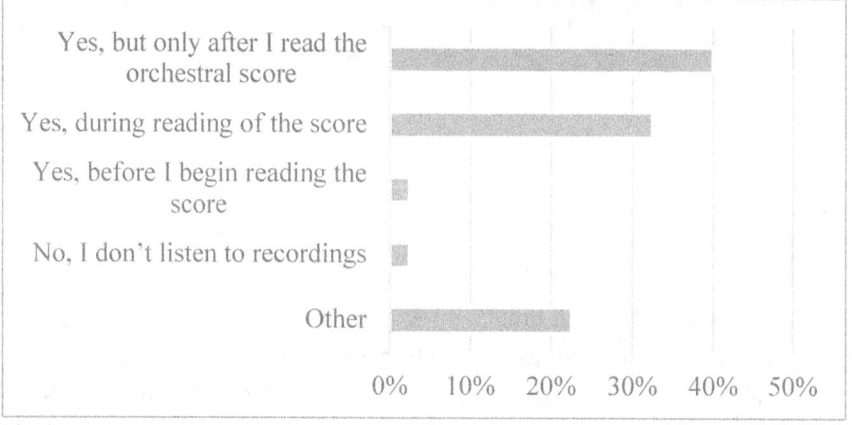

Fig. 3. (n=40)

Ninety-seven percent of conductors listen to recordings at some stage of their score reading process. Those who selected "Other" (twenty-three percent) provided additional comments, summarized below:

- The process of listening to recordings may extend from before to after reading the score.
- The amount of available time can affect how much listening is done.
- Conductors may have preferred recordings, such as "gold standard" recordings, or listen to as many versions as they can find.
- Some conductors listen to recordings while going through the score; others listen without the score.

Results of the Score Reading Questionnaire

"*After playing [a score] on the piano, it can be helpful to listen to contrasting recordings, especially if there are recordings conducted by the composer. Comparing recordings can give a good sense for different approaches, also in a historical context. For example, early Mahler recordings, Beethoven recordings by period ensembles, or Rachmaninov recordings of his time. I recommend against using recordings as a shortcut, as in the long run, it will decrease score reading skills. However, if a conductor is young and starting to build a repertoire, it might sometimes be necessary to cut corners. As an assistant conductor, you might face so many new scores that there is only the chance to learn them all by using recordings as a shortcut. However, in the long run, it is better to train your ear and score reading skills to be able to read scores quickly.*"[105]

"*I don't play recordings when analyzing a score, and I believe you should never 'conduct' a recording. You can get the bad habit of following instead of leading. However, I am a musician, and I like to listen to music! So, listening to recordings is part of my musical research, as well for enjoyment.*"[106]

Do you listen to recordings to get to know the performance traditions and/or explore performance issues?

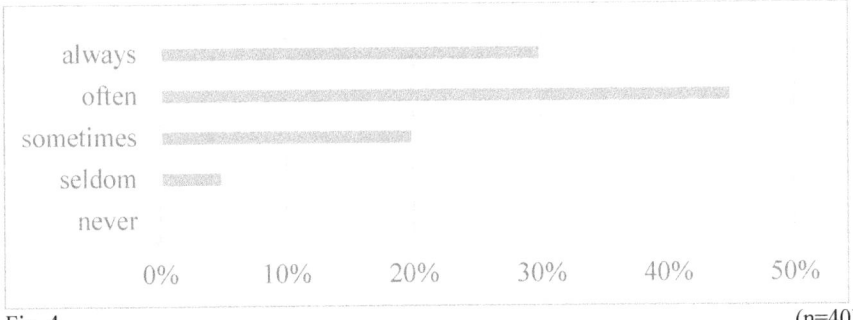

Fig. 4 (n=40)

All conductors, to some extent, use recordings to familiarize themselves with performance traditions and/or explore performance issues.

---

[105] David Danzmayr, in: Score Reading Questionnaire.
[106] Marcelo Lehniger, in: Score Reading Questionnaire.

Do you sing the solo vocal parts when reading an opera orchestral score?

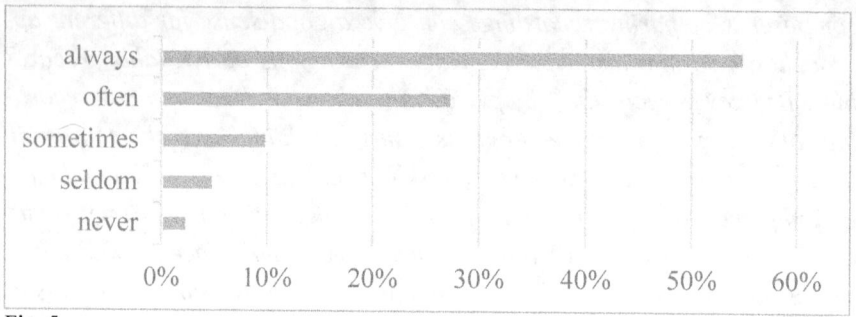

Fig. 5 (n=40)

Almost all conductors (ninety-seven percent) sing the solo vocal parts when reading an opera orchestral score, and among them, fifty-five percent always do this.

What elements of the score do you focus on when reading orchestral scores?

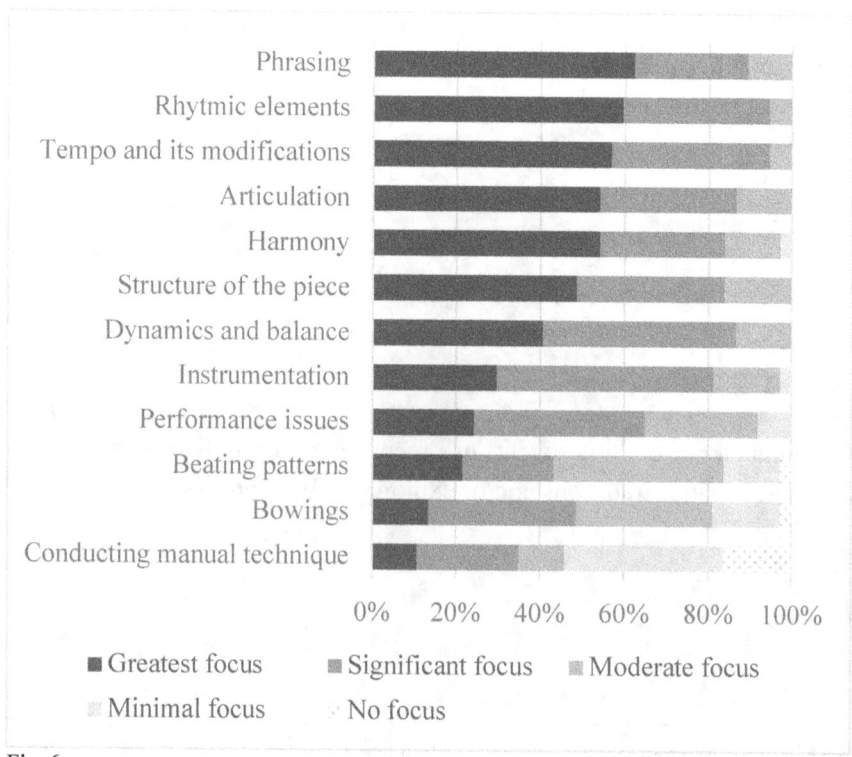

Fig. 6 (n=37)

When reading orchestral scores, conductors place the greatest emphasis on phrasing, rhythmic elements, tempo and its modifications, articulation, harmony, and structure. Secondly, they also focus on dynamics and balance, instrumentation, and performance-related issues. Most conductors give no or only minimal to moderate attention to beating patterns and manual technique.

Conductors also mentioned other aspects to which they give significant – or in some cases, primary – attention when reading scores. These include the proportions of and within movements, historical performance practices, rehearsal numbers and letters, errors and inconsistencies, decisions about where to lead or give space, character, emotional content, expression, and the overall meaning of the music.

One conductor left an additional comment:
"The score is only a shorthand for an aural language that existed at a specific time and place. Therefore, the relevant historical performance practices can greatly alter the meaning of the notation. The idea that 'everything is in the score' is the central tenant of contemporary mainstream conducting. But it is also a fallacy, manufactured by post-WWI composers and performers to distance themselves from past traditions, which they usually deemed degenerate or compromised by sentimentality. Not explaining this foundation for the meaning of the texts of different eras is the main failure of contemporary conducting education in conservatories worldwide."[107]

---

[107] Eugene Tzigane, in: Score Reading Questionnaire.

Do you learn the score by heart before conducting the orchestra?

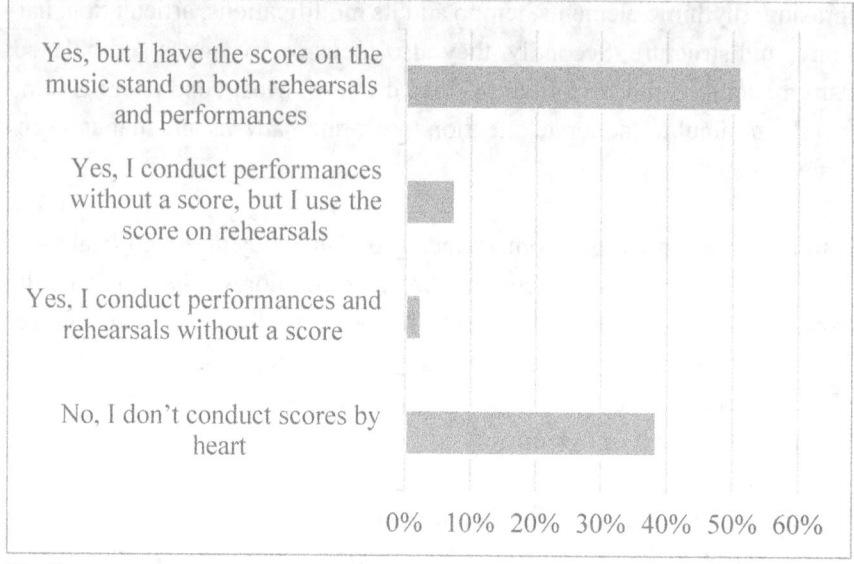

Fig. 7.   (n=40)

The responses revealed that sixty-two percent of conductors memorize scores before conducting the orchestra, while the remaining thirty-eight percent do not conduct by heart.

Do you research the background of the piece and the composer's aesthetic for the purpose of reading an orchestral score?

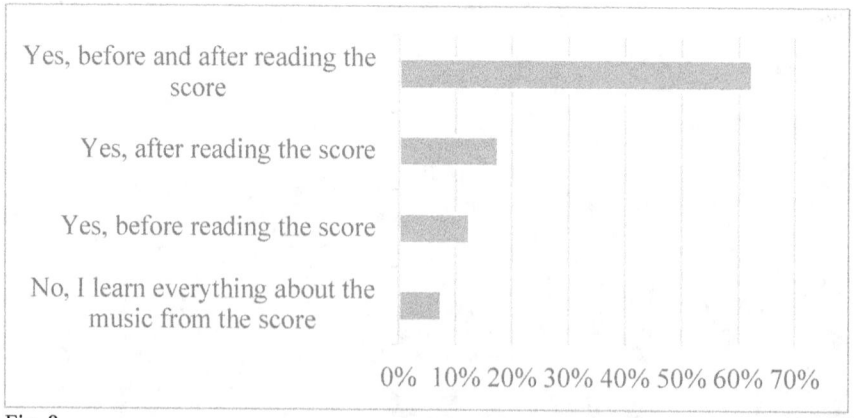

Fig. 8.   (n=40)

Ninety-two percent of conductors research the background of the piece and the composer's aesthetic for reading a score, while only eight percent rely solely on the score to learn everything about the music.

Do you mark bowings for the string parts while reading an orchestral score?

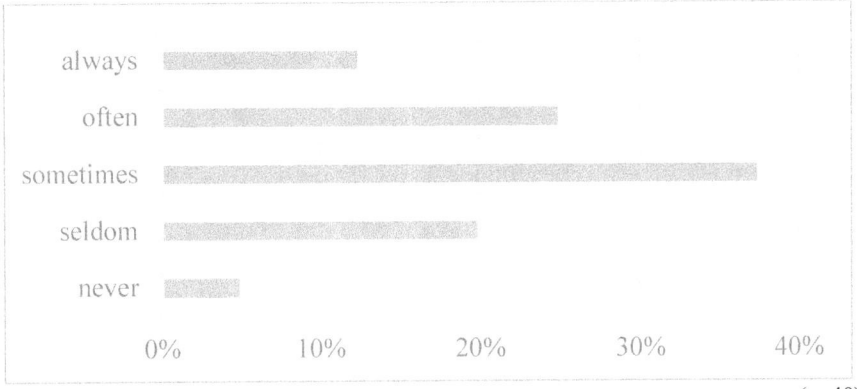

Fig. 9. (n=40)

Almost all conductors (ninety-five percent) add bowings to the string parts in some extent, with thirteen percent always doing so.

Do you prepare your own set of orchestral parts for use in rehearsals and performances?

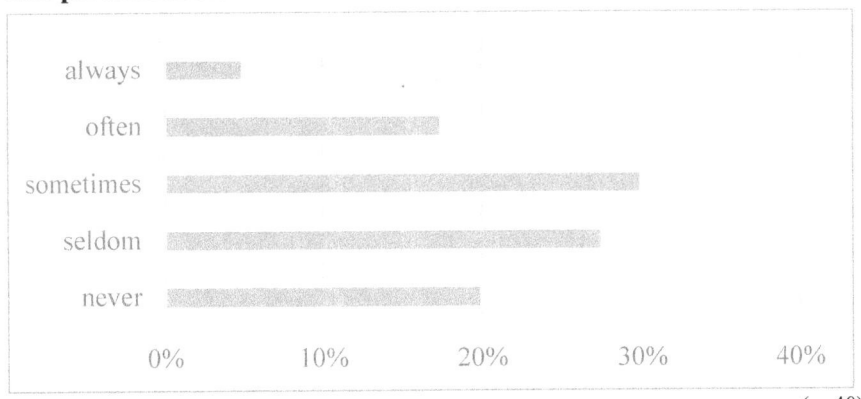

Fig. 10. (n=40)

While eighty percent of conductors prepare and use their own sets of orchestral parts, only five percent do this consistently.

Do you make a formal analysis of the score's structure while reading it?

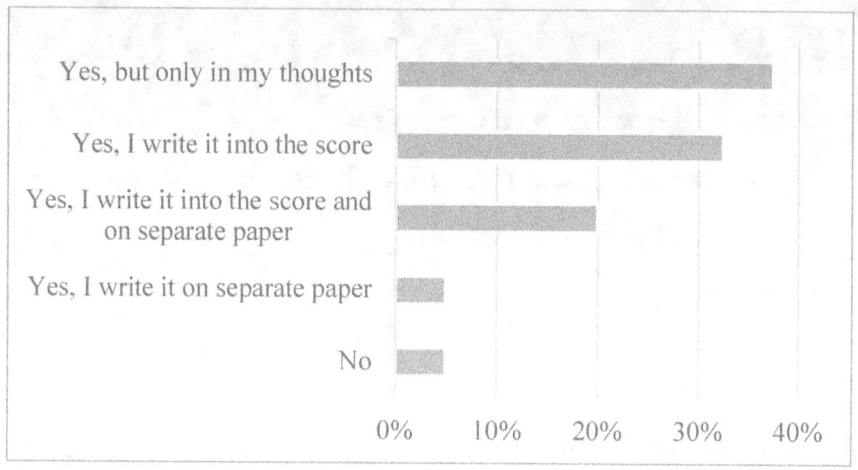

Fig. 11 (n=40)

Ninety-five percent of conductors perform a formal analysis of the score's structure, with fifty-eight percent writing it down either in the score or on separate paper.

Do you study individual instrument parts before reading the full score?

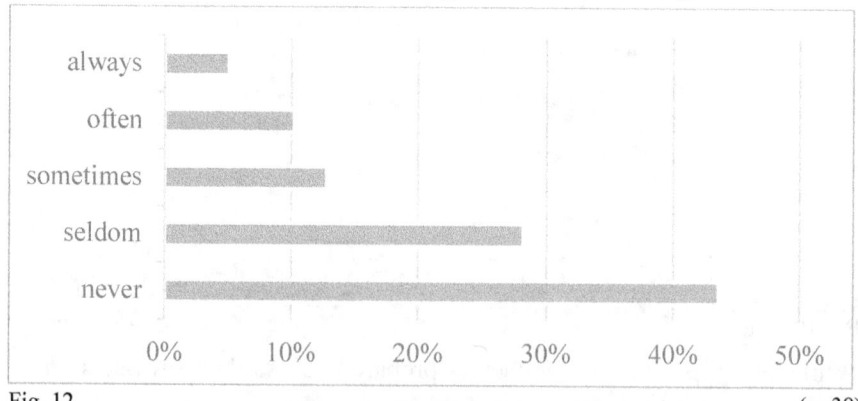

Fig. 12. (n=39)

Just over half of conductors (fifty-six percent) read individual instrument parts before studying the full orchestral score, while only forty-four percent always read the whole orchestra from the outset.

Do you make instrumentation retouches to the scores you conduct?

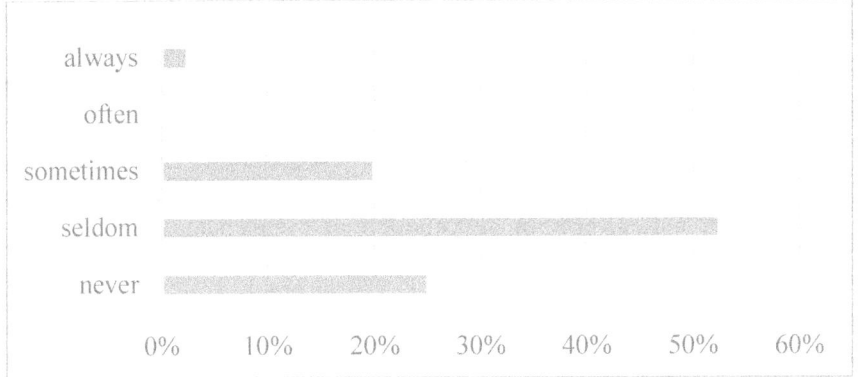

Fig. 13 (n=40)

Conductors are divided on this issue, but only twenty-five percent reported that they never alter the instrumentation.

Do you write markings in scores?

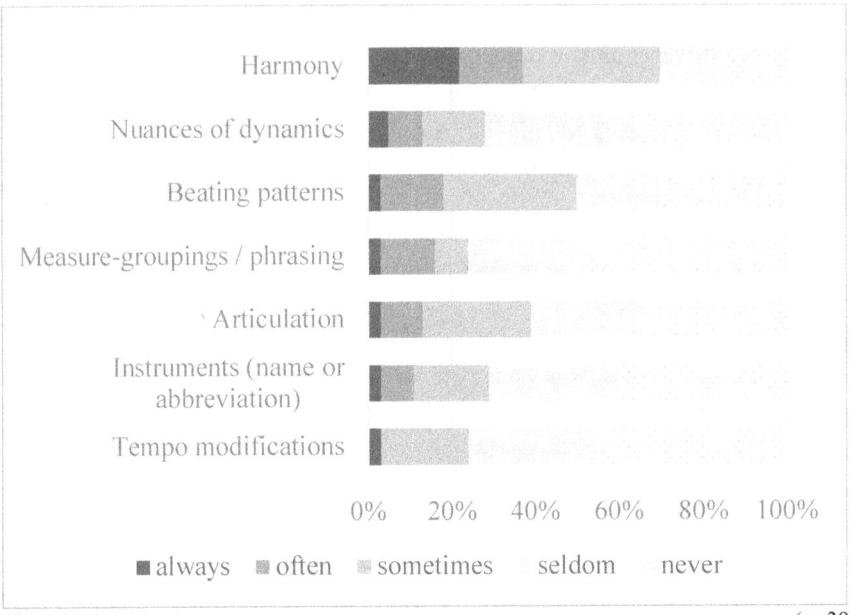

Fig. 14. (n=39)

When conductors write markings in the score, they often pertain to harmony, beating patterns, articulation, dynamic nuances, instrument names or abbreviations, tempo modifications, and measure groupings or phrasing.

Some conductors also mentioned other elements they mark in their scores:
- Musical ideas for interpretation
- Solutions to rehearsal problems
- Comments from composers – quotations, texts from letters, and other references
- Descriptive or poetic notes about character and emotion
- Personal tempo markings, sometimes supported by metronome indications or reminders about tempo tendencies
- Performance practices and unwritten traditions
- Bar numbers and rehearsal marks, if missing or inconsistent across editions
- Remarks on form
- Notes on balance
- Translations of text in opera, if needed
- Clarifications of instrumentation (e.g., Cor I vs Cor I. for first horn and English horn)
- Highlighting of important lines and melodies
- Breath marks
- Fun facts

Conductors differ in how extensively they mark their scores. Some are very reserved or minimalistic in this regard – or choose not to write in the score at all. One conductor noted that excessive markings can be distracting. Others make extensive annotations, using a regular pencil or incorporating color as well.

Results of the Score Reading Questionnaire

Do you use clef substitution for reading transpositions?

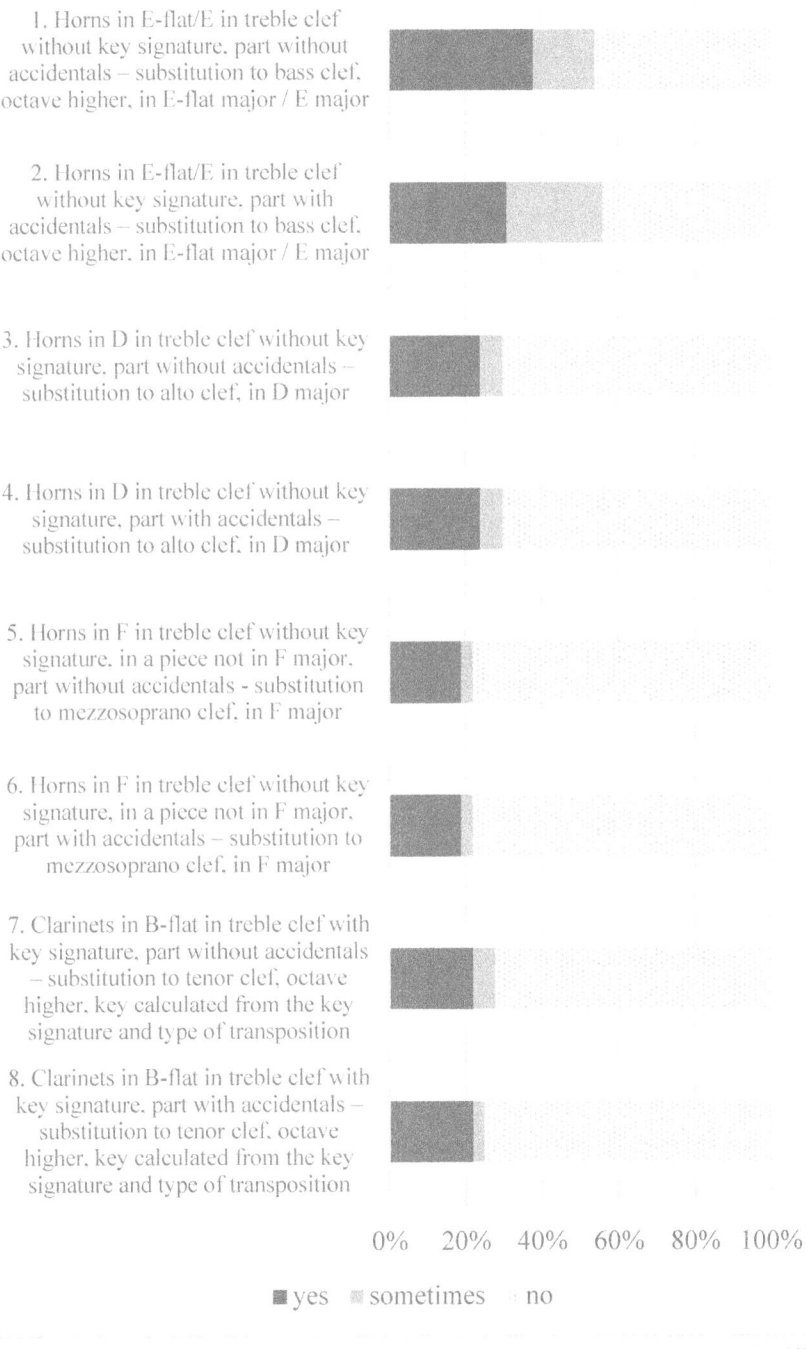

Fig. 15 (n=40)

Summary of clef substitution usage:

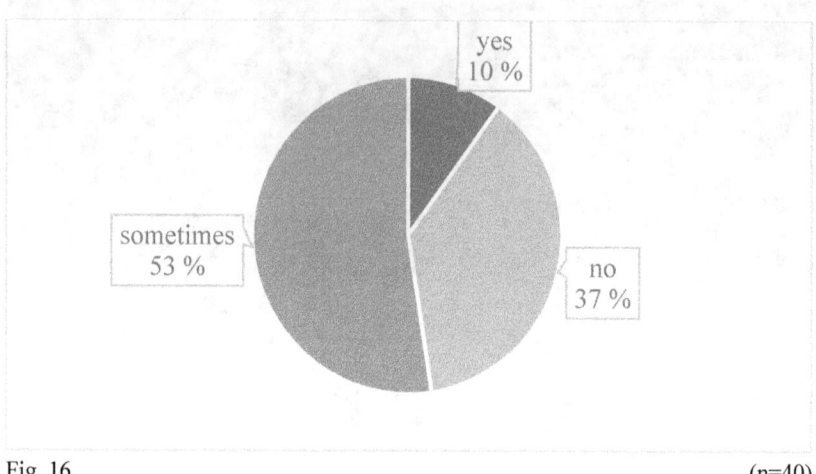

Fig. 16. (n=40)

Slightly more than half of conductors (sixty-three percent) use clef substitution for reading transpositions, and among them, ten percent do this consistently. Substituting E-flat and E transpositions in treble clef with bass clef is especially common.

One conductor remarked, "M*astering all clefs is the* key *to transposition!*"[108]

---

[108] Kornilios Michailidis, in: Score Reading Questionnaire.

What do you consider the greatest challenges in reading orchestral scores?

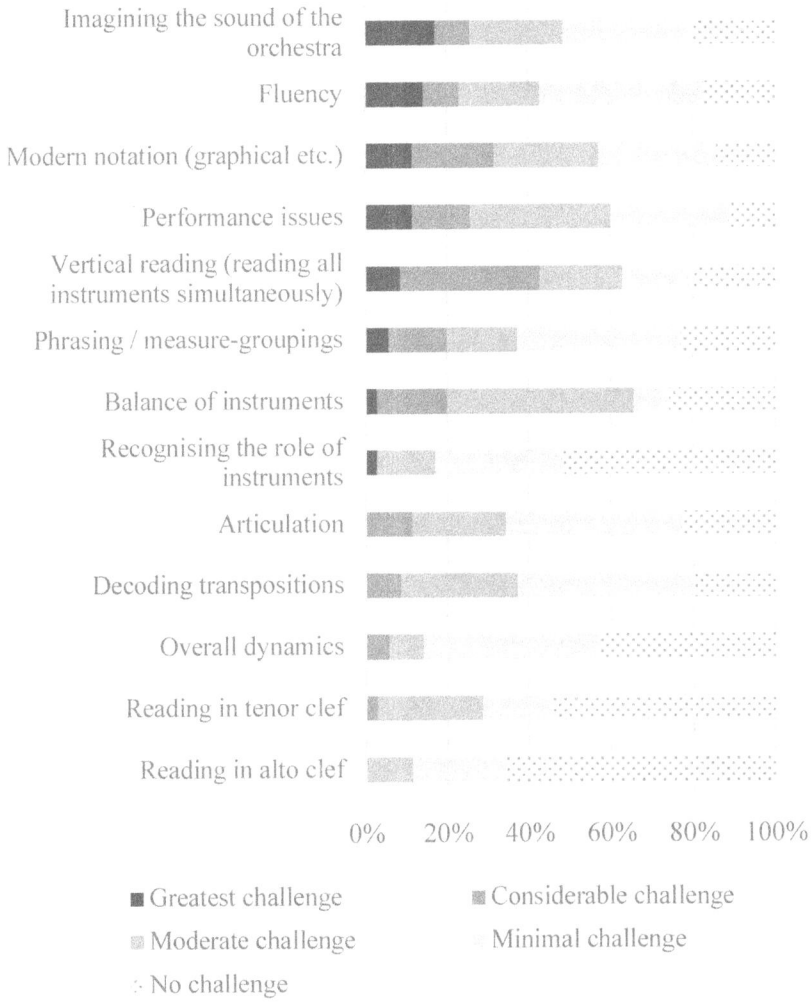

Fig. 17. (n=35)

Among the greatest challenges in score reading, conductors especially noted performance issues, modern notation, fluency, imagining the sound of the orchestra, vertical reading, and decoding transpositions. Some also identified articulation, phrasing or measure grouping, balance of instruments, overall dynamics, the role of instruments, reading in clefs as difficult aspects. Additionally, two conductors mentioned the layout of the score – for example, very small staves and notes, or too many measures in a single system. According to one conductor, challenges include finding the correct feeling of tempo and developing an inner hearing of the combined instruments. Another pointed out that challenges can vary depending on the repertoire.

Have you taken a course in score reading at a university, academy, or music school?

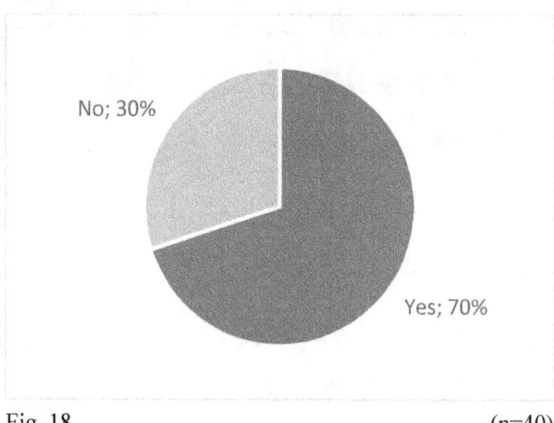

Seventy percent of conductors participating in the Questionnaire studied score reading at a university, academy, or music school.

Fig. 18. (n=40)

Would you like to share any additional comments or observations on score reading?

"The score is a map. It does not tell us how to get to our destination. It only gives us an abstract idea of the layout of the streets. And like most maps, scores don't even let you know what's actually there, what it will feel like to drive or walk those streets, the sights, sounds, smells. This is especially true for music written before the modernist revolution in the early 20th century. For musicians educated and raised before this radical paradigm shift, the score was understood as an approximation. For them, playing only what is written was not only inadequate, but could actually be considered incorrect. This dry, literal manner of execution, what Quantz called 'richtige Vortrag', went against the aesthetics and musical traditions of the time. The ideal was actually 'schöne Vortrag', in which the performer read between the notes and put their own stamp on the music, thereby reaching a more profound and beautiful truth. In contrast, modern and contemporary scores are generally written with the ideology of Objectivity and literal rendering in mind. We are expected to perform them more or less exactly as the composers wrote them. This is not only obligatory in this repertoire, but it produces superior results, precisely because it gets us closest to what the composers intended. The mistake comes when applying this modernist aesthetic to pre-modern music. It literally drains the music of life, precisely because the goal is perfectionistic and literal. Therefore, in music before the Modernist Revolution, my rule is, 'fidelity to the spirit of the music.' For as in Modern music onwards, the rule is 'fidelity to the text'."[109]

"I consider my score reading somewhat 'nonlinear'; for me, the process is not about reading the score from the first bar to the last bar and starting over again until I think I know it. I rather 'zoom in' by scrolling through and identifying the big blocks first, and only then examining the smaller units (i.e. single phrases and bars). I also often study the scores with the 'Memento method' (the film by Christopher Nolan); starting from the last rehearsal mark to the end, then from the second last rehearsal mark to the last, from the third last to the second last, etc. I feel that this is good for building the structure as you always know where the music should be leading."[110]

"1.) Practicing prima vista playing of easy piano scores, playing in D, in E-flat/E, in F, in B-flat, A, but in tempo with dynamics etc. Very useful. 2.) Playing a symphony in tempo with only one voice; also useful."[111]

"Score reading is fundamental for being a conductor. Each time I work on a score, I go through it at the piano to scan the score, detect mistakes, and analyze the way the composer wrote it. It's very helpful to understand an opus deeply. Working with a recording can often be helpful, but it will not give a strong understanding of the score."[112]

"Most importantly, start with the big picture and don't obsess over the details. This was something Mark Elder told us at a competition. I used to go too quickly into all the details, but it's very important on the first reads to get an outline of the score, by reading melodic lines, harmony and bass. Particularly in complex scores, don't overdo it; get a real feeling of the

---

[109] Eugene Tzigane, in: Score Reading Questionnaire.
[110] Eero Lehtimäki, in: Score Reading Questionnaire.
[111] Ilona Dobszay-Meskó, in: Score Reading Questionnaire.
[112] Cyril Englebert, in: Score Reading Questionnaire.

piece as a whole. Then, with every read-through, I try to pick up more details, look more at the instrumentation, add lines to my piano playing, think more about interpretation. Score learning takes a lot of time, I still study a lot, and it takes determination and time investment. Some people are quicker, some slower, but what counts is to really put in the work."[113]

"What is score reading? The ability to play what's written on some instrument? For me – I'm quite terrible at piano, but when I look at the score, I hear how it sounds. The more I look at the page, the more detailed the sounding picture in my head becomes. When I conduct, my aim is to make the orchestra sound like the sounding picture in my head, of course, being open to the musical suggestions and traditions by the orchestra and its members, demands of the soloist(s), and acoustics, etc. Another aspect: making your own scores and parts with music notation software (I use Dorico), especially from the material where the available material is bad (handwritten, printed in 19th century, etc.). One learns so much how the piece is written as you have to enter every detail, from notes to articulations, from slurs to dynamics."[114]

"Philosophically speaking, a challenge in score reading is to read 'between the lines.' Purely musical notation is very mathematical, but we need to pay attention to the musical meaning of the piece; the message the composer is telling us..."[115]

---

[113] David Danzmayr, in: Score Reading Questionnaire.
[114] Mikk Murdvee, in: Score Reading Questionnaire.
[115] Marcelo Lehniger, in: Score Reading Questionnaire.

4 Conclusions

Overview

This book explores both contemporary and traditional approaches to orchestral score reading, placing them within a broad historical and geographical context. It connects conductors and conducting schools across generations and around the world, offering a masterclass in the art of score reading and serving as a source of knowledge and inspiration for students and future conductors.

With deepest respect and admiration for the conductors whose insights are shared here, the author aims to highlight the richness of their approaches and achievements. To present a wide spectrum of methods and techniques, this book offers multiple perspectives on this essential aspect of the conductor's work.

The author has striven to establish a possible scientific foundation for understanding the art and phenomenon of orchestral score reading. While it has been observed that each conductor carves their own personal way of reading the score, some principles, methods, and techniques are shared by conductors. These observations may be especially valuable for conducting students, helping them develop skills and gain a deeper understanding of the conductor's art.

Through in-depth interviews carried out by the author, and by filling out a specially designed questionnaire, conductors shared their invaluable knowledge, experience, and nuances of their art. The responses revealed a breadth and diversity of perspectives on score reading, touching on aspects such as tempo, the composer's style and musical language, interpretation versus realization, phrasing, and technical considerations. Conversations covered topics ranging from decoding and understanding notation, performance practices and traditions, memorizing the score, and balancing dynamics, to the role of listening to recordings and emotional engagement with the music. Additionally, conductors addressed the practical steps of score preparation, using different editions, identifying mistakes, writing in rehearsal letters and numbers, and preparing materials for the orchestra.

For many conductors, creating a mental sound image of the music through score reading is the starting point of their work – they need to hear the notes internally in order to shape the music and make informed performance decisions. Some underline that for effective score reading important is knowledge of the composer's aesthetic, musical language, and stylistic characteristics, as well as the background, key elements, and purpose of the piece. Through reading the score, conductors connect with the world and thoughts of the composer and, in rehearsal and performance, guide the musicians toward their vision of the piece – adjusting it if needed.

The presented results confirm that score reading is about far more than simply deciphering the notes. It is a multidimensional process that integrates reading, analysis, interpretation, and performance considerations as inseparable activities, each informing and enhancing the others. It involves uncovering the composer's intentions, shaping the music, and forming a sounding image of the score in the mind. Through this process, conductors develop interpretative ideas and prepare for performance, bridging the gap between the composer's idea, the written score, the orchestra, and the realization of the piece for the audience.

Score Reading Methods

The evolution of score reading methods has been shaped historically by developments in the music itself – such as chromatism and atonality – as well as by technological advancements like recordings and digital manuscripts. Conductors today benefit from a wealth of resources, including musical treatises from various eras, digital tools, and recordings of composers' performances. Some prefer traditional techniques, while others incorporate modern tools, but the common goal remains the same: to bring music to life with the orchestra and communicate its essence to the listener.

Conductors recognize score reading as a creative process and emphasize that each develops their own individual method, which may evolve over the course of their conducting career. Many inventive approaches were presented, including "zooming in," "peeling the onion," "organizing," "Memento," "magnifying glass," "forest and trees," "x-ray," "eating soup," and "walking through a city." From the descriptions in this book, we can observe and appreciate both the similarities and differences in score reading methods of professional conductors. The ultimate test of score reading is the live performance with the orchestra.

It has become clear that a conductor's score reading method may vary depending on the repertoire. In the case of older music, the conductor may already be familiar with the piece through recordings or performances and may consult these sources for additional insight. When working on a new contemporary score, the conductor can often seek answers directly from the composer and request a MIDI file exported from the notation software such as Sibelius, Finale, or Dorico in order to hear the piece as a whole in digital sound.

In opera, conductors emphasize that they begin reading the score with the text and libretto. In this repertoire especially, the importance of language knowledge becomes evident, as the text is integrally connected to the music – affecting expression, tempo, articulation, and more – and understanding it is essential for a valid interpretation. When the text is in a foreign language, conductors may choose to translate each word or consult a language specialist to ensure they grasp the meaning, pronunciation, and nuance. Conductors also encounter verbal indications from composers in various languages across all types of scores, and it is crucial that they understand their implications for the music.

A particularly fascinating discovery is the close correlation between a conductor's score reading approach and their musical background. Whether trained as pianists, string players, wind players, percussionists, or vocalists, conductors bring distinct perspectives and methods to score reading. Some rely entirely on their inner hearing, while others use instruments like piano or violin, or sing through the score to deepen their understanding of the music.

Methods for reading transpositions and decoding score notation vary: some conductors prefer to read transpositions by interval, others by clef substitution, and some use both methods interchangeably depending on the musical situation. Conductors differ as well in how they mark scores – some prefer to conduct from a clean score, while others add (sometimes extensive) annotations related to analysis, interpretation, or gesture. For some, memorizing the score enhances musical freedom and communication with the orchestra; for others, having the score in front of them while conducting serves as an undisputed point of reference and a source of comfort in making music.

It was observed that, over time, some conductors' approaches to score reading have changed. For example, they stopped marking scores, switched from color-coded to pencil markings, shifted their focus to other elements – such as horizontal lines and phrases – or altered the order in which they read the score. Some conductors emphasize that their interpretation of a score depends on the particular moment, place, and stage of life they are in, striving to create a new interpretation each time they read and conduct a piece. Many noted that with experience, score reading becomes easier and more efficient. A conductor's engagement with a score is influenced by their personality, knowledge, and preferences; thus, the mental image and vision they form of a piece is always individual.

Contemporary conductors noted that today's composers' notation has become more detailed – more performance aspects are now determined in scores, leaving less open to interpretation. At the same time, performance trends have shifted, and greater personal freedom in interpretation seems to be once again accepted. Audiences seek excitement, deep emotions, and variety, among other impressions. Modern tools are now available to conductors, including digital scores, manuscripts, tuners, metronomes, pianos, audio and video recordings, and musical software. Conductors can also travel

Conclusions 217

with greater ease and hear orchestras perform local composers using performance practices that date back to the composers' own time. These evolving circumstances continue to influence how conductors read, understand, and interpret scores. Many stressed the importance of score reading and expressed the view that it should be taught more extensively at universities and music schools than it currently is.

The research for this book confirms that there is no single "best" or "correct" way to read a score that works for all conductors. Score reading is intimately tied to each conductor's personality, aesthetics, preferences, and background. Rather than conforming to one method, conductors develop personal approaches shaped by their training, experience, and artistic perspective. While some methods align and others diverge, all serve the ultimate goal of effective communication – with the orchestra and with the audience – of the musical ideas encoded in the score. The role of the conductor is therefore not merely to beat time, but to realize, shape, and interpret the music – to breathe life into the score.

This book has presented detailed accounts of personal methods of professional conductors, offering valuable insights and advice on how one might develop their own approach to score reading. As the content reveals, conductors employ a wide variety of methods and techniques to read scores, each shaped by their individual conducting work, personality, and context. Ultimately, fluency and proficiency in score reading come through practice and experience. The material presented here demonstrates that orchestral score reading can be taught and mastered, and that the challenges along the way can be overcome.

The Stages and Focus of Score Reading

As a very first step in score reading, conductors mention checking the instrumentation and the duration of the piece, usually listed on the front pages of the score. These are important not only for reading the score but also for programming concerts and planning rehearsals. Duration of many pieces can nowadays be reviewed easily through a YouTube video or other recording – without actually playing the piece. Before diving into the music, it is necessary to determine the key (in tonal music) and time signature. Several conductors begin score reading by simply flipping through the pages of the score to get a general overview of the piece.

Most conductors recommend starting score reading with the "big picture" – the overall structure – before moving into the infinite amount of details. This has been metaphorically described as going from the "forest" to the "trees", or from the "city" to the "buildings." This approach involves first examining the architecture of the piece – and of each movement, if there are any – by dividing it into larger and smaller sections. Some emphasize the risk of getting lost in the vast number of details and stress the importance of not being overwhelmed. Interestingly, some conductors prefer the opposite approach: beginning with details and building toward an understanding of the whole work.

When reading a score, conductors focus on a wide range of musical elements. They often prioritize tempo and its modifications, harmony and the bassline (as the foundation), structure and form, transpositions, dramatic flow, climaxes, key and meter changes, phrasing, and beating patterns. Special attention is also paid to balance, instrumentation (including doublings), articulation, the roles of instruments, bowings (especially among string players), and discrepancies or unwritten aspects of performance practice. The order in which these elements are addressed varies. Ultimately, conductors analyze the score with the goal of performing it. In the Classical and Romantic repertoire, much can often be inferred – such as voice leading, harmonic connections, and instrumental doublings – whereas contemporary music may require a more careful and literal reading.

Some conductors emphasize reading each note and harmony in order to fully understand the music, which also helps them in identifying potential errors in the score. Others find it sufficient to read only some of the notes and harmonies to grasp the composer's musical language, allowing them to deduce the rest. Conductors often pay special attention to difficult chord progressions. With experience, they become more adept at recognizing compositional solutions and parallelisms within the music.

Tempo is often a central concern, with many conductors focusing on it from the outset of their score reading – even before dividing the piece into sections. Tempo indications are usually treated as flexible guidelines rather than fixed values. If no metronome marking is provided, the conductor has greater freedom in determining the tempo. This decision is often linked to rhythm, phrasing, and texture, and some conductors arrive at it by singing through the score. Others "photograph" the score at tempo in their minds, while some only choose it later in the reading process, as a result of assessing the proportions of the entire piece. Conductors may deduce the tempo not from the opening of the piece, but rather from passages with shorter rhythmic values that occur later, in order to maintain a consistent tempo throughout. When everything comes together and the conductor hears the score internally – both as a whole and in detail – they may experiment with different tempos before settling on a final one. In repertoire involving soloists, such as opera or concertos, the tempo can often only be finalized during rehearsals and the performance. The acoustics of the performance hall and the orchestra's abilities also influence tempo choices.

Different conductors adopt different reading techniques. Some proceed measure by measure, like instrumentalists, while others read in larger sections, analyzing their content and interrelationships. A great deal can happen in just four measures of the score. Sometimes, both techniques are combined. Several conductors stress the importance of the score's visual layout for reading efficiency. Some prefer clear scores that don't require enlargement or excessive markings. Those with photographic memory, in particular, often favor using the same edition of the score repeatedly.

Sight-reading the score is rarely enough to fully grasp its meaning. Some conductors compare the score reading process to detective work – using a magnifying glass to uncover hidden truths beneath the surface. A useful strategy recommended by many is to read the score in several rounds, each time focusing on a different element, such as harmony, rhythm, instrumentation, or balance.

Approaches to vertical and horizontal reading also differ. Some conductors begin by reading the score as a vertical whole, focusing on harmonies and the blend of sound – even in polyphonic textures – before breaking it down by groups of instruments or musical elements. Others start with horizontal layers like melody, bassline, and accompaniment, or separate instruments and groups of instruments, gradually building the full image in their minds. Regardless of the order, conductors must combine vertical and horizontal dimensions of the score to form an integrated mental image of the music.

Throughout score reading, a conductor is engaged in the creation of a mental sound image of the score. This process involves not only the eyes and intellect but, perhaps most importantly, the ears. The image of the score is formed from the accumulation of details, not the other way around. In the final stage of score reading, the conductor works to shape their personal vision of the piece, taking into account interpretive and performance challenges. They seek out the inner logic of the composition – revealed only through thorough and detailed reading – and many recommend imagining a long musical line that runs through the piece.

It is widely agreed among conductors that having a vision of the piece is essential before stepping in front of an orchestra. Their reading of the score is affected by their own personality, knowledge, and preferences, making each conductor's mental vision of the piece unique. Anticipating potential challenges during performance and considering solutions to them is also part of the preparation. Some conductors practice conducting the score in silence, moving their hands to internalize the music physically. Others prefer to avoid gestures during score reading, finding the appropriate movements later in rehearsal with the orchestra. Several conductors stress that manual limitations should not constrain interpretation and that physical flexibility is essential for real-time response to the orchestra's sound. Experience working with orchestras seems to resolve such challenges.

Many conductors highlight the importance of putting the score aside for a while to let it "incubate" or "digest," then returning to it with fresh insight. This practice often deepens understanding and reveals new aspects of the music. They recommend beginning score reading as early as possible and working on it daily, with focused attention. Time is a crucial element in this process, as the music continues to settle in the mind between sessions. The earlier a conductor begins reading a score, the better their familiarity with it will be.

When returning to a piece they have previously conducted, some conductors prefer to start from scratch with a clean score, while others reuse their earlier marked-up scores. If the conductor has recorded the piece, they might also refer to the recording in addition to revisiting the score. As part of their score reading process, some conductors compare different editions or consult manuscripts when available. This helps clarify markings and resolve ambiguities in the score.

Memorization often occurs as a byproduct of score reading. Many conductors believe that memorizing the score – at least in terms of phrasing – is essential for conducting. Knowing what comes next allows the conductor to lead the orchestra and make eye contact with the musicians. Even when the score is memorized, some conductors still choose to have it present during rehearsals or performances, in case a reference is needed. Conducting from memory requires truly "owning" the music to manage any unexpected problems in the orchestra.

Conductors with photographic memory memorize more quickly and, in some cases, can even write the score down from memory. Repetition in reading the score and conducting experience aid memorization. For many, memorizing happens naturally, and they enjoy carrying the music in their minds. Others prefer conducting from the score, feeling more secure and confident with the orchestra. In opera and accompaniments, using the score is usually preferred to ensure the safety of the performance in case of changes or jumps by the soloist.

In discussing score reading, conductors also address the topic of interpretation. Many emphasize the crucial importance of faithfulness to the score, a solid understanding of its background and the composer's musical language, and the concept of interpretation as realization. Some note that each return to a score reveals something new and invites fresh interpretation, while others prefer to maintain their earlier choices.

Finally, some conductors emphasize that it may never be possible to know a score completely – there will always be unanswered questions and undiscovered details. This uncertainty keeps the process of score reading alive and creative. Still, the more a conductor reads a score, the fewer surprises they will encounter in rehearsal. Most agree that score reading should be learned by conductors as early as possible. With practice, it becomes faster and easier. The more scores one reads, the more fluent the process becomes.

The Composer's Language and Background of the Piece

Many conductors emphasize the importance of becoming familiar with the background of a piece before reading the score. This includes reading the composer's verbal texts – such as descriptions, letters, comments, treatises, and critiques. In their view, knowing about the composer and the context of the piece is a necessary condition for conducting. Music is often shaped by the composer's life experiences, and the more we understand the historical context, the better we can interpret their work. This type of research becomes especially important when conducting a piece by a composer who is unfamiliar to the conductor.

Sensitivity to style was also frequently mentioned, both in relation to the musical era and the individual composer. According to many, a conductor needs to become acquainted with these stylistic contexts to grasp the specific and personal language of the composer. Several conductors underlined that, in score reading, they strive to connect with the composer's mind – and that the conductor's responsibility is not to impose an interpretation, but rather to realize the music faithfully. This requires reading the score with knowledge, stylistic awareness, and sensitivity to the composer's musical language.

Conductors explain that every composer has their own unique musical language, and that this can best be discovered by reading and exploring many of their scores – not limited only to orchestral works. A composer may focus on a particular element, such as rhythm or sonority, and it is the conductor's task to identify and understand this emphasis. Knowing a composer's musical language can also assist in practical matters, such as spotting errors or inconsistencies in the score.

Many conductors also stress that no piece exists in isolation. It is essential for the conductor to explore the context in which the work was written. The same markings may mean different things depending on the composer. Even though some composers notate their ideas more precisely than others, uncertainties and ambiguities often remain in the score. In the case of contemporary music, many conductors value the opportunity to communicate directly with the composer, seeking clarification and insight before performing the piece.

A thorough understanding of performance styles and practices is also needed for effective score reading. Conductors recommend developing this knowledge by listening to orchestras that are historically or geographically connected to the composer, and by studying musical treatises. Awareness of performing traditions – especially in opera – is essential, though each conductor makes interpretive choices based on their own understanding.

At the same time, there are conductors who insist on beginning their work with just the score, without referring to external descriptive materials. They don't want their interpretation to be influenced by outside sources. Some believe that all the necessary information about the music is already written into the score by the composer, while others consult additional sources only after reading the score.

Score Reading Tools and Orchestral Imagination

Some conductors read scores in silence – without using a musical instrument or even singing. They focus entirely on imagining all aspects of the music simultaneously. This may be a personal preference or a necessity when no instrument is available. It is often assumed that conductors with perfect pitch do not need to play the score on a piano or any other instrument. However, some conductors always choose to read the score on the piano. Many conductors, especially when working on difficult scores, play through the music – or parts of it – on an instrument to hear the notes more clearly, both in tonal and, even more so, in atonal music.

Reading the score on the piano can help conductors further develop their inner hearing, train their ears, and support the creation of a sounding image of the piece in their mind. Most conductors who use the piano for this purpose emphasize that they imagine the sound of the orchestra while playing the score. Even if they are not pianists, many conductors use the piano to check harmonies and chord progressions – often at a slower tempo – as a way of clarifying the notation, understanding the music, and hearing how it sounds. It also helps in detecting wrong notes and identifying musical details. Playing a piano reduction (their own or someone else's), even slowly, can aid in imagining the score as a vertical whole.

Some conductors note that the inability to play the piano does not necessarily indicate poor score reading skills – just as being able to play a score on the piano does not guarantee strong score reading. There are many other aspects to consider. Nevertheless, pianist-conductors often enjoy reading scores on the piano, finding that it helps them uncover such elements as phrasing and discover the beauty of the music.

If a conductor plays a wind or string instrument, they can use it to explore not only notes and intervals, but also phrasing, breaths, musical direction, articulation, bowings, and technical considerations. Some conductors go through the score by playing each line on their instrument, then imagining them all together. This can provide the perspective of an orchestral musician. Others use tools like a tuning fork (especially singers and choir conductors) or an electronic tuner to focus on absolute pitch and harmony. In many cases, it is enough to imagine how it would feel to play a passage on an instrument in order to find the right solutions and form a mental sound image – without needing to play it physically.

Many conductors use a metronome for score reading, especially when working on contemporary music. It helps them check the composer's tempo markings, measure their own tempo preferences, and control their conducting speed. While many take the composer's metronome mark as a starting point – particularly in contemporary music – they may disregard it in older works, where it may have been added by an editor or reflect different performance conditions. A metronome, being mechanical, does not allow for agogic flexibility or breathing between phrases. For this reason, some conductors choose not to use it, or use it only to verify starting tempos. For some, tempo arises organically from the musical material and is checked with the metronome at the end of the score reading process. For others, tempo is the starting point, with the material adjusted around it.

Most conductors recommend learning score reading at the piano. This is often taught together with sight-reading skills. The primary aim of this is to develop fluency in reading notes. Students commonly practice Bach chorales to learn how to read in multiple clefs and to grasp the vertical dimension of the score. Transpositions can be taught through orchestral excerpts or by transposing instrumental parts and piano music. Vertical reading can be reinforced by comparing scores with piano reductions. Recommended exercises include playing simultaneously all lines slowly to decode transpositions, and only selected lines at full tempo to practice musical flow. Sometimes, score reading is taught in four-handed settings with a teacher or another student. The level of difficulty can be increased gradually. It is important that students learn to identify priorities and understand the interrelation of musical elements. Another aspect of learning score reading at the piano is finding enjoyment and building confidence.

Many conductors recommend singing as a tool to discover musical phrasing – identifying the direction of a phrase, its climax, and breathing points. Singing trains the ear, helps to find a natural tempo, and supports the feeling of musical flow. Some conductors sing through the entire score, changing instruments as they go, in order to follow a line from beginning to end of the piece. This can also be practiced while imagining the remaining orchestral parts. In rhythmic pieces, some conductors speak the rhythm to feel it in their body.

In case of contemporary pieces, some conductors find it useful to listen to MIDI files generated by a computer. Exceptionally conductors may use software to practice specific aspects of the score, such as tempo changes.

To develop orchestral sound imagination, conductors recommend playing in an orchestra or listening to orchestral rehearsals and performances. They advise always bringing a score to compare the written notation with the resulting sound. By listening closely during the first rehearsal, conductors can learn about the difficult spots in the score. Over time, the experience of listening to and conducting orchestras helps build more precise mental images of how orchestral music sounds.

Transpositions and Other Challenges in Score Reading

Conductors decode transpositions either by the interval of transposition or through clef substitution. The choice of method depends on the conductor's background, training, and personal preference, and some may vary their approach depending on the type of music. Wind-player conductors often read by interval if that is how they think on their instrument (e.g., horn, trumpet, clarinet), but some prefer the clef substitution method if they were trained in it. String-player conductors who use alto or tenor clef in their instrumental playing often find this helpful when reading in other clefs. Pianist-conductors may have learned to read different clefs through the traditional notation of early music, but only some choose to use clef substitution for transpositions, while others are more comfortable transposing by interval.

Some conductors combine both methods depending on the musical situation and the type of transposition. For example, they may prefer clef substitution in Classical period music but switch to the interval of transposition method in chromatic, enharmonic, or atonal music with many accidentals. Clef substitution is especially popular for decoding E-flat and E transpositions in treble clef, as they can be read in bass clef with adjusted key, accidentals, and, if needed, octave placement. Conductors who use clef substitution consistently mention that they think in terms of adjusting accidentals according to the type of instrument rather than the key of transposition, which allows them to use this method also in atonal music. For some, Zoltán Kodály's moveable "DO" method is a helpful tool for reading transpositions in tonal music.

Regardless of the method, conductors agree that experience and practice lead to fluency. Transpositions that appear frequently in scores (such as B-flat, F, A) become easier to read, while rarely used ones (especially the G transposition) remain more challenging. Although decoding transpositions may seem difficult at first, it becomes significantly easier with practice. Multiple simultaneous transpositions can still be demanding, and in such cases, some conductors choose to write chord names in the score. Several conductors have used score reading exercise books to improve their fluency. When using clef substitution, one must have mastered reading various clefs, which can be practiced, for example, with old editions of Bach chorales. Transposing by interval can also be practiced with simple piano pieces – by shifting them up or down by a given interval.

Most conductors prefer reading scores with transpositions rather than in C, because it helps them recognize instrument registers and see the same notation as the orchestral musicians with transposing instruments. This gives insight into the musicians' challenges and responses. However, a handful of conductors prefer scores in C, as this allows them to focus more easily on concert pitch.

Scores with many simultaneous transpositions – such as in music by Berlioz, Wagner, Strauss, or Verdi – are especially challenging to read. Scores with complex textures are also difficult; in these cases, some conductors recommend reading "step by step," focusing on instrument groups separately (e.g., strings, winds, brass) before imagining the full ensemble. Starting with foundational instruments such as cellos, double basses, bassoons, trombones, and tuba is also a helpful approach.

Interpreting the composer's markings can be complex. Dynamics, for instance, may refer to the overall balance of the orchestra rather than specific instruments, and often require adjustment. Articulation markings such as dots, lines, slurs, and accents carry different meanings depending on the musical era and the composer. Tempo and its modifications can also be difficult to interpret.

Score layout can present challenges for reading. If the notes or staves are too small, poorly positioned, or the score itself is too large for the music stand, the conductor's reading process may be slowed down. In such cases, conductors may need to enlarge or compress the score, change the edition, request corrections from the composer, or even re-engrave the score. The advantage of re-engraving the score oneself is that the conductor learns the score in detail, because it requires going through every note and every mark. A few conductors mention using iPads to read scores, but issues such as screen size and page-turning may be obstacles. Many still prefer printed scores and feel a personal attachment to them.

With new contemporary works, conductors often have to rely solely on the score – without recordings – to imagine the music and identify any potential wrong notes in rehearsal. Contemporary music may feature unconventional notations, which are challenging to read. Figuring out the language of a new composer and how they use notation is described by some conductors as the greatest challenge in reading scores. Through reading, singing, and listening to the notes, they aim to reach the composer's sound-world.

For some conductors, a challenge can be not being able to play the full score fluently on the piano. In such cases, they can, for example, prioritize instruments or slow down the tempo to grasp the full score. Not all conductors, however, use the piano for reading scores.

One modern challenge in score reading is the abundance of resources. Too many editions of scores (even several labeled "urtext"), recordings, books on the composer, theoretical materials, and guides to performance practice can be overwhelming. Since time is limited, conductors may be forced to prioritize and selectively engage with the available materials.

Marking the Score

Many conductors have personal methods for marking the score – ranging from minimal to extensive annotations. These markings may be limited to the use of a regular pencil and eraser, or expanded to include colorful markers of various kinds. Marking the score helps them in both reading and memorizing the music. Some markings are part of score analysis, while others serve practical purposes, acting as reminders when conducting from the score.

Conductors' markings often concern corrections, phrasing (groupings of measures), beating patterns, instrumental entries (cues), dynamic adjustments, articulation, bowings, and chord names. Some conductors write the structure and form of the piece directly in the score or on a separate sheet – especially in large works such as operas. Additional markings may include metronome indications, other conductors' solutions, attention signs, and many personalized notes. The scores of certain conductors may resemble "paintings" in their detail and color.

Some conductors make markings only in pencil, because these can be easily adjusted and modified. Others use color-coded systems to make the markings more visible. Colored markings are particularly popular in opera. When color is used, it is often to differentiate instruments or dynamics – for example, blue for *piano*, red for *forte*.

On the other hand, a number of conductors prefer to conduct from clean scores, avoiding markings altogether or limiting them to minimal notes. They find that excessive markings can be distracting and blur the composer's notation – and the music itself – referring to them as "graffiti" or "pollution" of the score. A clean score, in their view, allows one to reach a higher understanding of the music and a more direct connection to the composer's intentions. Several conductors note that, with experience, they have changed their marking habits – gradually reducing or abandoning them.

Certain conductors consider it necessary or beneficial to make retouches to scores. These retouches may involve adding articulation markings, adjusting balance, modifying instrumentation, or indicating cuts and repeats. Such adjustments are often made to clarify or enhance the composer's intentions. Dynamics, in particular, are difficult to predict before hearing the orchestra in the acoustics of the performance hall; they are relative and often need to be adapted – especially in older repertoire, due to changes in instrument construction and sound. Instrumentation changes may be required when dynamic adjustments alone do not achieve the desired effect. Scores frequently lack clarity in the range of articulation, which has to be specified by the conductor.

Those with string-playing backgrounds often prepare bowings for the orchestra in advance, as bowings significantly impact the sound of the orchestra. Others leave these decisions to the concertmasters. Many experienced conductors emphasize that bowings are specific to each orchestra, its characteristics, and level. Different orchestras may have different bowing styles, and it is not uncommon for players to prefer their own bowings over the conductor's suggestions. In any case, bowings are typically prepared before rehearsals and only slightly modified during them.

There are also conductors who prepare orchestral parts for pieces. While some believe everything can be communicated through conducting alone and see no need to write nuances into the parts, others argue that preparing the parts in advance saves time in rehearsal and aids in realizing their musical vision. These parts may include markings that clarify the composer's notation or address performance matters such as dynamics, articulation, phrasing, and bowings. Instead of editing the parts, some conductors choose to send errata lists to orchestras with detailed instructions.

Listening to Recordings

One of the most significant technological advancements influencing score reading is the widespread availability of recordings. Today, practically all conductors listen to recordings, and many use them to test or reinforce their knowledge of the score. Recordings are easily accessible through platforms such as YouTube, Spotify, and other digital services, as well as through more traditional formats like CDs and DVDs. Conductors usually recommend listening to recordings with the score in hand – reading and listening simultaneously.

Most conductors emphasize that it is crucial to first read and fully internalize the score before listening to recordings. This is because a recording can, even unconsciously, influence a conductor's personal vision of the piece. From this perspective, recordings should not be used as a substitute for score reading, but rather as a supplement – to be consulted only after a mental sound image has been formed. Listening to recordings can be a valuable way to quickly become familiar with a wide range of orchestral repertoire, but to learn, understand, and interpret a piece, reading the score remains essential.

The primary reasons conductors mention for listening to recordings are to confront their mental image of the score with the reality of the sound, to correct inaccuracies in that image, to refine their interpretation, and to reflect on performance decisions by asking questions such as, "Why did this conductor or orchestra play it this way?" or "Do I agree with it?" A common concern among conductors is the risk of adopting others' ideas and interpretations instead of developing their own directly from the score. They caution that relying exclusively or too heavily on recordings as a shortcut to learning music can lead to copying, "cloning," and producing caricatures or unsuccessful replicas of other performances – without truly understanding the music, creating one's own vision of the piece, or knowing why something sounds a certain way. These qualities can only be achieved through reading the score.

When conductors listen to a recording after reading the score, they become aware of interpretive differences and performance choices. This is why many recommend listening to a recording with the score in hand – following the two simultaneously. They emphasize that if you hear something in a recording and do not understand why it was done that way, you should not adopt it. The main aspect examined by conductors is tempo, because it is the element most directly influenced by the conductor and significantly affects the success of a performance.

For some conductors, listening to recordings helps them perceive the full vertical sound of the orchestra, whereas when reading the score, they focus more on details and individual instruments or smaller groups. However, in matters of balance, many conductors warn that recordings are not reliable, as microphones and post-production editing can distort the acoustic result. Notably, conductors do not consider recordings to be a way to learn conducting itself. This is especially true because, when listening to a recording, the conductor follows the sound – whereas one of the key elements of conducting is to lead it, to stay ahead of the music.

Many conductors prefer listening to historical recordings, as these can be a valuable source of information about a composer's preferences and expectations – particularly if the recording was made by the composer themselves, or by someone closely acquainted with them. It is important for conductors to be aware of performance traditions, and these can be discovered through recordings. Some conductors recommend listening to live recordings, as these typically involve less editing. Recordings can provide insight into performance practices associated with specific orchestras and the era in which the recordings were made, as well as highlight technical difficulties within the piece – challenges that may also arise in live performance. Video recordings, too, can offer useful observations, including ideas for the conductor's body language.

Listening to multiple recordings is considered more valuable than relying on just one. Comparing various interpretations helps reduce the risk of imitation and reveals stylistic trends, fashions, and traditions. For example, it is useful to compare how different soloists render vocal parts in opera. Many conductors consider listening to their own recordings or watching videos of their conducting to be an exceptionally valuable learning tool. It allows them to identify mistakes, plan improvements, and continue developing their interpretation of the piece. On the other hand, others prefer not to listen to their own earlier recordings, in order to preserve a fresh perspective on the piece, uninfluenced by their previous experiences.

In the case of new contemporary works, several conductors note the usefulness of listening to a MIDI file provided by the composer – unless non-traditional notation is used. Though abstract in sound, MIDI tracks can offer a helpful reference for imagining the overall picture of the music.

Finally, some conductors express the belief that a deep understanding of the score is not possible nowadays without listening to recordings. They stress, however, that recordings should be used reasonably – not as a shortcut, but as a complement to score reading. When approached in this way, recordings can be a useful tool in preparation for conducting, support the development of a conductor's personal interpretation, and deepen their knowledge of the music.

Score Reading and Conducting

The insights presented in this book highlight the intrinsic and strong connection between score reading and conducting. Many conductors describe score reading as the foundational stage of their work – where they uncover a piece's inner meaning, construct a sounding image of it in their mind, and develop a vision for the performance that they will later bring to life with the orchestra. For many, knowing the score is the first and most essential requirement for conducting.

A conductor is generally expected to have a mental image of the piece before stepping in front of the orchestra, and most conductors emphasize the importance of having a clear vision or concept for the performance. All of these – image, vision, and concept – are formed through thoughtful and careful reading of the score. Score reading is often described by conductors as a creative and endless process – homework done in solitude. A substantial portion of this preparatory work takes place before the first rehearsal with the orchestra. Although today's conductors can also familiarize themselves with a piece by listening to recordings, many caution that this way one gets to know only the outer characteristics of the music, without delving into its essence, details, and meaning.

Beyond technical proficiency, conductors point out that great conducting stems from a deep understanding of the music's meaning – its structure, emotion, and expressive possibilities. While notation has evolved and become more precise over time, it still requires interpretation; not all ideas can be fully captured in the form of notes and textual descriptions. A thoughtful reading of a score requires knowledge of the composer's musical language, as well as awareness of relevant performance practices, in order to decode the markings on the page. Every musical detail, including the tempo, phrasing, articulation, dynamics, rhythm, and color contributes to the shape and character of the music. Some conductors underline the importance of feeling an emotional response to the music while reading the score, in order to be able to transfer it through the orchestra to the audience.

From today's perspective, we can observe a shift in how conductors approach score reading and the role it plays in their work – driven by changes in leadership style, technological developments, and evolving audience expectations. In recent decades, conductors have increasingly emphasized collaboration with orchestras. Rather than rigidly – or "at any cost" – realizing a fixed vision formed during score reading, many choose to remain open to the orchestra's ideas, aiming to support rather than disturb its unique character, traditions, and collective expertise. In this more collaborative approach, interpretation becomes more of a team effort, with the conductor serving as an inspiring link – encouraging musicians to give their best rather than imposing a predetermined outcome. In reading the score, conductors are placing greater emphasis on aspects of leadership, and on anticipating potential situations that might arise during rehearsals and performances.

Some contemporary conductors describe their vision of a piece as flexible and responsive – shaped in real time through rehearsal. While they may begin with certain assumptions, they remain open to change, allowing their interpretation to emerge during work with the orchestra. In this view, the conductor's role centers on enabling music-making, not controlling it. The acoustics of the performance space, the orchestra's characteristics, and the conductor's emotional state in the moment all influence the final realization of the piece.

Because orchestras have their own traditions and ways of playing, they respond differently to different conductors and their interpretive ideas. As a result, the realization of a conductor's vision will sound different depending on the orchestra. Increasingly, discussions around conducting emphasize communication and dialogue between conductor and orchestra, rather than a one-way transmission of the composer's message – delivered by the conductor, through the orchestra, to the audience.

This shift has led some conductors to suggest that arriving at rehearsal less fully "prepared" on the score – at least in the traditional sense – can be beneficial, as it allows them to remain more open and responsive to adjust to the orchestra's ideas. They argue that genuine contact with the ensemble may matter more than rigid adherence to a predetermined vision. A fixed approach can sometimes lead to frustration or conflict if it clashes with orchestra's style and tendencies. In contrast, a more open attitude enables the conductor to support and inspire – to "do no harm" – rather than to control.

The technical abilities and stylistic knowledge of orchestral musicians have developed significantly over the past century. For conductors, the challenge may lie in respecting the orchestra's character and expertise while still unifying the ensemble and realizing the score and the composer's intentions. At the same time, there is always the risk that if a conductor is not sufficiently prepared or lacks a clear vision, they may end up merely following the sound of the orchestra rather than leading it. However, when conductors devote attention to score reading, they can, with experience and practice, achieve fluency, confidence, and joy in this process – to the benefit of the music, the composer, the orchestra musicians, and the audience alike.

Rehearsal time is limited, which means conductors need to clearly present and articulate their vision of the piece from the very beginning of their work with the orchestra – it is commonly done during the first rehearsal. In opera and accompaniments, the conductor's vision must be coordinated with the soloist's interpretation and performance style. If more rehearsal time is available, conductors can work more collaboratively with soloists and the orchestra toward a shared interpretation of the piece.

Despite changing expectations, the conductor's responsibility remains constant: to deliver the composer's creation – encoded in the notation of the score – to the audience through the orchestra. Today's audiences often seek "magic" in performances – something on top of just a realization of the score. Yet that magic is inseparable and grounded in the score. This is also why score reading continues to be a necessary and basic activity and step in the art of the conductor.

Score reading is only the beginning of the conductor's complex and multifaceted task of bringing music to life with the orchestra. With a vision of the piece, the conductor uses it to inspire the orchestra in both rehearsals and performance – while also embracing the ensemble's strengths. Making music together is a great and deeply rewarding experience. At the same time, the conductor has a duty to the composer – the creator of the music. Of course, some composers are known for being more open to varied interpretation of their music than others. The conductor's success and central goal lie in guiding the orchestra toward the best performance and presentation of the music – as a gift to the audience.

This book invites and engages the reader in an extended masterclass in orchestral score reading. The author is deeply grateful to the conductors who generously shared their wisdom, experience, and passion, and holds great admiration for their artistry. Their insights into both the personal and universal aspects of score reading are invaluable. Score reading remains an evolving art – rooted in tradition, yet continually enriched by new ideas, demands, and tools. It is the author's sincere hope that the knowledge and reflections presented here will serve as a resource for students, musicians, music lovers, and conductors seeking to deepen their understanding and proficiency in score reading. The conductor stands as a bridge between the composer's vision encoded in the score, the orchestra's performance, and the audience's experience of the music. Mastery lies at the heart of the conductor's art – and it begins with the act of reading the score.

Bibliography

Brooks, Jeanice, and Kimberly Francis, eds. *Nadia Boulanger: Thoughts on Music*. Rochester, NY: University of Rochester Press, 2020. Selections:
- Nadia Boulanger, "Concerts Colonne" (*Le Monde musical* 30, no. 11, 1919), 101–2.
- Nadia Boulanger, "Teacher's Lecture" (original English text, 1925), 391.
- Nadia Boulanger, "Lecture for the British Broadcasting Corporation, *Music of the Week*" (original English text, 1938), 418.

Boult, Sir Adrian C. *Handbook on the Technique of Conducting*. Oxford: Hall the Printer Limited, 1920.

Boult, Sir Adrian C. *Thoughts on Conducting*. London: Phoenix House, 1963.

Glass, Philip. *Words Without Music: A Memoir*. New York: Liveright Publishing Company, 2015.

Jochum, Eugen. *"About the Phenomenology of Conducting."* In *The Conductor's Art,* ed. Carl Bamberger, 257-264. New York: McGraw-Hill, 1965.

Leinsdorf, Erich. *The Composer's Advocate: A Radical Orthodoxy for Musicians*. New Haven and London: Yale University Press, 1981.

Malko, Nicolai. *Conductor and His Baton: Fundamentals of The Technic of Conducting*. Copenhagen: Wilhelm Hansen, 1950.

Malko, Nicolai, and Elizabeth A. H. Green. *The Conductor and His Score*. Englewood Cliffs, NJ: Prentice Hall, 1975.

Мусин, Илья Александрович. *Язык дирижерского жеста* [The Language of the Conducting Gesture]. Москва: Музыка, 2007.

Panula, Jorma. *Directives for conducting studies at Sibelius Academy,* 1992. Unpublished material.

Panula, Jorma. *A Masterclass for Conductors*. Unpublished material.

Panula, Jorma. *Some Hints to the Conductor*. Unpublished material.

Ormandy, Eugene. *"The Art of Conducting"*. In *The Conductor's Art,* ed. Carl Bamberger, 251-256. New York: McGraw-Hill, 1965.

Rosenstiel, Léonie. *Nadia Boulanger: A Life in Music*. New York: W. W. Norton & Company, 1998.

Rowicki, Witold. *Zapiski dyrygenta* [Notes of a Conductor]. Warszawa: Oficyna Wydawnicza przybylik &, 2014.

Scherchen, Hermann. *Handbook of Conducting*. Translated by M. D. Calvocoressi. Oxford: Oxford University Press, 1989.

Schuller, Gunther. *The Compleat Conductor*. Oxford: Oxford University Press, 1997.

Solti, Georg. *Memoirs*. Chicago: A Cappella Books, 1998.

Skrowaczewski, Stanisław. Byłem w niebie. w rozmowiez Agnieszką Malatyńską-Stankiewicz. FIX

Wit, Antoni. *Dyrygowanie – sprawa życia i śmierci – Antoni Wit w rozmowie z Agnieszką Malatyńska-Stankiewicz* [Conducting – A Matter of Life and Death: Antoni Wit in Conversation with Agnieszka Malatyńska-Stankiewicz]. Warszawa: Czytelnik, 2021.

www.ingramcontent.com/pod-product-compliance
Lightning Source LLC
Chambersburg PA
CBHW072142290426
44111CB00012B/1948